THE FEDERAL RESERVE

THE FEDERAL RESERVE
Lender of Last Resort

GILLIAN GARCIA
and
ELIZABETH PLAUTZ

BALLINGER PUBLISHING COMPANY
Cambridge, Massachusetts
A Subsidiary of Harper & Row, Publishers, Inc.

International Standard Book Number: 0-88730-324-2

Library of Congress Catalog Card Number: 88-19261

Printed in the United States of America

Library of Congress Cataloging-in-Publication Data

Garcia, G.G.
    The Federal Reserve : lender of last resort.

    Bibliography: p.
    Includes index.
    1. United States. Federal Reserve Board. 2. Federal Reserve banks. 3. Lenders of last resort—United States. I. Plautz, Elizabeth. II. Title.
    HG2562.L6G37 1988   332.1'1'0973   88-19261
    ISBN 0-88730-324-2

to
Gina, Andrew, and Jason

CONTENTS

List of Figures   xi

List of Tables   xiii

Preface   xv

Chapter 1
Crises, Insolvency, and Failure   1

The Lender of Last Resort (LLR)   1
Signs of Stress   3
The Causes of the Problems   7
Establishing the Criteria   8
Themes and Definitions   9
Costs and Benefits of Failure and Rescue   12
Public or Private Responsibility?   13

Chapter 2
The Origins of the Lender
of Last Resort   15

The Need for a Lender of Last Resort   16
Depository Institutions and Runs   17

Contagion	18
Periods of Monetary Contraction	20
The British Origins of the LLR Concept	21
Classic Admonitions	22
The American Lender of Last Resort Concept	28
Summary	39

Chapter 3
The Federal Reserve as Lender
of Last Resort   41

The Financial System Safety Net	42
The LLR Within the Financial System Safety Net	43
Money Creation	44
Lender-of-Last-Resort Operations	45
The Monetary Control Act of 1980	48
Special Industry Lenders	49
Collateral Requirements	49
The Cost of Lender-of-Last-Resort Assistance	54
Conclusions	57

Chapter 4
Trigger Areas   65

Sources of Economic Malfunction	66
Size and Concentration	68
The Speed of Transmission and Urgency of Regulatory Response	81
Complexity	84
Interdependency	87
Summary	89

Chapter 5
Evaluation Criteria   97

Establishing the Criteria of Effectiveness and Equity	97
Aspects of Effectiveness	99
Aspects of Equity	114
Trade-offs Between Effectiveness and Equity	118

Summary—The Relationship Between the Modern and
    Classic Criteria   123

        Chapter 6
        Handling Domestic Crises   127

Has the Federal Reserve's Assistance Been Effective?   128
Is the Federal Reserve's Assistance Equitable?   147
Fairness in Treatment   150

        Chapter 7
        Domestic Concerns and
        Resolutions   157

Equity   158
The Wrong Incentives   161
Accountability   173
Concerns for the Future   175
Extending Assistance Too Far   175
Should Assistance Be Extended Further?   177
Access to Information   183

        Chapter 8
        From Here, Where?   189

Periods of LLR Evolution   189
Future Directions   193
When Should LLR Action Be Taken?   194
The Costs and Benefits of LLR Action   197
A Social Accounting   205
Public or Private Provision of LLR Assistance?   206

        Appendices:
        Failure Case Studies   213

Case Study A: Franklin National Bank   217
Case Study B: The 1980 Silver Crisis   233
Case Study C: The S & L Crisis of 1985–87   257

References   281

Index   291

About the Authors   311

LIST OF FIGURES

5-1   Concentration in Commercial Banking   109
5-2   Core Deposits as a Percent of Assets   122
A-1   Dollar Subsidy, Franklin National Bank: May 9, 1974–
      October 9, 1974   227
C-1   FSLIC-Insured Institutions: Net New Deposits
      Received   258
C-2   Actual Versus Predicted FHLB Advances   267

LIST OF TABLES

1-1	Commercial Bank Suspensions Before the FDIC	2
1-2	Federal Deposit Insurance Corporation Bank Failures: 1934 to Present	4
1-3	Regulatory Resolutions for FSLIC-Insured Institutions	6
1-4	Number of Problem Institutions: 1975-87	7
2-1	Central Bank and LLR Functions in the United States: 1791-1987	30
3-1	Applicability of the Classic LLR Components to the Modern Domestic LLR Concept	58
4-1	Off-Balance Sheet Commitments: December 1986	76
4-2	Gross Standby Letters of Credit Issued by U.S. Commerical Banks: 1973-86	78
4-3	Core Deposits and Managed Deposits at Commercial Banks 1962-86	83
4-4	Core Deposits and Managed Liabilities by Bank Size, December 1986	84
4-5	Assets of Private Domestic Financial Institutions: 1946-85	91
4-6	Commercial and Industrial Loans: Dollar Volume and Percent of Short-Term Business Credit, December Average	92
5-1	Concentration Among the Nation's Superbanks	106

5-2   Comparative Statistics on Commercial Bank Concentration (Sample Includes All FDIC-Insured Commercial Banks for a Given Year)   107

5-3   Relationship Between the Modern and Classic LLR Criteria   124

8-1   Periods of U.S. Central Bank Evolution   190

8-2   Who Loses From Bank Runs?   198

8-3   Who Loses From Run Resolutions?   200

A-1   Interest Rate and Dollar Subsidy, Franklin National Bank, May–October 1984   224

A-2   Minimum Replacement Cost of Funds for Franklin National Bank   226

B-1   Estimated World Silver Production, Consumption, and Stock Liquidation: 1969–79   236

B-2   Estimated Silver Contract Ownership by Hunt-Related Accounts   241

B-3   Estimated Silver Contract Ownership by Conti-Related Accounts   242

B-4   Hunt Silver-Related Loan Balances   248

C-1   Incidence of Insolvencies by State, December 1986   260

C-2   FSLIC Insurance Fund Reserves 1980–86   263

C-3   Federal Home Loan Bank System, Member Institutions, Regulatory Net Worth, and FHLBank Advances: 1940–86   266

C-4   Deposits and FHLBank Advances, All FSLIC-Insured Institutions, Fourth Quarter 1986   270

C-5   FHLBank Advances, FSLIC Guarantees, and Collateral Deficiencies: 1985-87   272

C-6   Dollar Values of Deposits and FHLBank Advances, All FSLIC-Insured Institutions, 1986   274

PREFACE

Much has been written about financial crises, failures, and rescues. Academics and policymakers alike have recently attributed many of these problems to deficiencies in the U.S. federal financial safety net and have suggested legislative and regulatory reforms. Academic attention has focused on one of the safety net's three facets—deposit insurance. The system of examination, supervision, and regulation has also been criticized, particularly in U.S. General Accounting Office reports of the past four years. There has been less discussion of the third facet—the lender of last resort (LLR), which provides liquidity support to troubled financial institutions. Yet the LLR's role in the federal financial safety net is both more fundamental and more venerable than the other two.

Some progress is being made toward understanding how the LLR contributes to preserving financial stability. Recent works by Professors Edward Kane and George Kaufman in Benston et al. (1986) and by Anna Schwartz (1987b, c) are particularly notable in this regard.

The Federal Reserve: Lender of Last Resort extensively examines the subject. The first three chapters explore the LLR's history, its rationale, and the procedures adopted by the Federal Reserve, the principal lender of last resort in the United States. Chapter 4 asks how the recent rapid and continuing changes in the world financial system are altering the need and procedures for successfully meeting the LLR's responsibility of providing immediate liquidity in a financial crisis.

Chapter 5 presents a set of criteria for evaluating the operations of the LLR. The authors developed these principles, which encompass both effectiveness and equity, using an iterative procedure. We first studied the LLR concept developed by classic British nineteenth century writers and applied by modern U.S. authors to handling contemporary crises. It became clear that in today's environment, a reconfiguration of the classic analysis is needed.

Next, the authors developed numerous case studies of financial crises that have occurred during the 1970s and 1980s. Three of these studies (on the failure of Franklin National Bank in 1974, the silver crisis of 1980, and the current S&L crisis) demonstrate the scope and recent evolution of LLR activities; they are presented in the Appendices.

The authors then established a tentative set of modern principles for executing the LLR function. They discussed these principles with experts in the field, both practitioners and academics. Staff workers at the Federal Reserve Board, the Federal Reserve Banks of New York, Chicago, and San Francisco, and the House and Senate Banking Committees, who were knowledgeable about how financial crises had occurred and rescues had been handled, were of invaluable assistance in refining these principles.

In Chapter 6 the revised criteria are used to evaluate the Federal Reserve's performance during crises since the 1970s. This chapter also includes some commentary on the Federal Home Loan Bank System's handling of the recent liquidity and solvency problems at S&Ls. Chapter 7 discusses issues relating the present and future execution of LLR activities.

The final chapter asks who benefits from LLR actions and who should conduct them. It concludes that the public-good aspects of LLR activities—those that reflect the generalized impact of, and are most commonly executed through, monetary policy open-market operations—must be conducted by the nation's central bank. They cannot be reallocated to the private sector.

But a stronger case can be made for using either private institutions or public facilities that charge fair market prices to support individual institutions. Even here, however, there is dispute over whether the public, currently subsidized benefits of LLR action outweigh their costs. If a full social accounting, beyond the scope of this book, were to show that the national benefits do exceed the costs, then the provision of LLR support should remain a public responsibility. That issue remains to be resolved. In the meantime, it is unlikely that LLR activities will be detached, in the foreseeable future, from the Federal Reserve's mandate.

As in any undertaking of this scope, the authors are indebted to many people. This study began as a self-initiated project at GAO, then was subordinated to congressionally requested work, and abandoned in mid-1987. The authors are grateful to the General Government Division, and Senior Associate Director Craig A. Simmons, in particular, for granting permission to carry the study to completion in their spare time during the next year. (They also thank their families for putting up with their single-minded evening and weekend preoccupation with completing the work.)

Many colleagues at the GAO contributed to the study by discussing, researching, and reading sections of the manuscript. The authors thank Anindya Bhattacharya, Larry Cluff, Drew Dahl, Benny McKee, John O'Keefe, R. G. Steinman, Elizabeth Mays, Norm Miller, Rob Sheppard, Rob Strand, James Thomson, and Kevin Yeats in these regards. They are particularly grateful to Michael Polakoff of Syracuse University who wrote the appendix on the silver crisis and Kim Staking, now a doctoral candidate at The Wharton School, for the first of several drafts of Chapter 4.

The authors benefitted from stimulating discussions with Don Kohn, Garry Gillam, Oliver Ireland and Walker Todd of the Federal Reserve and Kenneth McLean of the Senate Banking Committee.

The authors owe substantial debts to Professor Robert Aliber of the University of Chicago, Professor Edward Kane of Ohio State University, and Dr. Anna Schwartz of the National Bureau of Economic Research, three of the nation's experts on the financial safety net. Each commented extensively on a draft of the study. Many of their comments are cited and quoted with permission throughout the book.

The authors are grateful to Georgetown University's Business School for typing much of the manuscript and to Jana Datillo, Yolanda Musgrove, and Lee Alvis Samuels for typing other sections. Carolyn Casagrande and the team at Ballinger were enthusiastic, supportive, and patient throughout the production of the book.

THE FEDERAL RESERVE

1 CRISES, INSOLVENCY, AND FAILURE

Changes in the structure of the domestic and international economy during recent years have caused serious adjustment problems in the financial sector. High, variable rates of interest and inflation, deregulation and increased competition in the financial services industry, and the effects of a serious worldwide recession in the early 1980s have all placed increased pressure on financial institutions. The very visible signs of strain in the financial sector have led to three major pieces of financial legislation since the Great Depression—the Depository Institutions Deregulation and Monetary Control Act (DIDMCA) of 1980, the Garn-St Germain Depository Institutions Act (GSGDIA) of 1982, and the Competitive Equality Banking Act of 1987. Prior to the 1987 act, proposals for substantial, further financial legislation had been stalled in Congress for five years. In the meantime, parts of the federal depository institution's safety net—bank examination, supervision, regulation, and deposit insurance—have come under close scrutiny. Yet, throughout the current debate, one important facet of the safety net, the role of the lender of last resort (or, LLR), has received remarkably little attention. This text aims to redress this imbalance.

THE LENDER OF LAST RESORT (LLR)

The concept of the lender of last resort developed (mostly during the nineteenth century) as a way to protect the public and its financial

1

institutions from waves of panic which periodically occurred during episodes of financial stress. These panics, it was observed, could cause sharp decreases in the availability of money and credit, bankruptcies, and economic recessions or depressions.

Classical economists in England argued that it was the Bank of England's responsibility to prevent these calamities by providing liquidity when none was available elsewhere. And after the crisis of 1866, the Bank, then a private corporation, accepted that responsibility. In the United States, the provision of liquidity assistance to troubled financial firms remained mostly a private responsibility until the Federal Reserve (hereinafter also referred to as the Fed) was created in 1913.

During the 1930s, however, the Federal Reserve failed to protect the banking system and the economy and so caused, or at least contributed significantly to, the severity of the Great Depression.

The extent of the catastrophe that occurred during the 1930s is illustrated in Table 1-1, which shows the numbers of bank suspensions that occurred in the thirteen years before the creation of the Federal Deposit Insurance Corporation (FDIC) in 1934. At the end of 1932, just before the declaration of the infamous "bank holiday"

Table 1-1. Commercial Bank Suspensions Before the FDIC.

	Number of Banks Suspended	Deposits at Suspended Banks ($ millions)
1921	506	172.8
2	366	91.2
3	646	149.6
4	775	210.2
1925	617	166.9
6	975	260.2
7	669	199.3
8	498	142.4
9	659	230.6
1930	1,350	837.1
1	2,293	1,690.2
2	1,453	706.2
3	4,000	3,596.7

Source: Friedman and Schwartz (1963, 438, table 16).

in March 1933, there were 18,074 commercial banks in existence. They held $34 billion in deposits (Friedman and Schwartz 1963). During 1933 alone, 4,000 of these banks (22.1 percent) failed. They held $3.6 billion (10.6 percent) of the nation's deposits.

To prevent a recurrence of this calamity, the U.S. Congress created an extensive Federal financial safety net to oversee U.S. financial institutions. The safety net had, and still has, three arms—deposit insurance, a system of oversight and regulation, and a lender of last resort. Deposit insurance was much less readily (and much later) accepted by other Western economies—France in 1979, Italy in 1974, and the United Kingdom in 1982 (Dale 1982a). British financial institutions, for example, had a less disastrous set of experiences during the Great Depression than did their U.S. counterparts.

The United States has been proud of its financial system and the safety net that has guarded that system. The protective system was almost unanimously regarded as highly successful until quite recently. However, during the 1980s, it has become increasingly clear that something is seriously wrong with the incentive signals that the safety net is sending to the protected institutions.

SIGNS OF STRESS

The safety net was designed to prevent a recurrence of the large number of bank failures that occurred during the 1930s. The data in Table 1-2 show that in 1943 the number of failures among banks insured by the FDIC declined below double digits for the first time (at least) since 1921. Failures did not reach double figures again until 1975. Since 1975, however, ten or more banks have failed every year except 1977 and 1978. Since 1984, there have been more than 100 failures each year.[1]

A similar deterioration has occurred in the condition of savings and loan associations (S & Ls or "thrifts"), as the data in Table 1-3 reveal. For many years, the Federal Savings and Loan Insurance Corporation (FSLIC) was able to preserve its preferred policy of avoiding S & L closures by merging troubled associations with healthier members of the industry. The acquiring firm was often given financial and regulatory inducements to take on a weak partner. Consequently, S & L closures were almost unknown until the 1980s. As the decade progressed, the numbers of supervisory and assisted merg-

Table 1-2. Federal Deposit Insurance Corporation Bank Failures: 1934 to Present.[a]

Year	Number of FDIC-Insured Banks	Failed Banks[b] Number FDIC-Insured	Failed Banks[b] Total Assets In FDIC-Insured Banks ($ millions)	Largest Failed Insured Bank Assets ($ millions)	Largest Failed Insured Bank Bank Name
1934	Unk.[c]	9	2.7	1.4	Bank American Trust, PA
1935	14126	26	17.2	4.6	Unk.
1936	13973	69	31.9	2.0	Union Bank, OH
1937	13797	77	40.4	2.0	Perth Amboy Trust, NJ
1938	13661	74	69.5	22.6	Camden Safe Dep., NJ
1939	13538	60	181.5	48.8	Unk.
1940	13442	43	161.9	48.3	Unk.
1941	13482	15	34.8	11.0	Unk.
1942	13403	20	22.3	2.7	Unk.
1943	13458	5	14.1	4.2	Unk.
1944	13460	2	2.1	1.5	Unk.
1945	13494	1	6.4	6.4	Unk.
1946	13550	1	0.4	0.3	Unk.
1947	13597	5	6.8	1.8	1st Ntl. Bk. Evnstn, WY
1948	13612	3	10.4	7.9	Columbus Trust Co., NJ
1949	13628	5	4.9	3.2	First Ntl. Bk. Dyer, IN
1950	13640	4	4.0	1.3	Fm Fst. NtlBk. Minooka, IL
1951	12243	2	3.1	2.9	Parnassus Ntl. Bk., PA
1952	13645	3	2.4	1.0	Thomasvile Bk&Trust, AL
1953	13651	4	18.8	17.5	1st StBk., Elmwood Pk, IL
1954	13541	2	1.1	1.0	Bank Whitesville, KY
1955	13457	5	12.0	6.0	Frontier Trust Co., ME
1956	13441	2	12.9	7.7	Home Ntl. Bk., Ellenvl, NY
1957	13404	2	1.3	1.3	1st St Bk Yorktown, TX
1958	13365	4	8.9	4.5	Rushville Bank Co., OH
1959	13382	3	2.9	1.3	First State Bank, TX

1960	13451	1	7.5	7.0	Unk.
1961	13445	5	9.8	4.4	Sheldon Ntl. Bank, IA
1962	13445	1	Unk.	3.0	1st Ntl Bank, Exeter, PA
1963	13820	2	26.2	19.1	Chatham Bk., Chicago, IL
1964	13820	7	25.8	7.9	Crown Savings Bank, VA
1965	13876	5	58.8	54.1	San Francisco Natl, CA
1966	13873	7	120.6	110.1	Public Bank, MI
1967	13850	4	12.0	4.3	Bank of Pineapple, AL
1968	13822	3	25.2	13.4	Central National, FL
1969	13804	9	43.6	11.4	First State Bank, TX
1970	13840	7	62.1	21.4	Eatontown National, NJ
1971	13939	7	206.0	109.7	Birmgham Bloomfld Bk, MI
1972	14059	2	1278.9	1256.8	Bank Commonwealth, MI
1973	14298	6	1309.7	1265.9	U.S. National Bank, CA
1974	14550	4	3822.6	3655.7	Franklin National Bk, NY
1975	14714	13	420.0	147.6	American City Bank, WI
1976	14740	17	1399.3	412.1	Hamilton National Bk, TE
1977	14741	6	232.6	190.3	Banco Economias, PR
1978	14716	7	994.0	712.5	Banco Credito, PR
1979	14688	10	133.0	32.8	Fidelity Bank, MISS
1980	14758	11	6403.0	6166.8	First Pennsylvania, PA
1981	14913	10	4859.1	2491.1	Greenwich Savings Bk, NY
1982	14994	42	11632.4	3403.0	New York Bk for Sav, NY
1983	14763	48	7026.9	2500.0	Drydock Savings Bk, NY
1984	14833	80	44727.2	41450.8	Cont Illinois Ntl Bk, IL
1985	14808	120	8741.3	5278.8	Bowery Savings Bank, NY
1986	19209	145	7686.4	1616.8	First National Bk&Tr, OK
1987	14212	203	9473.0	1240.0	Syracuse Savings Bank

Source: Information for most years came from *FDIC Annual Reports*. The number of 1984, 1985, 1986, and 1987 FDIC-insured and non-FDIC-insured banks came from the FDIC Librarian.

a. Data include both commercial banks and FDIC-insured mutual savings banks.

b. Data include banks that failed and those that were given FDIC financial assistance to avoid failure.

c. Unk. = unknown.

Table 1-3.   Regulatory Resolutions for FSLIC-Insured Institutions.

	Numbers of Institutions	Numbers Closed[a]	Numbers of Assisted Mergers[b]	Numbers Required to Merge[b]	Numbers Placed in MCP[c]
1980					
1	4,005	0	11	21	0
2	3,785	1	23	56	0
3	3,349	1	46	166	0
4	3,183	9	17	13	0
5	3,136	10	22	11	25
6	3,246	21	23	4	29 (17)[d]
7[e]	3,220	4	3	0	3

Sources: Federal Home Loan Bank Board (1982); FSLIC Public Information Department, GAO (1987d), Cargill and Garcia (1985).

a. Between 1960 and 1980 only six S & Ls were closed, one in each 1985 and 1971, and two each in 1966 and 1968.

b. Sometimes more than two S & Ls were combined in a merger. For example, in 1981, 1982 and 1983, twenty-seven, sixty-five, and forty-six troubled S & Ls, respectively, were merged with assistance.

c. Numbers of institutions placed into the Management Consignment Program (MCP).

d. Seventeen S & Ls originally classed as MCPs were reclassified out of the program at the end of 1986.

e. At the end of the first quarter 1987.

ers increased to peak at 166 and 46, respectively, in 1982. Closures continued to rise through 1986, when they reached twenty-one in total.

After 1982, the Federal Home Loan Bank Board (FHLBB) had increasing difficulty finding merger partners for troubled S & Ls, and was forced to place some in its Management Consignment Program (MCP) to contain their losses while a resolution was sought for the problem of allowing troubled S & Ls to continue in business.

Table 1-4 shows that the numbers of banks and thrifts that continued to operate in a weak or insolvent condition rose each year from 1975 through 1986, despite the increase in the number of closures and the improving health of the economy in the midyears of that period. At the end of 1986, there were 1,457 banks on the FDIC's problem bank list and 460 insolvent but still operating S & Ls. These S & Ls were insolvent under generally accepted accounting principles (GAAP).

Table 1-4. Number of Problem Institutions: 1975–87.

Year End	Commercial Banks on the FDIC's Problem Bank List	S & Ls Operating	
		Although GAAP-Insolvent[a]	RAP-Insolvent[b]
1975	349	U[c]	U[c]
6	379	U[c]	U[c]
7	368	14	14
8	342	10	13
9	287	15	16
1980	217	16	17
1	223	53	36
2	369	222	80
3	642	281	52
4	848	434	71
1985	1140	449	122
6	1457	460	252

Sources: Data for commercial banks from 1973 through 1983 were obtained from the *FDIC's Annual Reports*. The FDIC Librarian supplied figures for 1984, 1985 and 1986. Data for S & Ls were derived by the authors from FSLIC reports of condition.

a. S & Ls that had zero or negative net worth according to generally accepted accounting principles at the end of the year.

b. S & Ls that were operating although insolvent under regulatory accounting principles.

c. U = Number unknown.

THE CAUSES OF THE PROBLEMS

A coincidence of three factors appears to have led to the present unhappy situation. First, financial institutions have been observed to get into difficulties during periods of tight money that follow several years of inflation. (The reasons this happens are explored in the following chapter.) However, even in difficult times, many or most financial institutions are able to survive unaided. When large numbers of the institutions get into serious difficulties, it is natural to ask (1) whether they had been encouraged to take risks that contributed to their difficulties, and (2) why the system of examination, supervision, and regulation had allowed them to indulge in risky activities and/or fraud and mismanagement.

These questions have already been asked. However, those seeking answers have focused particularly on the present misalignment of the deposit insurance guarantees (Kane 1986) and the problems of the deposit insurance system in the context of a flawed safety net, including the LLR and an inadequate supervisory and oversight system (Benston et al. 1986). Nevertheless, to date, relatively little has been written about the role of the lender of last resort and its contributions to causing and resolving the current concerns.

Consequently, this text focuses on the lender of last resort in the context of the federal financial safety net. Chapters 2 through 5 examine, in turn, evolution of the LLR, current applicable laws and regulatory procedures, the rapidly changing financial environment in which it operates, and criteria for assessing LLR performance.[2]

ESTABLISHING THE CRITERIA

An iterative approach was adopted in choosing the criteria to judge current LLR performance (in isolation or as an integral part of a federal depository institution guarantee) that are presented in Chapter 5. First, the classical and contemporary writings on the subject were studied. Second, various domestic and international case studies were developed to show how, when, and where lender-of-last-resort assistance has been provided (or not provided).

From this experience, an initial set of criteria was developed for assessing LLR performance in the United States. These criteria fall into two broad groups of effectiveness and equity, and were then discussed with knowledgeable academics, U.S. Congressional staff, and Federal Reserve officials. The criteria were then revised and are presented in Chapter 5. In Chapter 6, the criteria are applied as yardsticks against which Federal Reserve performance in handling U.S. crises can be described and assessed. Chapter 7 discusses the problems that have been discerned in current Federal Reserve policies and procedures; this chapter also contains comments on the Federal Home Loan Bank System's performance as a LLR in the S & L liquidity crisis of 1985–87, which is described at the end of Appendix C. Conclusions for the entire study and recommendations for the future are presented in Chapter 8.

THEMES AND DEFINITIONS

Some themes and phrases recur repeatedly during this text, so some preliminary definitions and ground rules will be established in the remainder of this chapter about the terminology utilized throughout the study.

The Lender of Last Resort

In times of financial stress when, for example, monetary policy is tight and/or the economy is in recession, businesses and individuals often curtail their expenditures and draw on their liquid financial resources. They may also seek loans, often from their bank. At such times, the banks may also be under similar pressures. Torn between curtailing their activities and meeting their customers' demands, they may turn to their banker—the lender of last resort—for accommodation. This is the origin of the phrase that dominates this text.

It is worth noting that because of their role in providing liquidity to the rest of the economy, commercial banks are sometimes called the "lenders of *next* to last resort."

Crisis

The LLR's responsibilities are to prevent, or cope with and contain, financial crises. There is no general agreement on what constitutes a crisis. The lay person's reaction is that like illness, those affected by a financial crisis recognize it when it happens. Nevertheless, as Andrew Carron (1982) points out, there are at least three extant definitions of the term "financial crisis."

For Hyman Minsky (1977), a crisis is serious situation in which the public is unable to raise cash by the usual means and so is forced to liquidate assets. This liquidation causes a sharp drop in asset prices and a breakdown of the financial system, which in turn leads inevitably to a depression. Carron comments that this phenomenon almost never occurs although it did occur several times in the last century and also in the 1930s. Moreover, the phenomenon is characteristic of the financial debacle in the energy and agricultural regions of the troubled states in the United States in the mid-1980s. Here, the experience to date differs from that of the 1920s and 1930s, mainly in that the depression has been confined to the directly affected regions and industries. At this time of this writing (September 1987), this depression has not spread to the rest of the U.S. economy although asset prices have plummeted and there have been many failures of financial institutions, businesses, and persons in the affected areas.

For Alan Sinai (1976), a financial crisis is a milder misfortune. It is a cyclical, "credit crunch" that occurs at the end of a period of economic expansion, when monetary policy becomes restrictive, interest rates rise, credit rationing may occur, businesses and consumers curtail their expenditures, and a recession ensues. The recession reduces the demands for money and credit, interest rates fall, and recovery follows.

Carron defines a financial crisis of intermediate severity between the Minsky and Sinai extremes. In normal times, borrowers pay interest rate premiums according to their economic circumstances. During a Carron-defined financial crisis, however, borrowers may be forced to pay an additional premium—one related to the adverse financial environment and unrelated to the borrowers' circumstances. Interest rates may become very high, and where there are legal caps on interest rates, some borrowers may be suddenly rationed out of the credit markets. The unusually high borrowing costs can precipitate liquidity and solvency problems and an unnecessarily severe recession.

Insolvency

Analytical confusion can be caused by the word insolvency, which can be interpreted in different ways. For an economist, insolvency occurs when the market value of the firm's net worth falls to zero. Net worth, for the economist, measures the difference between the market values of assets and liabilities. Asset values include both on-balance sheet and off-balance sheet items, including any goodwill arising from the value of the firm's charter, and the value of any government guarantees which should be recorded as a separate item.[3]

The market value of liabilities should include both "bookable" and off-balance sheet, contingent claims.

For the accountant, insolvency occurs when the book value of liabilities exceeds that of assets. Book values are often, but not always, historical cost-of-acquisition values. For reasons explained in Chapter 2, accounting insolvency for depository institutions often occurs at a later point than economic insolvency. Consequently, if a troubled firm is not closed until it is insolvent vis-à-vis book value, there will often not be enough money obtained by selling the firm's assets to meet all the creditors' claims. Losses are then passed on, upon liquidation, and the solvency of other firms or individuals may be threatened.

For a lawyer, failure means formally declared bankruptcy. Bankruptcy proceedings are typically started by creditors unable to obtain repayment of their principal and interest who are attempting to establish a claim to the firm's assets, or by the firm seeking protection from its creditors' claims. Bankruptcy is usually acknowledged when a firm cannot obtain funds (net income from its operations, new borrowed funds from creditors, or additional equity from its owners) to continue to pay its bills. The firm is "cash insolvent."

Cash insolvency may occur well after economic and book-value insolvency for an insured depository institution. A large proportion of a bank's or thrift's costs of doing business is interest expense on deposits and borrowed money. Interest on deposits typically does not have to be paid out in cash since interest is usually credited to the depositors' accounts. The depositor does not withdraw the funds unless it needs the funds or fears for their safety. It is therefore possible for a depository institution, with a credible guarantee, to continue in business well after it is book-value insolvent. In December 1986, 460 S & Ls—14.3 percent of the thrifts in the industry—were GAAP-insolvent. Putting heavily insolvent thrifts into liquidation can eventually leave the insurer with a large bill payable to insured depositors and secured creditors.

Regulators are well aware that insurance can hold off the run that in pre-insurance days was likely to force a bank into receivership. If they wish, regulators can allow book-value and market-value insolvent firms to continue to operate. At the same time, if desired, to obscure the institution's condition from the public, regulators can measure net worth on more lenient, regulatory accounting principles

(RAP). In the S & L industry in the 1980s, RAP net worth included deferred losses, goodwill, and FSLIC promissory notes as well as the more usually accepted equity components.

Failure

For most people, "failure" is "insolvency." But the previous section reveals that failure, like beauty, is in the eye of the beholder–economist, accountant, lawyer, or regulator.

A regulator, especially an S & L regulator, has been unlikely in recent years to declare a thrift to have failed until it is insolvent under RAP. Moreover, as Table 1–4 reveals, even RAP-insolvent thrifts have been allowed to continue operating in the 1980s.[4] Thus, failure is a regulatory decision. In this text usage of the term failure is confined to the formal, chartering agency's declaration of a financial firm's insolvency and the appointment of a receiver (who liquidates the institution to pay its depositors and creditors) or a conservator (who preserves the ongoing value of the firm's assets for its creditors and shareholders).

COSTS AND BENEFITS OF FAILURE AND RESCUE

The classical and post–Depression writers tended to stress the costs and calamities that financial failures, particularly of banks, impose on depositors, borrowers, and their contacts. The post–Depression lessons were well learned by Congress, the regulators, and the public. Failure prevention and rescue were seen to carry benefits that always exceeded their social costs.

Today, however, the pendulum has swung the other way. Many economists now emphasize the costs of rescue more than the benefits. In a situation where financial institution owners and managers know that the authorities fear failure above all else and will go to considerable lengths to prevent and conceal it, and finally bail out, other institutions may become anti-socially risk-prone.

Some authors (Benston et al. 1986; Kane 1986a; Kaufman 1987) stress the cathartic, market-disciplining benefits of allowing failures to happen. For them, the costs of failure have been exaggerated and the costs of rescue underestimated.

PUBLIC OR PRIVATE RESPONSIBILITY?

Yet, others (Schwartz 1987b, c; Goodfriend and King 1987; Ely 1985; England 1985) point out that the financial safety net does not have to be a public responsibility. In the past, deposit insurance, examination, supervision, regulation, and lender of last resort facilities have all been provided, at one time or another by private agents. Sometimes, these authors claim, the privately provided facilities have functioned better than the present publicly provided ones. But on other occasions, private facilities have proved to be inadequate, as in Ohio and Maryland in 1985.[5]

NOTES

1. The FDIC predicts 200 failures, approximately, for 1987.
2. Changes in the financial system—domestic and international—are described in greater detail in Appendix A.
3. Firms that have zero accounting worth sometimes have positive stock prices because federal guarantees (implicit or explicit) hold bankruptcy at bay and give a chance for recovery and future profitability.
4. Interesting work is being done to discover what makes a regulator close a particular one of many troubled S & Ls (Barth et al. 1987).
5. The crises in these two states are described in Garcia (1987a).

2 THE ORIGINS OF THE LENDER OF LAST RESORT

As indicated in Chapter 1, the lender of last resort is responsible for ensuring the smooth functioning of the economy by maintaining liquidity in the financial sector. Historically, liquidity assistance has been provided directly or indirectly to those institutions which, while solvent, were temporarily unable to tap alternative sources of funding. Lender-of-last-resort assistance has not been intended to subsidize failed firms. Nevertheless, as case studies in the Appendices show, today assistance is granted to institutions that are insolvent although they have not been formally declared to have failed.

LLR assistance in the United States evolved historically when private institutions realized that it is often in their self-interest to aid a stricken competitor to prevent its demise from having repercussions on their own viability. Later it was judged that the "externalities" (effects on others) caused by bank failures made bank runs a public, not private, responsibility. Today, because of its control over money creation, the role of lender of last resort is normally undertaken by the central bank and is a complement to its control over monetary policy. Due to the structure of the U.S. financial system and the close relationship between the Federal Reserve and the banking system, lender-of-last-resort liquidity was provided mainly to banks until recently. However, since 1980, LLR assistance has been available to all depository institutions.

This chapter will first show why banks may need liquidity assistance. It will then examine the classic lender of last resort concept as it developed in England in the nineteenth century. Finally, it will describe how the LLR concept was applied in the United States until the Great Depression. The following chapter describes the ways in which the Federal Reserve has executed its liquidity assistance role in the United States since the Depression.

THE NEED FOR A LENDER OF LAST RESORT

Several academic writers have discussed the role of the lender of last resort in a financial crisis.[1] Historically, crises have occurred during periods of monetary contraction. At such times interest rates rise and the values of interest-sensitive assets fall. Investors (depositors) may perceive that the increase in returns on certain assets is accompanied by a more than commensurate increase in financial risk. The source of increased risk can be external to the financial institution (for example, real or expected defaults by some of the institution's customers), or internal (for example, concerns regarding fraud or mismanagement). The liquidity of assets maintained at troubled institutions may become impaired.

In response to changes in risk perceptions, investors may rationally attempt to convert their ready assets into even more liquid forms and to shift their deposits (especially those at questionably solvent banks) into higher quality, likely-to-remain liquid assets such as U.S. government obligations, cash, or precious metals. In rational financial markets, it is both normal and desirable for investors to shift their funds to those institutions that offer the highest return for a given amount of risk. However, when investors suddenly and simultaneously attempt to shift funds away from a number of financial institutions, a crisis may develop.

Because of the nature of their assets and liabilities, banks and other depository institutions have been particularly prone to these problems. If a bank or some other important segment of the financial sector is unable to attract new funds to replace outflows and is forced to sell assets, its liquidity crisis can evolve fairly quickly into insolvency; especially as banks and thrifts typically have lower capital-to-asset ratios than do commercial and industrial firms. Insolvency is hastened if the bank can sell its assets only at "fire sale" prices.[2] The illiquidity and insolvency of the crisis-initiating financial institution can put similar pressures on other financial firms. Then the initial crisis can spread. One of the fundamental roles of the lender of last resort is to contain the effects of runs on financial institutions which were solvent before the crisis began.

Diff bet. illiquidity of bank vs. uun into non-bank assets!

DEPOSITORY INSTITUTIONS AND RUNS

The nature of a depository institution's liabilities makes it especially susceptible to runs by depositors. Transactions accounts (legally) and most saving accounts (*de facto*) can immediately be withdrawn at par (that is, at their face value), without notice and without substantial penalty. When a depositor fears for the continued viability of its bank, the major cost in protecting itself from loss is the time spent and inconvenience of withdrawing funds from the troubled bank and relocating them to a sound institution. While the cost of protecting the investment is low, the penalties for delaying action are potentially very high. Those who withdraw their funds quickly from a potentially insolvent institution are paid in full, while those who delay may never be fully reimbursed or may experience considerable delay and inconvenience before recovering their funds.

Both depositors and managers at a troubled depository institution are aware of the "first come, best served" reality which can lead to a run at a suspect bank.[3] Federal deposit insurance offered by the FDIC and FSLIC has been instrumental and until recently, very successful, in reducing uncertainty and eliminating runs by small insured depositors. However, the run experienced by Continental Illinois National Bank was electronic. Kane (1987b) calls such runs "teleportations." Today these runs may develop among large, professionally managed institutional investors (the uninsured depositors). Electronic runs can be just as, if not more, formidable as were (and still are) the lines of individual depositors waiting outside a bank to withdraw their funds.

A run occurs when many depositors attempt to withdraw their funds from an institution simultaneously. The nature of their assets makes it difficult for depository institutions to survive a run without assistance. In a fractional-reserve banking system, depository institutions back only a small proportion of their total obligations with cash or reserves.[4] These immediately available assets are the first line of defense against a run. However, today most cash and reserves are already pledged to meet reserve requirements and therefore, must be replaced even during a run. There is only a limited capacity to meet unexpected depositor requests. Once cash reserves are depleted, if depository institutions cannot raise additional new deposits or acquire purchased funds, they will be forced to sell other assets, ultimately even illiquid assets, to meet cash demands.

In the absence of lender-of-last-resort assistance, financial institutions undergoing extensive withdrawals will typically next sell their more liquid non-cash assets, those traded in active secondary markets. However, only a small proportion of depository institution assets are actively traded or easily securitized.[5] Loans to consumers and to businesses are normally illiquid and long-term in nature. Moreover, these loans are of particular value to the originating institution because it has specific knowledge, not readily available to others, concerning the creditworthiness of its customers. Such loans are not readily saleable at face value and can be disposed of quickly only at a discount. If asset sales continue, the necessary discount may grow and the realized value may be substantially below long-term equilibrium economic value. Without liquidity support the crisis will, of necessity, deepen. Moreover, if several banks in any area are simultaneously seeking to sell illiquid assets, there may be very few buyers. Values may become doubly depressed. The institution may become "fire sale" insolvent.

CONTAGION

Runs and bank failures are particularly feared because they can be contagious. Contagion can occur in four ways. First, the circumstances judged to have caused the failure at one depository institution may be applicable to its colleagues and competitors. Their viability may then be questioned and runs may occur against them.

Second, the firm that failed may also bring down its depositors and creditors. If these entities then default on loans from other financial firms, the insolvencies may spread within both the real and financial sectors of the economy. Moreover, some of these depositors and creditors may themselves be depository institutions. If their losses due to the initial insolvency are sufficiently severe, these depository institutions also may be brought down.

The U.S. system, with its large number of small institutions, appears to be particularly exposed to contagion in this second instance. Many banks are too small to be able to efficiently provide all the internal services they need and typically buy these services from other large (correspondent) banks. Some larger banks may specialize in the provisions of check clearing, settlement, loan origination, and other services for small banks. The correspondents could charge fees for the services provided; but instead they often require their customers (respondent) banks to maintain non-interest bearing demand deposits (called compensating balances) with their correspondent. These balances may well be larger than would be required solely to facilitate settlement.

Consequently, if the correspondent bank fails it can bring down a chain of its respondent banks. (This was one of the reasons the regulators gave in testimony for rescuing Continental Illinois National Bank. See Conover 1984, Volcker 1984.)

Tiering is the third source of intrabank contagion. The public makes deposits at institutions that appear safe. If these institutions cannot use the funds to make loans directly, they may pass the funds on to other institutions to make loans. Alternatively, the deposit-receiving bank may participate in a loan initiated by another, riskier bank. In either of these cases, the bank trusted by depositors becomes at least somewhat dependent on the professional conduct of the bank using the funds or initiating the syndicated loan.

Aliber (1985) has pointed out that internationally there is a tiering of banks, with funds passing from the safest banks (who receive the public's deposits) to the riskiest banks which make loans, for example, to Third World countries. If one of these risky, loan-generating banks fails, it can bring to failure those banks supplying it with funds or sharing in its loan participations. The 1982 failure of Penn Square National Bank in the United States, for example, was contagious and had adverse repercussions on Continental Illinois, Seattle First, Michigan National Banks, and other depository institutions.

The fourth source of contagion comes from decreases in the money supply which can occur as a result of liquidity squeezes and bank runs. If a depositor withdraws its funds as cash, it reduces the quantity of bank reserves. Fearing runs when the financial system is under stress, depository institutions may choose to hold additional reserves. Both of these influences reduce the amount of bank reserves available for lending and creating money. The stocks of money and credit can then fall and the economy will go into recession or depression. Not accommodating these demands was a major failing of the Federal Reserve during the Great Depression. The Fed did not accommodate either the public's increased demand for cash or the banks' additional demands for excess reserves (that is, reserves held above minimum, required levels).

George Kaufman (1987) has pointed out that runs to cash are almost unheard of today. Deposit insurance has reduced small depositors' needs to run. And when a small depositor becomes concerned enough about the status of its bank to move its funds, that depositor typically relocates them to another institution. Moreover, large depositors, while uninsured, cannot run to cash, which is not a practical medium of exchange for large, non-criminal, transactions today. So depositors who "run" merely relocate their funds somewhere else. Even if they run to quality—by buying a Treasury security—their deposit gets transferred to a new owner, possibly at another bank. So, bank runs today have far fewer consequences for the money supply than they did in the days before deposit insurance.

Nevertheless, runs do cause liquidity problems for those institutions experiencing deposit withdrawals. Consequently, contagion remains a problem for depository institutions, but in the United States today, the difficulties arise primarily from the first three causes discussed above—similarity in circumstances, correspondent relationships, and tiering.

PERIODS OF MONETARY CONTRACTION

Because many bank liabilities can be withdrawn at par, while the market values of both liquid and illiquid assets vary from one period to another as interest rates change, banks are particularly vulnerable to runs which tend to occur during or following periods of monetary contraction. During such times, the values of bank assets are depressed relative to those of bank liabilities. With its net worth at a lower market value, the institution is less able to survive a run unaided.

This observation is reinforced by the fact that bank income is also likely to be low during periods of monetary contraction when interest rates are high, or in the ensuing periods of recession when some assets are in default. The rates of return earned on bank assets are often less responsive to changes in market interest rates than are the rates paid on liabilities. This is the typical "mismatch" problem at S & Ls, which historically have funded fixed rate mortgages with more variable rate liabilities. In this situation, during monetary contraction/high interest rate periods, banks' profit levels are reduced. Bank income may also be low in a recession, when default rates rise as a result of strains in the real sector. These reductions in income make depository institutions more vulnerable to a run.

The central bank has advantages over other institutions, public or private, in the provision of lender-of-last-resort assistance. It has, for example, the power to create money and is often in a good position to strike a balance between public and private interests in the provision of aid. Some economists (Schwartz 1987b, c; Goodfriend and King 1987) question whether LLR facilities would be better provided by a private rather than a public body, however. This issue is discussed further in Chapter 8.

THE BRITISH ORIGINS OF THE LLR CONCEPT

The need for LLR assistance was recognized early in Great Britain. Consequently, the modern U.S. lender of last resort has its roots in the classic concept developed during the nineteenth century in England. Henry Thorton first defined the lender of last resort in *An Enquiry into the Nature and Effects of the Paper of Great Britain* in 1802. Sixty-five years later, Walter Bagehot expanded and refined the concept in his book *Lombard Street*, in which he clearly outlined the Bank of England's lender of last resort function. Bagehot's *Lombard Street* has come to be generally accepted as the definitive classic work on the subject (Brimmer 1984; Humphrey 1975; Barth and Keheler 1984).

The classic concept was developed in response to a series of British financial panics in 1825, 1847, 1857, and 1866. Bagehot believed that each of these financial panics was more severe than necessary because the Bank of England did not immediately provide sufficient liquidity, in the form of "advances," to the financial sector and therefore, was unable to restore public confidence in the financial system. Bagehot described the situation as follows:

> and though the Bank of England certainly does make great advances in time of panic . . . it naturally does it hesitantly, reluctantly and with misgivings. In 1847, even in 1866, there was an instant when it was believed that the Bank

would not advance (funds) or at least hesitated. To lend a great deal, and yet not to give the public confidence that you will lend sufficiently and effectively, is the worst of all policies, but it is the policy now pursued.
(Bagehot 1921, 63)

In response to the apparent ineffectiveness of the Bank of England in containing the spread of these four financial panics, Bagehot outlined the actions that the Bank of England should follow during a crisis. He advised that in general, lender-of-last-resort actions should be designed to prevent the proliferation of a localized panic into a widespread crisis in the financial sector, which could lead to a sharp reduction in the money supply and thereby trigger a depression in the real sector. By immediately supplying sufficient funds to the financial sector, Bagehot maintained that the lender of last resort would be able to contain a financial crisis and, more importantly, restore public confidence in the viability of the financial system. Thorton and Bagehot agreed that the central bank's lender-of-last-resort function should not interfere with long-term monetary policy objectives.

The following section will review the classic lender of last resort concept, and examine nine major prescriptions for classic lender-of-last-resort assistance. The last section will examine the evolutions of the LLR in the United States up to the time of the Great Depression.

CLASSIC ADMONITIONS

The classic lender-of-last-resort concept emphasized the need for stability of the whole financial system. This macroeconomic emphasis conferred on the central bank (as sole issuer of legal tender) the responsibility for controlling the spread of financial panics. In his 1975 article "The Classical Concept of the Lender of Last Resort," Thomas Humphrey outlines nine major components of the classic lender of last resort doctrine. These classic components are reviewed in the remainder of this section. Differences between the two classic writers, Thorton and Bagehot, in their conceptions of the role of the lender of last resort will be noted. It is Bagehot's fully defined classic lender-of-last-resort concept which is accepted in academic literature (Brimmer 1984; Humphrey 1975; Barth and Keheler 1984; Meltzer 1986) and is employed as such in this study.

Liquidity Assistance Should Not Conflict
With Monetary Policy

Thorton believed that the primary responsibility of the central bank was to regulate the money stock so that the economy would grow steadily and in line with long-term policy goals. When the lender of last resort provides liquidity assistance to banks, the possibility exists that it will lead to an unintended increase in the money supply. Thorton and Bagehot believed that the lender-of-last-resort function is vital, but that it should be managed so as to interfere as little as possible with the steady growth of money supply thereby not upsetting the attainment of longer term policy objectives.

Assistance Should Be Speedy and Short-Term

Thorton and Bagehot believed that the central bank should take actions which respond quickly to a liquidity crisis, thereby averting a panic. Bagehot considered that the Bank of England acted appropriately in 1866 when the House of Overend failed and caused a crisis. He quotes the Governor of the Bank "and before the Chancellor of the Exchequer was perhaps out of his bed we had advanced one half of our reserves." (Bagehot 1873, 81) Later, Bagehot commented "Theory suggests, and experience proves, that in a panic the holders of the ultimate Bank [of England] reserve should lend to all that bring good securities quickly, freely, and readily." (Bagehot 1873, 85).

At the same time, the assistance should be only temporary, to insure that deviations in the level of the money supply from monetary policy goals remain small and inconsequential.

Responsibility to the Whole Financial System

Bagehot believed that the central bank bears the responsibility for guaranteeing the liquidity of the entire economy. Classic lender-of-last-resort actions should counteract general financial emergencies, not bail-out individual bank failures. The systemwide orientation of lender-of-last-resort assistance was designed to minimize the possibility of excess risk-taking by individual banks. Bagehot (1921, 97) cautioned that the lender of last resort "should never lend to unsound people." He feared that if the lender of last resort were to lend to unsound individual institutions in order to prevent the escalation of a crisis, excessive risk taking would be encouraged. For many commentators, both classic and contemporary, the concern regarding the elimination of this tendency, referred to as moral hazard, is a recurring theme.

Prevent Systemwide Financial Shocks, Neutralize the Effects of Individual Failures

In keeping with the macroeconomic orientation and the desire to avoid moral hazard, Bagehot and Thorton agreed that the lender-of-last-resort actions should prevent panics and a series of systemwide failures: "In wild periods of alarm, one failure makes many, and the best way to prevent the derivative failures is to arrest the primary failure which causes them." (Bagehot 1873, 25)

The lender of last resort should not engineer a bailout of a mismanaged institution after economic failure has occurred. Moreover, the concealment of a bank failure runs counter to the spirit of the classic LLR concept. Concealment or rescue could result in an increase in risky activities at the troubled firm and other institutions. "Arresting the primary failure," without bailing out the original owners or managers, was accomplished by quickly selling the failing firm to new owners who were required to recapitalize it. (This procedure contributed to the highly concentrated nature of British banking.)

Forestalling contagion was also helped by providing the entire market with sufficient liquidity to "weather the storm" caused by the primary failure at one or several unsound institutions.

Lend Freely During a Crisis

Bagehot maintained that once a financial crisis occurs, the lender of last resort must be ready to immediately supply the market with sufficient liquidity to minimize the spread of the panic. He believed that the temporary provision of large amounts of funds to any needy, sound borrower was essential to maintaining public confidence in the financial system. Bagehot described appropriate lender-of-last-resort action as follows: "What is wanted and what is necessary to stop a panic is to diffuse the impression that . . . money is to be had. If people could be convinced that utter ruin is not coming, most likely they would cease to run in such a mad way for money." (Bagehot 1921, 64)

Assist Any and All Sound Borrowers

For the lender of last resort to effectively contain a panic and protect the entire financial system, it must be ready to advance funds to *any* sound borrower. Bagehot maintained that there should be no distinctions made about the type of business of a troubled institution during a crisis (Humphrey 1975, 7). The only consideration should be whether the potential borrower has sufficient collateral to support a lender-of-last-resort loan. Meltzer (1986) quotes Bagehot in stating that the objective "is to stay alarm, and nothing therefore should be done to cause alarm. The way to cause alarm is to *refuse some one who has good security to offer.*" (Bagehot 1873, 97), (*emphasis added*) Bagehot also favored the Governor of the Bank of England's proposal: "The Bank agrees, in fact, if not in name, to make unlimited advances on proper security to anyone who applies for it—to the mercantile community, or to the bankers." (Bagehot 1873, 83)

The primary emphasis here is to lend to anyone with acceptable collateral. Public confidence and the lender of last resort's effectiveness would be seriously undermined if some specific institutions were singled out for support while others were arbitrarily refused it. The admonition to lend only to sound borrowers appears to be a secondary one, put there to remind the central bank not to promote moral hazard.

Acceptable Collateral

According to Bagehot, every kind of security or paper on which money is normally lent by the markets should be deemed acceptable collateral for lender-of-last-resort loans. That is, the central bank should not be constrained by precedent by what collateral it has accepted in the past. Humphrey (1975, 4) states that "the basic criterion was that the paper be indisputably good in ordinary or normal times." By accepting customary assets, at pre-crisis values, as collateral for lender-of-last-resort support, a borrower would not be penalized for the depression of illiquid asset's market prices during a crisis (Barth and Keheler 1984). Bagehot expressed his view that "The only safe plan for the Bank is the brave plan, to lend in a panic on every kind of current security, on every sort on which money is ordinarily and usually lent." (Bagehot 1873, 97) Bagehot praised the Bank of England's actions in the 1866 crisis, which are characterized as follows: "we lent money by every possible means, and in modes which we had never adopted before,—by every possible means, consistent with the safety of the Bank." (Bagehot 1873, 99) Nevertheless, only sound assets should be discounted, "That in a panic the bank, or banks—should refuse bad bills or bad securities will not make the panic really worse; the unsound people are a feeble minority. . . ." (Bagehot 1873, 97) Unfortunately, as discussed in Chapters 1, 6, and 7 and in the Appendices, today unsound institutions have become widespread.

Assistance Should Be Given at Penalty Rates

While Bagehot urged the Bank of England to lend freely during a crisis, he cautioned that such loans should carry a penalty rate. His reason was threefold. First, by charging a penalty above market rates, the lender-of-last-resort loan would be sought only as a last resort. This charge would preserve lender-of-last-resort assistance for crisis, not regular, use. Additionally, a penalty rate would further discourage undue risk taking and encourage banks to develop better techniques of money and risk management. Third, since the Bank of England was privately owned at that time, the imposition of above market rates would help encourage it to lend freely during a crisis.

By lending freely and accepting collateral at pre-crisis value, the lender of last resort would be taking on a risk—the risk that the problem institution would default despite assistance, and that the value of the collateral would prove insufficient to compensate the central bank for the liquidity assistance provided. At that time, the Bank of England was a private corporation, so it needed to be encouraged to undertake that risk. Charging above market interest rates would compensate the Bank of England for the risk it undertook. If properly set, the rate would compensate the Bank for the potential losses inherent in accepting collateral at its higher pre-crisis, economic value.

Assure the Markets in Advance

Bagehot argued that in order for the lender of last resort to maintain the public's confidence in the financial sector, the central bank should not only lend freely during a crisis but should also state its principles in advance and adhere to them. Humphrey and Meltzer elaborate on this point, to argue that the lack of a well-publicized lender-of-last-resort policy could result in a loss of confidence during a crisis since the public would be unaware of what steps the critical bank would take to minimize the crisis. In Bagehot's words:

> the Bank has never laid down any clear and sound policy on the subject. . . . The public is never sure what policy will be adopted at the most important moment: it is not sure what amount of advance will be made, or on what security it will be made. . . . And until we have on this point a clear understanding with the Bank of England, both our liability for crises and our terror at crises will always be greater than they would otherwise be. (Bagehot 1873, 101)

Bagehot believed that deviations from market assurances could irrevocably damage the public's confidence in the willingness and ability of the central bank to react during a crisis. Any deviation would increase uncertainty, whereas the lender of last resort's objective should be to reduce that uncertainty. To counteract any potential increase in moral hazard inherent in prestated policy assurances, under the classic concept, the prestated assurance of lender-of-last-resort support would stipulate that aid would *not* be available to prevent individual failures or be given to insolvent institutions, and would be available only at a penalty rate.

Summary of the Classic LLR Concept

As evidenced by this review, the classic lender-of-last-resort concept is geared to maintaining public confidence in the financial sector, avoiding systemwide crises, and preventing the spread of a localized financial crisis to the entire financial system. Bagehot's prescription for the provision of lender-of-last-resort support was designed to (1) afford the greatest support to the entire financial market, while (2) avoiding the problems of moral hazard resulting from aiding individual, insolvent institutions.

The classic lender-of-last-resort concept was intended to facilitate economic activity in nineteenth century Britain. However, the United States is very different from Britain. Consequently, the lender-of-last-resort role evolved differently in the United States.

THE AMERICAN LENDER OF LAST RESORT CONCEPT

The American LLR concept evolved haphazardly, in reaction to changes in the financial environment, sporadic shocks which threatened the stability of the financial system, and more recently to efforts of the federal government to provide a supporting safety net. The evolution began as the nation first experimented with central banking in the late 1700s, when advocates of an extensive system of large, nationally-supervised banks competed with those who preferred local control and a minimum of constraints. The concept continued to evolve with the establishment of the Federal Reserve system in 1913 and was significantly influenced by extensive regulatory and other changes instituted after the Great Depression.

While the Federal Reserve has emerged as the ultimate guarantor of financial security, private institutions have provided varying degrees of LLR assistance throughout U.S. history. Principal among these institutions are the early quasicentral banks and the bank clearinghouse associations, which were prominent in the late 1800s. During the Depression the Reconstruction Finance Corporation (RFC) and the Home Owners' Loan Corporation (HOLC), both formed by the U.S. Congress, assisted financial institutions, businesses, and homeowners separately from the Federal Reserve. The functions and operating dates of organizations undertaking LLR actions are shown in Table 2–1.

Early Central Banking

Shortly after the U.S. Constitution was signed in 1787, a charter for the First Bank of the United States was granted for twenty years.

This bank, funded by the capital provided by both the federal government and private sources, was created to spur capital investment and economic growth in an environment short of loanable funds. The First Bank and its branches actively participated in the purchase and sale of gold and silver bullion, dealt in bills of exchange, acted as a fiscal agent for the federal government, as does the modern Federal Reserve, and it also operated as a privately owned enterprise that competed directly with other commercial banks.

The First Bank also performed significant central banking and LLR functions. It was, for instance, able to influence the money supply by expanding or contracting the amount of the state bank notes held among its assets. These notes, issued by the growing number of state-chartered banks, were left at the First Bank as reserves to facilitate settlement. They could be presented by state banks to the First Bank for redemption in gold or silver specie. The First Bank also provided liquidity to state banks by making specie loans during economic crises.

Despite its achievements, the First Bank generated considerable political opposition from various groups which favored a more liberal expansion of credit, or feared creation of an overly powerful financial institutions. The First Bank's charter was allowed to expire in 1811.

The federal government chartered the Second Bank of the United States in 1816 to cope with debts resulting from the War of 1812 and to resolve a banking panic brought on by volatile economic conditions associated with the war and its financing. The Second Bank was similar to its predecessor, having many of the same powers and an identical twenty-year charter. It grew more powerful in the execution of its responsibilities, however, and by 1830 had become "a central bank, controlling the quantity of money in the economy and rendering services to the Federal government as well as to commercial banks. At times it also acted as a lender of last resort to commercial banks." (Robertson 1968, 19).

Like the First Bank, the Second Bank was also politically controversial. Andrew Jackson vetoed a bill to recharter it following his election to the presidency in 1832. Consequently, the Second Bank ceased to exist when its federal charter expired in 1836.

Table 2-1. Central Bank and LLR Functions in the United States: 1791–1987.

Time Period	Institution	Central Bank Functions	LLR Functions
1791–1811 and 1816–1836	First Bank of the United States Second Bank of the United States	• Limited influence (with Treasury) over money supply. • Some fiscal-agent-for-the-federal government actions. • Dealt in gold and silver. • Discounted bills of exchange. • Issued bank notes always convertible into specie. • Settlement and clearing.	• Not understood. • But could make specie loans to banks in times of stress and discount bills.
1853–1907	Clearinghouses	• Settlement and clearing. • Clearinghouse certificates. • Clearinghouse Loan Certificates. • Supervised banks' daily condition reports. • Set reserve requirements.	• Provided some (but inadequate) liquidity assistance to members. • Suspended convertibility.
1913–1933	Federal Reserve System	• Det. quantity of money subject to the gold standard. • Issued currency. • Ended seasonal cash shortages. • Influenced currency-deposit composition of money supply. • Fiscal agent for federal govt. • Dealt in gold (not silver).	• Conducted open market operations. • Rediscounted bills for member banks. • Made advances to member banks.

		• Discounted bills of exchange. • Set discount rate. • Cleared checks, facilitated payments. • Supervised banks. • Influenced bank powers. • Held commercial member bank reserves. • Public body not concerned with earnings.
1932–1953	Reconstruction Finance Corporation	• Provided liquidity assistance to financial institutions and others. • Provided capital assistance to financial institutions and businesses.
1933–1954	Home Owners' Loan Corporation	• Bought delinquent mortgages from S & Ls and banks. • Rescheduled loans to help people keep their homes. • Made loans to lenders.
1932–Present	Federal Home Loan Bank System	• Examines, supervises, and regulates FSLIC-insured S & Ls. • Insures S & Ls. • Provides advances to member thrifts.

(*Table 2–1. continued overleaf*)

Table 2-1. continued

Time Period	Institution	Central Bank Functions	LLR Functions
1934–Present	Federal Reserve System	• Determines quantity of money • Monitors and influences credit conditions. • Fiscal agent for fed govt. and its agencies. • Handles nation's gold reserves. • Monitors and influences foreign exchange rates. • Discounts bills. • Sets discount rate. • Settlement and clearing (inc. electronic system). • Examines, supervises and regulates state-chartered member banks, bank holding companies. • Maintains stability of the financial system. • Monitors and supports health of the economy.	• Open market operations. • Discounts for member banks pre-1980, and DIs since MCA. • Makes advances to DIs. • Crisis management and co-ordination. • International cooperation.
1934	Federal Deposit Insurance Corporation		• Insures banks.
1970–Present	NCUA Central Liquidity Authority		• Examines, supervises, and regulates credit unions. • Insures credit unions. • Provides liquidity.

Banking Without an LLR

After the Second National Bank went out of existence, U.S. banking entered an era in which only limited central banking functions were provided. Those functions which existed, moreover, were provided by states and private organizations rather than by the federal government. By 1825 many banks in New England held reserves at the Suffolk Bank of Boston, for instance, which enabled the Suffolk Bank to prudently restrain the level of local note issuance. Moreover, in the 1830s the New York Safety Fund required that each member bank deposit a percentage of its capital to the fund, which became a source of liquidity for the member, but not for other banks during periods of stress.

Reforms were also instituted by other individual states during this period. Although the reforms strengthened the state banking systems that adopted them, they provided no means of liquidity assistance through an LLR. The reforms were ineffective in stemming bank failures, which continued to occur as an increasing number of banks gained state charters with easy entry requirements. Another problem was that each bank could issue its own notes, which resulted in an amalgamation of more than 7,000 different currencies by the time of the Civil War.

The U.S. Congress passed the National Bank Act of 1863 to reinstate order in the state banking system. The act was intended to (1) encourage state banks to shift to national charters, (2) establish a uniform currency, and (3) reduce the banking system's vulnerability to bank runs. It permitted nationally chartered banks to operate under a similar, but more stringent, set of guidelines than their state bank counterparts. These guidelines included capital requirements; reserve requirements; restrictions on loans and borrowed funds; and bank supervision and regular examination by the Comptroller of the Currency.

However, state banks did not shift immediately to national charters because of the more rigorous regulation of the national charter system. It was not until 1866, when a 10 percent per annum tax was imposed on state bank notes, that state-chartered institutions converted to national charters. With the imposition of the tax, state bank notes disappeared. Notes issued by national banks, along with "greenbacks" issued by the U.S. Treasury, became the prevalent currencies. State banks began to offer checking accounts and so remained popular, however, and by 1890 overtook national banks in both numbers and total assets.

The national banking system was intended to provide a flexible money supply and to stabilize the financial system. But the system was deficient in two specific areas: (1) it failed to provide an elastic currency that could fluctuate in response to seasonal needs or to demands for conversion of deposits into cash during financial panics; and (2) it failed to publicly provide LLR functions.

The Clearinghouses

Regional clearinghouse associations[6] were formed in New York and such secondary money centers as St. Louis, New Orleans, Baltimore, and Atlanta in an attempt to remedy some of the inadequacies of the U.S. financial system that existed in the mid nineteenth century. Originally, each clearinghouse was organized by a small number of institutions to improve the efficiency and lower the settlement costs of interbank debts. Each bank kept part of its stock of specie or greenbacks as a reserve at its clearinghouse to facilitate settlements. The clearinghouse issued large denomination certificates (to the value of a bank's reserves) to expedite the clearing process.

The financial panic of 1857 encouraged two clearinghouse innovations. Banks usually met a currency drain by curtailing loans, but on this particular occasion they agreed to reduce their reserve ratios below unity. In so doing banks moved to a fractional reserve system— the first clearinghouse innovation. During the liquidity squeeze, the rural banks reduced the balances they held at urban banks, to enable the rural banks to redeem their notes. Following the reduction, urban banks refused to accept rural bank notes. To overcome the impasse, the New York Clearing House Association (NYCHA) agreed in 1857 to accept country bank notes from their members as collateral against clearinghouse loan certificates. The second innovation had occurred—thus, temporarily irredeemable notes were converted into as usable a medium of exchange as specie.[7]

The NYCHA made a third important advance in financial stabilization when it provided liquidity assistance in advance of a foreseen panic in 1893. The clearinghouses began to issue loan certificates in small denominations to meet the needs of individual depositors. These notes then served as a medium of exchange for depositors as well as for clearinghouse members.

As time elapsed, the clearinghouses took over the responsibility for supervising individual banks and acting to protect their members in general. For example, during panics, banks would suspend convertibility of their notes in order to protect their cash reserves.[8] The clearinghouses took over the role of coordinating suspensions, which allowed banks to retain reserves while continuing their payment-system settlement services for depositors and their lending function for borrowers. Thus, suspensions were less disruptive to the economy than the bank holidays that were declared, for example, during the Great Depression and the crisis in Ohio in 1985. Moreover, banks and the public trusted clearinghouse certificates more than the notes of individual banks whose strength was difficult to assess. So, certificates came to circulate as currency, allowing banks to convert illiquid assets (such as irredeemable country bank notes) into liquid assets during panics.

These and other innovations were helpful; they were not sufficient to resolve the panic of 1907, when LLR assistance in the form of loan certificates, suspensions of convertibility, and other restrictions failed to calm the runs which then spread across the United States. The financial debacle sharply and negatively affected real economic activity, and provided the impetus for Congress to undertake major banking reform legislation with passage of the Aldrich–Vreeland Act in 1908.

The Early Federal Reserve

The Aldrich–Vreeland Act called for the voluntary association of ten or more national banks to act as clearinghouses for participating banks, with powers similar to those of their private clearinghouse counterparts. The act also created a National Currency Association, which was empowered to issue emergency currency to banks, and established the National Monetary Commission, which stated "that during a period of distress the central bank should follow the Bagehotian principle of extending credit liberally to everyone whose solvency and condition entitles him to receive it." The commission's reports prompted the passage of the Federal Reserve Act of 1913.

The early Federal Reserve had three major goals, to: (1) provide money in a flexible way to allow the economy to expand in a non-inflationary manner; (2) provide liquidity during panics to prevent runs; and (3) supervise the banking sector. The preamble to the Federal Reserve Act expressed these goals as "to furnish an elastic currency, to afford a means of rediscounting commercial paper, and to establish a more effective supervision of banking in the U.S."

The Federal Reserve system, consisting of twelve regional Federal Reserve banks, headed by the Federal Reserve Board in Washington, DC, was established as an independent entity with the capability to correct deficiencies in the monetary system. Membership was compulsory for national banks and optional for state banks which met certain entrance requirements. Upon joining the system, a bank was required to buy shares of the capital stock of one of the Federal Reserve banks. The Reserve banks, in turn, were required to provide funds from their earnings to meet expenses of the central Federal Reserve Board. This structure was intended to ensure some degree of decentralization and independence from congressional funding.

The original Board, then consisting of seven members (five appointed by the president of the United States, was empowered to supervise banks and to control the volume and use of bank credit. The powers to examine member banks, admit state banks into the system, and under certain conditions, approve mergers of banks or the establishment of branches (both foreign and domestic) were also granted to the Federal Reserve.

Federal Reserve Monetary Policy Before the Great Depression

The Federal Reserve Act of 1913 was intended to produce the "elastic currency" that had proved elusive earlier. The authority to issue Federal Reserve notes also allowed the Federal Reserve system to increase one kind of money (currency) relative to another kind (deposits) without changing the total amount of money available to the economy. Rediscounting bills of exchange was the means whereby Federal Reserve notes would be put into circulation and later retired.[9]

The total amount of money in circulation was determined by the country's stock of gold under the gold standard. However, in the

United States, World War I ended that function of the gold standard. Thereafter, rediscounting and open market operations (described in Chapter 3) became the two mechanisms used to control both the composition and the quantity of money available in the country.

In the early period of the Federal Reserve, individual Federal Reserve banks held autonomy over credit policies in their respective districts. This meant that each Reserve bank had the authority to buy and sell securities through open-market operations and to set the rate of interest, or discount rate, on loans it made to member banks in its district. (Although the actions of the Reserve banks were subject to review by the Federal Reserve Board, only rarely were their proposals rejected.)

A critical shortcoming of the early Federal Reserve system, which became apparent during the Depression, was its failure to serve effectively its intended function as LLR. This failure is underscored by the view of the Federal Reserve Advisory Council, which after observing months of declining economic activity, recommended in 1931 that "the situation will best be served if the natural flow of credit is unhampered by open-market operations or changes in the rediscount rates."[10] Friedman and Schwartz (1963) have also criticized the Federal Reserve's inappropriate policies as contributing importantly to the severity of the Depression in the United States.

One reason for the Fed's inaction during the worst financial crisis in the nation's history was the previously mentioned autonomy of the Federal Reserve banks. Kennedy (1973) attributes a "surprising lack of coordination" among credit policies to "an unresolved tug-of-war" between the Federal Reserve Board and the presidents of the twelve Reserve banks.

Early in 1933, bank customers, having lost faith in the banking system following the failures of thousands of commercial banks in the late 1920s and early 1930s, withdrew their funds and in so doing, reduced bank reserves. At the same time, banks wanted to hold more reserves in case they were needed to face a run. The Federal Reserve did not accommodate the public's additional demands for cash or the banks' demands for precautionary reserves above minimum, required levels. Consequently there was a dramatic plunge in the money supply.[11] The stock of currency plus commercial bank deposits dropped by 32.9 percent from $45.9 billion in December 1929 to $30.8 billion in December 1933 (Friedman and Schwartz 1963, Table A-1).

In legislation passed during the later part of the Depression, a federal financial safety net was created to prevent bank runs. Policy coordination among the previously, relatively autonomous, Reserve banks was achieved by centralizing policymaking at the Federal Open Market Committee (FOMC). The FOMC was usually dominated by the reconfigured Board of Governors in Washington. In the future, only the New York Reserve Bank would conduct open-market operations; the New York Fed merely acted as the Reserve System's agent to execute Board policy.

Other Lenders of Last Resort

During the Great Depression, the U.S. Congress and the Hoover administration created other bodies to help illiquid and even insolvent persons and businesses. The Federal Home Loan Banks were created in 1932 (see Appendix C) to assist thrifts. The Reconstruction Finance Corporation and the Home Owners' Loan Corporation were also formed in 1932 by the Hoover Administration to aid troubled financial institutions, and homeowners.

The Reconstruction Finance Corporation.   In order to provide a separate channel for expanding credit during the Depression, Congress established the Reconstruction Finance Corporation (RFC) in January 1932. Although the RFC did not have the power to issue currency, it provided significant liquidity and capital to the financial system.

The RFC initially provided only liquidity assistance by making low interest loans to commercial banks, savings banks, savings and loan associations, mortgage companies, credit unions, and railroads.[12] Its purpose was defined by President Hoover, who believed that the Depression was being prolonged by the unwillingness of bankers to make commercial loans because of bank failures. By the time Hoover left office early in March 1933, the RFC had extended more than $2 billion to thousands of financial institutions.

The capabilities of the RFC soon became dwarfed by the magnitude of the banking crisis, which culminated in the "banking holiday" declared by President Roosevelt later that March. Congress responded by expanding the powers of the RFC to give capital infusions to troubled financial institutions and businesses by purchasing, for example, preferred stock in commercial banks. The RFC eventually disbursed nearly $4 billion in assistance to financial institutions through loans or purchases of preferred stock, capital notes, or debentures. This amount represents about 10 percent of the approximately $40 billion in deposit liabilities of the banking system in the early 1930s (Jones 1951).

Although the RFC was not disbanded until 1953, three-quarters of its lending to financial institutions occurred before 1935. After this time, the partial economic recovery and creation of the financial safety net reduced the importance of the RFC. Late in the 1930s, the RFC turned to encouraging defense production; after the second World War it focused attention on direct lending to business, which proved to be the most politically controversial and corrupt part of its activities.

The contribution of RFC lending to financial institutions to economic recovery was questionable. Despite infusions of capital, the total value of commercial bank loans dropped from $38 billion in 1930 to $20 billion in 1935. Bernanke (1983) argues that the reduction in the availability of credit exacerbated the Depression. Some authors, however, contend that the RFC played a "cushioning role," which helped prevent further declines in the economy.

Home Owners' Loan Corporation. In 1933, 40 percent of the nation's home mortgages (valued at $20 billion) were in default. The HOLC[13] helped homeowners and lenders by buying delinquent mortgages and rescheduling the loans, with lower interest rates and monthly payments plus an extended period of repayment. The HOLC bought $2.8 billion in loans over a three-year period, also bought other mortgages from S & Ls, made loans to lenders and in total provided $6.2 billion assistance and allowed 1 million homeowners to avoid foreclosure.

The agency made loans for three years. For the following twenty years it auctioned off its mortgage portfolio until it ceased to exist in February 1954, after repaying all the money it had received from the federal government.

SUMMARY

The classical LLR was intended to maintain public confidence in the financial sector and minimize the spread of localized financial crises. Under Bagehot's conception of the LLR, this support to the entire market should be achieved while avoiding problems associated with assistance to insolvent institutions.

As the history of the LLR through the Great Depression illustrates, the U.S. application of the classic system left much room for improvement. The following chapter describes the Federal Reserve's role in post-Depression LLR arrangements in the United States.

NOTES

1. See for example, Aliber (1987a); Barth and Keheler (1984); Benston et al. (1986); Humphrey (1975); Guttentag and Herring (1983); Brimmer (1984); and Meltzer (1986).
2. Kaufman introduced the "fire sale" terminology into the literature. He develops the analysis fully in Benston et al. (1986, 42–45).
3. Cone (1982) provides an excellent, technical analysis of the potential instability at depository institutions. This concept is reiterated in Benston et al. (1986, 4).
4. Cash equivalents kept by the bank will include legally required reserves, working reserves, and some level of precautionary reserves. See, for example, Havrilesky and Boorman (1976). Since, with the exclusion of legally required reserves, an important proportion of these cash equivalents are invested in the federal funds market, one bank's demand for increased liquidity will reduce the liquidity available to other banks.
5. The movement towards securitization of mortgages, credit card receivables, and car loans is increasing the marketability of bank assets.
6. This section is based on Timberlake (1984).
7. The rural banks paid interest at a 6 percent annual rate to the money center banks on their notes until they were redeemed, so they were a profitable proposition for the city banks.
8. During supervision of convertibility, currency traded at a premium over deposits.
9. The analysis in this and the next paragraph is from Anna Schwartz (1987a).
10. See Beckhart (1972, 264).
11. The process of monetary expansion and contraction is explained in introductory texts and is discussed briefly in the next chapter.
12. Failures among the railroads would have weakened the banks that had invested heavily in railroad securities.
13. This section is based on Federal Home Loan Bank System (1987).

3 THE FEDERAL RESERVE AS LENDER OF LAST RESORT

The economic structure of the United States today differs both from nineteenth century Britain and the pre-Depression United States in many ways. One important difference is that the United States today possesses an extensive, financial sector safety net. The safety net, developed since the Great Depression to prevent and contain financial crises, is still evolving and expanding. This chapter begins by briefly describing the safety net system and the implementation of the Federal Reserve's lender-of-last-resort role in the context of that safety net. In particular, this chapter describes the use of open market operations to provide systemwide liquidity and the circumstances associated with access to the discount window—the mechanism by which the Federal Reserve aids individual banks and thrifts. The following chapter discusses some recent developments which prompt questions about the adequacy of the present LLR arrangements.

The Federal Reserve plays several roles in the economy. It conducts monetary policy, adjusts reserve requirements, regulates state-chartered member banks, oversees bank holding companies, acts as a leader of last resort, and studies, advises Congress on, and takes actions to promote the well-being of the economy. Naturally, all of these roles are interrelated. This chapter will discuss how the Federal Reserve currently executes its lender-of-last-resort responsibilities, which is dependent on the Federal Reserve's ability to create money. The money creation process and the tools used by the Federal Reserve to implement monetary policy and provide lender-of-last-resort assistance are also briefly reviewed.

THE FINANCIAL SYSTEM SAFETY NET

There have been many changes in the structure of the financial system since the lender-of-last-resort concept was originated in nineteenth century England. Principal among these changes has been the establishment and explanation of a financial system safety net. In the United States, most of the development of the federal financial safety net has taken place since the Great Depression.

The creation of the Federal Deposit Insurance Corporation as part of the Banking Act of 1933 was perhaps the most important step taken in the evolution of this safety net in the United States. As Representative Steagall stated in 1933:

> The purpose of this legislation is to protect the people of the United States in the right to have banks in which their deposits will be safe. They have the right to expect of Congress the establishment and maintenance of a system of banks in the United States where citizens may place their hard earnings with reasonable expectation of being able to get them out again on demand.[1]

The federal safety net has grown far beyond a system of examination, supervision, regulation, and the provision of deposit insurance to commercial banks. Regulators for other depository institutions have been established along with special industry lenders and deposit insurers. The Federal Home Loan Banks and their Board, created in 1932, serve as the regulator and special industry lenders for S & Ls. The FSLIC, established in 1934 as part of the National Housing Act, insures S & L deposits. The National Credit Union Association (NCUA) was set up in 1970 to afford credit unions the same regulatory and support framework available to banks and S & Ls. The NCUA's Central Liquidity Facility is the special LLR lender for credit unions. The Securities and Exchange Commission (SEC) was also created in 1934 to monitor the activities and disclosures of publicly traded corporations in order to protect the interests of individual investors. More recently, protection for pension plan participants (the Pension Benefit Guarantee Corporation under the Employment Retirement Income Security Act (ERISA) in 1974) has been established.[2]

At the state level, many of the states (with varying degrees of success) have been active in establishing their own, more limited, financial sector safety nets. These include state-sponsored deposit insurance to protect depositors at state-chartered depository institutions, and state-sponsored guarantee funds for the customers of insurance companies that are all currently state (but not federally) regulated. State supervision of banking, insurance, and investment activities exists as well.

In addition to the agencies instituted to protect depositors and investors from fraud and mismanagement of individual financial institutions, the federal government has also been active in attempting to maintain financial and economic stability. The U.S. Congress has taken steps to support large failing municipalities and corporations when it determined that the public interest would best be served by such intervention.[3,4] Currently, Congress may be extending similar protection to the agricultural sector.

THE LLR WITHIN FINANCIAL SYSTEM SAFETY NET

Within this overall financial sector safety net, the Federal Reserve continues to play an important role as lender of last resort. As determined by the classic writers, in order to fulfill the full extent of its obligations as the lender of last resort, the central bank must have the ability to meet any and all liquidity needs. This in effect requires the ability to issue legal tender. In the United States, only the Federal Reserve has the ability to create money, and therefore provide the massive assistance that would be needed in the event of a major financial crisis.[5] All other agencies are limited by the size of their respective guarantee funds and their lines of credit from the U.S. Treasury.[6] The Federal Reserve therefore provides the ultimate liquidity backstop for all other members of the safety net.[7] The special industry lenders such as the Federal Home Loan Banks and NCUA's Central Liquidity Facility, for example, are designed to provide the primary source of assistance for their industries. When funds are not readily available, however, the Federal Reserve, in coordination with the special industry lender, can and will provide liquidity assistance to FHLBB and NCUA members.[8] Coordination is also necessary with the Office of the Comptroller of the Currency (for nationally chartered banks) and the respective regulators (for state-chartered banks) that oversee the banks, but do not provide assistance to them.

This chapter will concentrate on the special role of the Federal Reserve as lender of last resort within the overall financial system safety net. Several authors have already written about, and criticized, the system of federal deposit insurance. (See for example, Kane 1986; GAO 1986e). Therefore the present focus is different.

MONEY CREATION

Commercial banks accept deposits from their customers. Under a fractional-reserve banking system, as exists in the United States, a proportion (determined by the Federal Reserve within the range established by Congress) of each deposit received by a commercial bank must be retained as reserves.[9] Reserves can be held as vault cash, as deposits maintained directly at a Federal Reserve bank, or as balances held at another institution which passes them through to a Federal Reserve Bank.[10] The remainder of the deposit that was initially received can be used by the bank to make consumer, commercial, or mortgage loans or to purchase government securities or other permissible assets.

In several different ways, the Federal Reserve manipulates the banks' need to hold reserves in order to control the stock of money in the economy.[11] For example, open-market operations are the Federal Reserve's favored method of administering monetary policy. This process entails the purchase of Treasury securities to increase bank reserves (and the money supply) or the sale of securities from the Fed's portfolio to decreases reserves (and the money supply). When buying Treasury securities for its portfolio, the Federal Reserve incurs an obligation to provide funds in payment for these securities and then issues a Federal Reserve check in payment or electronically credits the seller's account at a Federal Reserve bank. In so doing, the Federal Reserve adds to the stock of bank reserves, which means that the stock of money in the economy is able to grow roughly proportionately.[12]

Two other tools are used to control the money supply. First, the Federal Reserve can, but rarely does, change legal reserve requirements. The lower (higher) these requirements, the greater (smaller) will be the supply of money available to the economy for any given stock of high-powered money (which is also called the monetary base, consisting of reserves plus currency). Second, the Federal Reserve can increase borrowed reserves and the banking system's total reserves by making "discount window" loans. Moreover, the overall level of borrowed reserves responds in aggregate value to the discount rate. In general, the stock of borrowed reserves, total reserves, and the money supply will increase (decrease) when the discount rate is lowered (raised).

LENDER-OF-LAST-RESORT OPERATIONS

Conceptually then, the Federal Reserve can provide lender-of-last-resort assistance in the same three ways—through open market operations, discount window loans, and changes in reserve requirements.[13] (However, in practice, the Fed uses only the first two techniques and it emphasizes the second when discussing its LLR role.) The Federal Reserve can also use these instruments to provide generalized liquidity support to the economy. Overall financial system liquidity increases when the Federal Reserve purchases securities in the open market, or reduces reserve requirements. Finally, the Federal Reserve can target funds directly to individual entities experiencing liquidity pressures by providing advances or discounts through the discount window. Discount window advances have historically been the Federal Reserve's preferred lender-of-last-resort mechanism for aiding individual depository institutions. However, open-market operations are used to contain the transmitted effects of failure among non-depository institutions and to provide systemwide liquidity support.

Discount Window Loans

Individual Federal Reserve banks are empowered to offer discount window loans under Section 13 of the Federal Reserve Act.[14] The provision of such loans is governed by Regulation A.[15] Reserve banks can offer discount window loans for several reasons, including assisting institutions to: (1) meet unusual creditor demands, (2) avoid temporary reserve account overdrafts, and (3) overcome the effects of temporary, severe deposit withdrawals. According to the 1980 booklet *The Federal Reserve Discount Window*, two types of discount window credit are provided to depository institutions (DIs)—adjustment credit and extended credit. These are defined as follows:

> Adjustment credit is available on a short term basis to assist borrowers in meeting temporary requirements for funds or to cushion briefly more persistent funds outflows while an orderly adjustment is being made. Extended credit is provided to assist depository institutions in meeting somewhat longer term needs for funds. (Board of Governors of the Federal Reserve, 1980, 2)

Adjustment credit has become part of the day-to-day operations of banking and the Federal Reserve's conduct of monetary policy. Discount window loans for adjustment credit are, therefore, not considered part of the Fed's lender-of-last-resort operations.

Extended Credit

Extended credit for depository institutions is broken down into three categories, two of which constitute lender-of-last-resort assistance. Seasonal credit is available to small banks with limited access to the funds market when they experience seasonal fluctuations in liquidity. As seasonal requirements can be anticipated, the need for seasonal credit does not constitute a crisis, although it did before the creation of the Federal Reserve (Miron 1986).

Extended credit, in exceptional circumstances, is available to individual institutions adversely affected by threatening circumstances that inhibit an institution's ability to raise funds. Finally, other extended credit is available to institutions experiencing difficulties in adjusting to changing money market conditions. The last two categories of extended credit are classified as lender-of-last-resort loans, partly because they are given in unexpected and possibly emergency situations. The Federal Reserve can also provide discount window assistance to non-depository institutions, but since the late 1950s, it has chosen not to do so.

Discount Window Access

For the purpose of discussing access to the discount window, potential applicants are divided into five categories: member banks, non-member banks, thrifts and credit unions, non-depository financial institutions (NDFIs) and other individuals, partnerships, and corporations (IPCs). Since the creation of the Federal Reserve in 1913, one of the benefits of membership in the Federal Reserve system has been access to the credit facilities of the Federal Reserve banks. Other entities, not carrying the costs and burdens of membership, did not have regular access (Hackley 1973). The Federal Reserve gave the following interpretation of its role during the 1970s:

> the immediate responsibility of the system is directly to the member bank. This is one of the benefits of Federal Reserve membership—paid for in a sense by the maintenance of non-earning assets in satisfaction of reserve requirements—and a basic source of confidence in the banking system. (Board of Governors of the Federal Reserve 1971, 19)

The preferential treatment of member banks ended in 1980, when the Monetary Control Act extended legally mandated reserve requirements and discount window access to all depository institutions.

Access by Nonmember Depository Institutions

For most of the post-Depression period, until 1980, nonmember banks could not obtain discount window assistance directly from Federal Reserve. Nor was liquidity assistance even indirectly available, through Federal Reserve advances made to correspondent member banks that were passed on to nonmember banks.

The original Federal Reserve Act specified that no member bank could act as an agent to pass discount window assistance through to nonmember banks without the specific approval of the Federal Reserve Board. Hackley (1973) reports that such approval was granted in the stressed periods of 1921, 1926, 1933, 1966, 1969, and 1972.

During the Great Depression, the Federal Reserve Act was amended to allow the Fed to provide liquidity assistance directly to IPCs. Section 13.3, added to the Act in July 1932, allowed Reserve banks, with approval of the Board, to discount eligible paper for IPCs when unable to obtain such accommodation from the commercial banking system. Nevertheless, the Board immediately chose to exclude nonmember banks from this provision, even though they were legal corporations.[16] The Board ended this exclusion thirty years later (during the credit crunches of 1966 and 1969) when it activated Section 13.3 to allow Reserve banks to discount paper for nonmember banks and thrifts. This authorization was not utilized, however (Hackley 1973).

In March 1933, Section 13.13 was added to the Federal Reserve Act. It allowed Reserve banks to make advances secured by U.S. Treasury or agency obligations to IPCs for periods not to exceed ninety days. In this case, the Board interpreted "corporation" to include nonmember banks. Nevertheless, Federal Reserve regulations discouraged use of this provision. Rates charged under this provision were higher (by two percentage points in 1972) than those charged to member banks. Hackley reports that use of this section was very limited.

Congress and the Board of Governors believed that the Federal Reserve's responsibilities were primarily to its member banks. For example, the most recent extensive Federal Reserve reconsideration of its lender-of-last-resort responsibilities was conducted in 1971. At that time, the Board wrote:

> The role of the Federal Reserve as the lender of last resort to other financial sectors of the economy may, under justifiable circumstances, require loans to institutions other than member banks. The apparent general approval of recent instances of lending and offering to lend to nonmember institutions has strengthened the belief that the system's ability to carry out this need. In contrast to the case of member banks, however, justification for Federal Reserve assistance to nonmember institutions must be in terms of probable impact of the failure on the economy's financial structure. It would be most unusual for the failure of a single institution or small group of institutions to have significant repercussions as to justify Federal Reserve action. (Board of Governors of the Federal Reserve 1971, 20)

As the deregulation of the financial sector proceeded during the 1970s, however, it became increasingly apparent that the concentration of Federal Reserve efforts on members banks had become obsolete. The Depository Institutions Deregulation and Monetary Control Act of 1980 (DIDMCA) acknowledged this change.

THE MONETARY CONTROL ACT OF 1980

The Monetary Control Act (MCA) of 1980 required all depository institutions offering reservable transaction accounts and/or nonpersonal time deposits, to maintain reserves directly at the Federal

Reserve or indirectly via a pass-through arrangement with a bank holding an account at a Federal Reserve bank. The MCA also gave all depository institutions access to all Federal Reserve services; including direct access to the discount window. MCA was enacted, in part, as a reaction to declining Federal Reserve membership. Federal Reserve Chairman Volcker and others argued that the Federal Reserve would be unable to effectively execute monetary policy if the declining membership trend continued.[17] The requirement to maintain reserves at the Federal Reserve and the extension of the ability to offer transactions accounts demanded an extension of lender-of-last-resort access to nonmember banks and non-bank depository institutions.

SPECIAL INDUSTRY LENDERS

In the world after DIDMCA distinctions remain in the access to the discount window between differing types of nonmember depository institutions. The evolution of a financial institution safety net since the 1930s, has included the introduction and growing use of special industry lenders designed to provide support to specific classes of institutions such as thrifts and credit unions. As a result, an additional source of funds is available to these institutions. The best example of the additional funding layer is the Federal Reserve regulation that troubled, federally insured savings and loan associations (S & Ls) first obtain advances from their Federal Home Loan Bank. Similarly, credit unions are expected to use the resources of NCUA's Central Liquidity Facility before turning to the Federal Reserve in a crisis.

COLLATERAL REQUIREMENTS

All depository institutions, regardless of classification and the need to seek assistance from a special industry lender, are subject collateral requirements for Federal Reserve loans. Section 201.4 of Regulation A defines satisfactory collateral as generally including "United States government and Federal agency securities, and, if of acceptable quality, mortgage notes covering one to four family residences, state and local government securities, and business, consumer and other customer notes."

When the Federal Reserve accepts an asset as collateral for a discount window loan, the par value of the collateral exceeds the value of the loan. That is, the Federal Reserve discounts the value of the collateral in making the loan. The ratio of the loan value to the collateral value can be called the "collateralization ratio." The amount of the collateralization ratio varies, depending on the quality and/or maturity of the underlying asset. The ratio amount can be viewed as risk-insurance imposed on a loan recipient by each Federal Reserve bank to protect itself from loss should it ultimately need to take legal possession of collateralized assets and sell them to cover a loan that is not repaid. The list of acceptable items in Regulation A serves mainly as a guideline; in practice, during a crisis, Federal Reserve banks accept a much wider range of assets as eligible discount window collateral.[18]

As it accepts assets of decreasing quality and longer maturity, the Federal Reserve decreases the collateralization ratio. However, there are several sets of guidelines that determine the amount of collateralization ratio that can be applied to specific classes of assets.

Collateral Guidelines

The Federal Reserve Act gives the Federal Reserve Board broad powers to interpret what is eligible as collateral. The Board has delegated these powers to the regional Reserve banks. The district banks each have some general guidelines concerning collateral that is acceptable in exchange for extended credit, regular, and emergency adjustment credit. While the guidelines do not differ substantially across districts, there is not complete uniformity across regions. Moreover, the guidelines tend to be jettisoned in a crisis.

The Cleveland Federal Reserve Bank does not publish valuation guidelines for collateral acceptable for extended credit because it wants to maintain maximum flexibility. At the Richmond Bank, in contrast, decisions are guided by a list of permitted valuations that is based on past precedent. For problem banks in its district, the Dallas Reserve Bank accepts U.S. government agency and state securities at 90 percent (and municipals at 80 percent) of the lesser of market or face value. If credit is needed immediately, the Dallas Reserve

Bank offers funds up to 50 percent of customer notes, pending a credit review. It takes good quality paper first, and accepts successively lower quality notes, preferably in large denominations, at increasing discounts.

At the Kansas City Reserve Bank, government securities are accepted at 100 percent of par value, mortgage participation certificates at full market value, municipals at 90 percent of book value, customer notes in healthy banks in good standing at 70 percent of outstanding balance (but at 50 percent at problem institutions). Where the primary regulator is trying to effect a resolution for a troubled bank's problems, that bank's valuation ratio for customer notes may be raised to 80 percent and substandard notes may become acceptable.

At the San Francisco Reserve Bank, the criteria are marginally different. Loans are granted to 100 percent of face value for government securities, 90 percent of the market value for state securities, and 80 percent for municipals. Commercial notes are acceptable at between 50 and 90 percent of outstanding balance, depending on their quality.

The Federal Reserve Bank of New York staff stated that they had not made extended credit loans since those granted to mutual savings banks in 1981 and 1982. However, faced with a potential crisis such as that at the Bank of New York (BONY) in November 1985, the staff said that the N.Y. Fed will take *all* of the institution's assets and will lend whatever is necessary to contain the situation. In BONY's case the Bank executed a "failed security agreement," under which it took possession of all the securities which BONY owed but could not deliver to its customers because of its computer malfunction at that time.

Early in 1986, the Fed formed a Collateral Work Group (CWG) that is charged with putting together a handbook of collateral guidance. The group is identifying types of assets (particularly, newly innovated assets) that may be accepted as collateral. It is also suggesting legal arrangements that can assist a Reserve bank in perfecting its legal claim to these assets and making suggestions for valuing collateral for adjustment, but not extended, credit. In the case of extended credit, aid may need to be so highly individualized that any guidelines could become irrelevant.

Adherence to the guidelines being established would be voluntary. Moreover, as of July 1987, no attempt is being made to regularize collateral practices across districts.[19] Therefore, the individual Federal Reserve banks retain flexibility in determining not only the types of assets which are acceptable as collateral, but also the discount that is to be applied to each asset. The application of the discount makes the Fed deviate from the classic prescription to lend on the full pre-crisis value of collateral. The practical execution and the equity of these flexible arrangements are discussed in Chapters 6 and 7, respectively.

Loans to Non-Depository Financial Institutions and IPCs

The Federal Reserve Act of 1913 did not provide access to the discount window for individuals, partnerships and corporations (IPCs), including non-depository financial institutions (NDFIs).[20] However, in July 1932, Section 13.3 was added to the Federal Reserve Act, which allowed that "In unusual and exigent circumstances, the Board of Governors of the Federal Reserve System, by the affirmative vote of not less than five members, may authorize any Federal reserve bank ... to discount for any individuual, partnership, or corporation, notes, drafts, and bills of exchange of the kinds and maturities made eligible for discount for member banks." (Federal Reserve Act 1913, Section 13.3.) This section is today implemented in Federal Reserve regulations. According to Section 210.3(c) of Regulation A:

> In unusual and exigent circumstances, a Reserve Bank may, after consultation with the Board, advance credit to individuals, partnerships and corporations that are not depository institutions if, in the judgement of the Reserve Bank. credit is not available from other sources and failure to obtain such credit would adversely affect the economy.

In 1933, the Federal Reserve's ability to provide discount window assistance to IPCs was further, permanently, expanded by the addition of Section 13.13 to the Federal Reserve Act. This section, which allows IPCs to discount for up to ninety days either a direct obligation of the United States or its agency, effected two expansions to LLR access. First, the scope of the two sections was interpreted differently. Although nonmember depository institutions were considered IPCs at that time, the Federal Reserve had interpreted Section 13.3 of the Act to exclude nonmember depository institutions. Section 13.13, on the other hand, was viewed as including nonmember banks and thrifts. Second, implementation of this section was not limited to emergency situations. Therefore, the 1933 addition of Section 13.13 provided, in principle, limited discount window access to nonmember depository institutions.

Despite the ability to provide discount window assistance to IPCs, the Federal Reserve, typically, does not lend today in the form of discounts or advances to an IPC. During 1933–1937, however, 123 loans in modest amounts were granted to IPCs. Since then, lending under Sections 13.3 and 13.13 has been virtually non-existent. However, the use of another part of the Federal Reserve Act, Section 13b, provides an aberration in the Federal Reserve history. Between June 1938, when it was added to the Federal Reserve Act, and August 1959, when it was repealed, Section 13b was used to make numerous working capital loans to established commercial and industrial businesses.

IPCs may be deterred from requesting aid from the discount window under Sections 13.3 or 13.13. The strict collateral requirements of Section 13.13 and the imposition of a penalty rate above the member bank's borrowing rate may make discount window loans unattractive to an IPC or NDFI. (The penalty rate will be discussed further in the next section.) Also, as will be discussed in Chapter 6, the Federal Reserve prefers to provide indirect assistance to IPCs by funneling assistance through depository institutions instead of aiding the IPCs directly. Senior Federal Reserve staff members expressed the opinion that the Board would be very reluctant to lend to a non-depository institution experiencing a crisis. Of course, the Fed could still use open market operations to provide generalized liquidity and endorse private initiatives to aid illiquid institutions (Garcia 1988).

Non-Uniform Access to the Lender of Last Resort

This discussion has demonstrated that access to the Federal Reserve's preferred mechanism for LLR support—the discount window—is not uniform across financial institutions. Commercial banks maintaining reserves directly at the Federal Reserve have the most direct access. Since 1980, other commercial banks can receive assistance channeled through a directly reporting bank or they can make arrangements (even in advance of an emergency) to receive assistance directly. Savings and loans, and credit unions must first seek support from their special industry lenders but can ultimately turn to the Federal Reserve, directly or indirectly, like nonmember banks. Finally, while non-depository financial institutions and non-financial firms have access in principle to the discount window in "unusual and exigent" situations, in practice they have not received direct access under Sections 13.3 and 13.13 since the 1930s or under Section 13b since the 1950s. They have, however, been aided indirectly where the Federal Reserve has lent to their commercial banks, and by generalized open-market operations.

THE COST OF LENDER-OF-LAST-RESORT ASSISTANCE

The basic interest rate charged by the Federal Reserve on all types of discount window loans is called the discount rate. According to the 1974 booklet *The Federal Reserve System Purposes and Function*, each Reserve Bank's board of directors sets its Bank's discount rate. Today, the rate is then quickly subject to review and final determination by the Board of Governors. It is the Board of Governors that announces any changes in the basic discount rate that it is charged on adjustment credit.

The Federal Reserve assesses penalties over the basic discount rate as the duration of an institution's borrowing increases. The discount rate structure was recently restated as: "Credit for 1 to 60 days is charged the discount window rate; that from 61 to 150 days is charged the discount window rate plus 100 basis points and that for over 150 days is charged the discount window rate plus 200 basis points." (Board of Governors of the Federal Reserve 1985, 31)

The basic discount rate tends to be a subsidized, below market rate. Normally, it is below the federal funds rate which is the rate that banks pay for very short-term funds in the interbank market. Kaufman (1986) argues that even after the 200 basis points penalty is assessed for borrowing over 150 days, the rate an institution pays for lender-of-last-resort assistance can be below market rates. It is almost always lower than the rate the institution would have to pay for funds in the market, were it able to raise funds on its own. For example, the authors estimate in Appendix A that Franklin National Bank received a minimum subsidy of 278 basis points on its lender-of-last-resort loan. Over the full duration of the loan, this amounted to a subsidy of $2 million on Franklin's $1.7 billion loan.[21]

The Federal Reserve imposes no direct charge for the emergency line of credit it offers, rather it offers access as an implicit benefit in compensation for any costs imposed by the need to maintain reserve requirements.

Changes in the Basic Discount Rate Structure

The classical writers indicated that subsidized lender-of-last-resort assistance leads to moral hazard, and this concern remains today. The Federal Reserve has introduced deviations from the basic discount rate structure to correct for potential interest rate subsidies in the two situations where potentially large subsidies would arise: (1) very long-term borrowings (particularly beyond 150 days) and (2) unusually large borrowings. With the exception of these two circumstances, the basic discount rate structure remains in effect.

Long-term Borrowings

As the duration of an institution's borrowing increases (particularly beyond 150 days), the potential dollar subsidy also increases. In order to counteract this, the Federal Reserve has most recently introduced a market-sensitive rate on long-term borrowing. According to a Federal Reserve Bank of Chicago *Operating Circular* (1985) the new, flexible, less-subsidizing rate policy allows the Federal Reserve to charge an institution a rate which takes into account rates that would be payable on market source of funds "when the institution is borrowing for unusually long periods and in unusually large amounts (Federal Reserve Bank of Chicago 1985)." While the new rate policy did not become effective formally until November 21, 1984, the Federal Reserve Bank of Chicago began applying the market-sensitive rate to Continental Illinois' borrowing as early as May 16, 1984.[22]

Unusually Large Borrowings

The 1985 computer malfunction at the Bank of New York (BONY) again raises questions about the appropriateness of subsidizing troubled institutions. At the time of the $23.6 billion overnight loan to BONY from the Federal Reserve Bank of New York, the federal funds rate was higher than the discount rate, as is usual. BONY was charged the overnight, basic discount rate, without penalty. Consequently, BONY received a subsidy on its discount window assistance.[23]

In response to the concern about BONY's subsidy, the Federal Reserve announced a new rate policy "to deal with exceptionally large borrowings from the discount window that arise from computer breakdowns or other operating problems associated with the payments mechanism" (from a Federal Reserve press release, May 19, 1986). Under this new policy, effective on May 22, 1986, the highest rate within the structure of discount rates (currently the discount rate plus 200 basis points) "will be applied to loans of unusual size, which result from a major operating problem at the borrower's facility, unless the problem is clearly beyond the reasonable control of the institution." The policy is designed to allow the Federal Reserve to charge rates approaching market rates. Additionally, it is intended to encourage institutions to put in place better precautionary and backup systems to prevent another computer problem such as BONY's.

Rates for Non-Depository Financial Institutions and IPCs

The rates applied to loans or advances made to IPCs and NDFIs are higher than the rates charged to depository institutions. In reference to assistance for NDFIs and other IPCs, Regulation A states "the rate applicable to such credit will be above the highest rate for advances in effect for deposit institutions." The higher rate is imposed as a penalty on such borrowing, since these entities do not maintain non-interest bearing reserves with the Federal Reserve. The Federal Reserve is conscious that reserve requirements can impose a financial burden on depository institutions, which may put them at a competitive disadvantage with respect to other firms that do not face this requirement.[24] Access to the discount window, and other Federal Reserve services, has been viewed as a form of partial compensation.

CONCLUSIONS

Chapter 2 set out the classical admonitions for lender-of-last-resort behavior. From the information provided in this chapter, it is clear that the Federal Reserve adheres to some of the classic precepts, but ignores others. The summary of the findings with respect to the nine principles is presented in Table 3–1.

First, Table 3–1 notes that the Federal Reserve follows the precept of not letting discount window assistance interfere with the long-term goals of monetary policy. In the deliberations of the Federal Open Market Committee (FOMC), which determines Fed monetary policy, the projected paths for non-borrowed reserves are adjusted downwards to reflect extended credit takedowns. This adjustment, if complete, will keep the money supply on course, even in the short run. During a widespread crisis, however, the Fed may decide to ease the credit reins. Additional systemwide liquidity may be provided through the discount window and/or through open-market operations.[25] Chapter 6 shows that this joint approach was adopted during credit crunches in the 1960s and 1970s. The policy of leniency can be reversed after the crisis is over in order to restore long-term monetary policy goals.

Under the second precept, the classicists maintained that aid should be provided speedily, but only temporarily. The modern Fed places great emphasis on the need to provide assistance immediately. It does not provide only short duration aid, however. As described in the case studies and Chapters 6 and 7, the Fed is willing to provide long-term assistance as part of the federal financial safety net, to give the regulators time to successfully dispose of failing institutions.

The third classic admonition directs LLR responsibility to the entire financial system rather than to individual institutions. However, the 1971 Federal Reserve statement clearly indicates that the Fed believed that it had obligations at that time to individual member banks experiencing difficulties, but not to others. Since 1980, the Federal Reserve interprets this responsibility to apply to all DIs, collectively and individually.

Table 3-1. Applicability of the Classic LLR Components to the Modern Domestic LLR Concept.

Classical Prescriptions	Modern Interpretations	Issues to be Discussed in Later Chapters
LLR actions should not conflict with monetary policy.	Applicable.	Can potential need for large-scale assistance interfere with monetary policy?
Speedy and short-term assistance.	Applicable. Assistance sometimes long-term.	Assisting and subsidizing problem institutions long-term.
Responsibility to the whole financial system.	DIs: Immediately applicable, NFDIs: and IPCs: aid provided through the banking system.	Will the indirect approach to LLR assistance to NDFIs continue to be effective?
Prevent both individual and systemwide runs even while allowing the insolvent to fail.	DIs: practice both prevention and neutralization for individual DIs and the system by avoiding failure. Others: avoid spill over.	Is there a tradeoff between containing an immediate problem and exacerbating future crises?
Lend freely during a crisis.	Applicable.	Are there practical limits to Fed aid that might be reached in a future crisis?
Lend to any and all sound borrowers.	DIs: freely; but also to insolvent institutions in some circumstances. Others: indirectly, freely, only to solvent institutions.	Aid to insolvent institutions.
Lend on all collateral at normal economic value.	Not applicable in principle: Discount is applied. Execution is obscure.	Fairness.
Impose a penalty rate on all borrowing.	Fed has subsidized aid in the past. Is now reducing the subsidy.	What is an appropriate penalty?
Assure markets beforehand.	DIs: applicable in principle, in practice, there is some uncertainty.	Should more advance information and greater *ex post* accountability be required?

The fourth element of classic advice argues that the Federal Reserve should avoid systemwide financial catastrophes, by preventing even individual runs, but the LLR should not prevent individual banks from failing. In contrast, the modern Federal Reserve works to prevent systemwide financial panics and individual failures. It believes that it has a greater responsibility to DIs than to NDFIs or IPCs, however.

[handwritten marginal note: at any bank size?]

The Federal Reserve departs from the fourth classic prescription in two ways. First, its emphasis on maintaining confidence extends to bailing out failures at individual (particularly large) DIs, rather than containing them. From its inception, the Federal Reserve appears to have had a preference for preventing rather than neutralizing financial panics at depository institutions. For example, in its first annual report, the Federal Reserve wrote "What is the proper place and function of the Federal Reserve Banks in our banking and credit system? . . . Its duty is not to await emergencies, but by anticipation, to do what it can to prevent them. (Federal Reserve Board 1914, 17)[26] While Bagehot advised against allowing runs to happen, he would not have supported the modern permission for insolvent firms to keep operating.

Following the fifth classic recommendation, the Federal Reserve is prepared to, and does, lend freely and speedily during a crisis, directly to DIs and indirectly to others through the banking system. Chapter 7 shows that the concerns that are sometimes expressed (about practical limits to the extent of aid that the Federal Reserve can provide in the form of dollars) are misplaced.

The central bank does not follow the sixth Bagehotian precept that it should lend to all solvent institutions and only to solvent institutions. At present it lends directly only to DIs. Moreover, as Chapter 6 shows, it is also prepared to lend, as part of the financial safety net, to insolvent institutions in certain circumstances. It does so by delaying the recognition of insolvency and the declaration of failure.

The seventh piece of nineteenth century advice concerns collateral. The Federal Reserve booklet and the individual Reserve bank rules lay out the limitations on the set of assets it is prepared to accept as collateral. The set is not as all-encompassing as the classicists recommend. However, the Appendices and Chapters 6 and 7 reveal that the Fed denies this classic principle of spreading the net wide for collateral, but sometimes approaches it in the execution of its LLR responsibilities. The Federal Reserve applies a sometimes substantial discount to the normal economic value of the collateral it accepts and in so doing departs from classic rules.

The eighth classic precept is to impose a penalty rate. Nevertheless, the Fed subsidized rather than penalized discount window borrowing until recently. Since 1984, it has taken steps to reduce the subsidy, but a penalty is still not systemically applied.

The ninth classic recommendation is to assure the markets about the conditions of LLR aid in advance of any crisis. The Federal Reserve, however, likes to retain maximum discretion over its LLR operations. Exercising discretion would be hampered by the publication of the rules that determine aid. Some, but not all, of the rules governing eligibility for, and the characteristics of aid for DIs are laid out in the Federal Reserve booklet *The Federal Reserve Discount Window* (1980). However, flexibility is apparent in their implementation.

There are several examples of departure from the set of published LLR rules. The most noticeable omission is an operational definition of solvency used by the regulators in determining eligibility for aid.

Thus, those charged with implementing the federal financial safety net retain discretion in determining when an institution becomes insolvent and ceases to be eligible for aid. Hence, there is some uncertainty among DIs about their eligibility for aid. There is more uncertainty among other organizations. Furthermore, the Federal Reserve appears to have flexibly applied both its stated and unstated rules in the past. Yet it is reluctant to discuss to whom and in what manner it has granted aid. These actions increase uncertainty and deny the pre-crisis assurance that the classical writers recommend.

The Fed's manner of implementing its LLR responsibilities had implications for the incentives offered to banks and others. These implications are discussed further in Chapter 7.

NOTES

1. Representative Steagall was quoted from a discussion of banking in general and the Glass-Steagall Act in particular. His comments, however, are indicative of the change in attitude from the laissez-faire, non-interference stance of prior decades.

2. Anna Schwartz (1987a), observes that this paragraph "lists federal guarantee programs without comment. Should not the paragraph refer to the dif-

ficulties of the deposit insurance agencies and the losses of the programs including the Pension Benefit Guarantee Corporation? Each of the programs suffers from serious design flaws that produce incentives for the insured to take excessive risks with the resulting losses passed on to the insurance or guarantee agency."

3. For information regarding congressional support, see U.S. General Accounting Office (1984b).

4. Many economists question whether the benefits of these programs have outweighed their costs (Kane 1987b; Schwartz 1987b, c).

5. The power to create money is granted by the Constitution to the U.S. Congress which has appointed the Federal Reserve to discharge this responsibility.

6. In the event of a major financial crisis, it is likely that even the U.S. Treasury would have to issue new debt obligations in order to provide the necessary funds to other members of the financial system safety net who were taking down their lines of credit at the Treasury. See U.S. General Accounting Office (1987a).

7. William Isaacs, while Chairman of the FDIC, during the Continental Illinoise crisis, expressed his opinion that the FDIC, not the Federal Reserve, was the lender of last resort, because the Fed receives collateral for its aid but the FDIC does not. U.S. Congress, House of Representatives (1984).

8. This policy was publicly announced in a Federal Reserve statement of policy released on September 1, 1980. The statement of policy is based on an exchange of letters between Federal Reserve Chairman Volcker and FHLBB Chairman Pratt, dated August 19 and August 29, 1980.

9. Banks need to hold cash reserves in order to meet their customers' demands. These needs have been formalized into reserve requirements. Currently, depository institutions maintain at least a marginal 12 percent of their transaction accounts and 3 percent of their short-term nonpersonal time deposits and eurocurrency liabilities as reserves (Federal Reserve Board of Governors 1986a, A7, table 1.15).

10. The Monetary Act of 1980 substantially increased the number of institutions formally required to hold reserves. To accommodate them, nonmember banks were allowed to hold their required reserves as balances at a depository institution which maintains reserve balances at a Federal Reserve bank, in a Federal Home Loan Bank, or in the National Credit Union Administration's Central Liquidity Facility, if the designated institution "maintains such funds in the form of balances at a Federal Reserve bank. . . . " (MCA, Section 104B)

11. The Federal Reserve uses several definitions of money. The most well-known is MI, which consists of cash in circulation, transactions deposits, and travelers checks. The broader definitions of money used by the Federal Reserve add a succession of other less liquid deposits and savings

instruments to MI. The precise definitions of the money aggregates are given in footnotes to tables in the *Federal Reserve Bulletin*. For example, see Board of Governors of the Federal Reserve 1986a, A14, notes to table 1.21).

12. For more detail on the money creation process see any standard money and banking text.

13. Technically, discount window assistance can be granted as advances or discounts. Advances, the more common form, are simply loans. Discounts involve the temporary purchase of some security at a discount from the illiquid bank holder. Before the security comes due, the Fed presents it back to the original holder for repurchase.

14. 12 U.S.C.; Chapter 6, 38 Stat. 251 (December 23, 1913).

15. 12 C.F.R.; Chapter 11, Part 201.

16. For one year during the Great Depression, until March 24, 1934, Congress authorized Federal Reserve banks to make advances to nonmember banks explicitly on the security of any security that would have been acceptable from a member bank.

17. Many economists disagreed with this assessment, however. They point out that banks need to maintain reserves in order to conduct business. The Fed could conduct monetary policy by influencing the level of reserves banks voluntarily hold.

18. For example, the Federal Reserve has accepted the foreign assets of Franklin National Bank's London branch and the fixed assets of the Bank of New York as collateral for discount window loans. (See the Appendix.)

19. Any such attempt would be made at a higher level, for example, by the Subcommittee on Discounts and Credits, which consists of senior vice presidents from four regional banks and reports to the Committee on Discounts and Credits (comprised of four Regional Bank presidents).

20. NDFIs and IPCs are treated similarly in the access laws. In this text, however, financial crises are held to be potentially more severe than nonfinancial crises. The differences are discussed in Chapters 6 and 7.

21. The subsidy was estimated by subtracting the interest rate on Franklin's discount window loan from a weighted average replacement cost of funds. The replacement rate represents the cost to the Franklin of replacing lost funds in the market. The rate does not, however, reflect any risk premiums which Franklin would have had to pay to replace lost deposits in the market.

22. Nevertheless, Kaufman (1986) estimates that Continental received a subsidy—of approximately 200 basis points—on its early assistance from the Fed.

23. However, Corrigan (1985) notes the Federal Reserve did not incur any losses as a result of BONY's computer malfunctions. However, "losses"

should be interpreted as expenditures in this context. While the loan was repaid in full, the Fed did incur an opportunity loss.

24.   This position is stated in Board of Governors of the Federal Reserve (1971, 21).

25.   Anna Schwartz (1987a) notes that Fed emphasizes its use of the discount window to combat financial crises rather than the execution of the open-market operations.

26.   Anna Schwartz (1987a) observes that this statement is ironic given the Fed's poor LLR performance during the Great Depression.

4 TRIGGER AREAS

As pointed out in Chapters 2 and 3, there have been some basic changes in the structure of the financial system since the days of Henry Thornton and Walter Bagehot. However, despite changes in the structure of the financial system, the basic thrust of the lender of last resort—the provision of liquidity assistance to troubled financial institutions and the prevention of financial panics—has remained unchanged. In recent years, the financial system has become increasingly complex and interdependent. Technology has dramatically changed the business of banking and has created a true world market for many financial products (Kaufman, Mote, and Rosenblum 1983). To assure the smooth functioning of the economy, the Federal Reserve must, therefore, be able to fulfill its lender-of-last-resort obligations within this new context.

This chapter will review some of the changes that have taken place in the world financial markets, with an emphasis on those activities which may increase the likelihood that a crisis involving vast amounts of funds might develop and where lender-of-last-resort assistance would be applied, appropriately or inappropriately. It will also discuss some market developments which may prevent the Federal Reserve from successfully fulfilling its critical role.

Kane (1987a) and Schwartz (1987b) both argue that unintended incentives have encouraged at least some of the market developments that now threaten the financial system. If this assessment is accurate, it would be better to change the incentive system and so reduce the threat of catastrophe, rather than gear up the Federal Reserve to deal with any resulting crisis. However, Congress and the regulators do not appear to be taking the steps necessary to change the incentive structure. Consequently, the Fed may find itself carrying the burden of supporting the economy during a crisis before the essential changes are made. Indeed, typically, even needed changes are not made until a crisis develops to reveal that they are unavoidable. In the interim, managing the crisis would most likely fall to the Federal Reserve at a time when it is less able than in the past to handle such a crisis. The Fed's problem would be that the banking system is losing market share to other segments of the financial services industry. This situation could make the Fed's policy of indirectly funneling aid to the economy through commercial banks less effective than it was when banks played a more dominant role in the economy.

SOURCES OF ECONOMIC MALFUNCTION

The potential for a significant malfunction in the financial system which might precipitate a lender-of-last-resort response has increased in recent years. This potential arises from four basic factors: (1) the increased size and concentration of economic activities, (2) the effect of technology on the speed of funds transfers, (3) the increased complexity and sophistication of financial transactions, and (4) the growing interdependency within the financial system. Kane (1987a) argues that unduly restrictive regulatory policies have contributed systematically to the development of these four basic factors.

First, increased size per se may not raise the probability of a crisis. In fact, large firms, if they are well diversified, may have a lower risk of bankruptcy. However, large banks and thrifts behave differently— in ways that are more risky—from other banks. For example, they typically rely on uninsured, large, managed liabilities to a greater extent than do small firms. Deposit insurance has made it unnecessary for small depositors to run from federally insured institutions as long as the public believes that the full faith and credit of the United States backs the funds. Today, large banks are, therefore, more exposed to liquidity crises of potentially greater magnitude than are small firms. In addition, regulators are more concerned about a crisis at large firms. The fear of contagion is greater, and so is the probability of a bailout if the firm becomes insolvent as well as illiquid. Moreover, large banks are also more exposed to losses from off-balance sheet activities and their international debt portfolios than are other banks.

Higher levels of concentration make it easier for examiners and supervisors to monitor an industry's performance, which should reduce the likelihood of a malfunction in the financial system performance. However, concentration also raises the likelihood of a bailout when one does occur because of a "too big to fail" approach by the regulators.

Second, the high speed transfer of funds can help a well-run firm to obtain funds quickly to enhance its liquidity when needed. But high speed transfers can be dangerous when a normally well-run firm makes a mistake or when a fraudulently run organization wants to take advantage of an opportunity to gain at others' expense. Alan Greenspan, in 1987 named chairman of the Federal Reserve to replace Paul Volcker, before his appointment described the potential dangers forcibly:

> The nature of the increased risk is caused solely by the speed at which markets now move. It is a question of high-technology and telecommunications. The ability now of funds to move has sharply reduced the time span in which a crisis can lead to a disaster. (Nash 1986, D.1, D.5)

The frequency of crises in this situation is likely to be greater where the technology available to the regulators does not keep up with that of market participants. Moreover, regulators may not have sufficient staff to adequately monitor the potential for abuse. When these abuses do occur, lender-of-last-resort assistance may be needed to aid firms incurring losses.

That the financial markets have used technology to advance beyond the purview of the regulators is a view expressed by Kane (1986a). The two parties (the regulated and the regulators) can be seen as playing an extended game of "tag" when the markets are almost always ahead of the regulatory agencies (Kane 1987b). Roberta Karmel (a former SEC commissioner and currently a law professor), expresses her concerns about the damage to the markets and the economy that can be caused by people who abuse their unregulated advantage: "There are now so many areas of the market that are unregulated, there is a growing danger that unscrupulous

people will be able to take advantage of the lack of regulation."
(Nash 1986, D1, D5)

Third, increased complexity and sophistication can be a source
of strength to market participants who want to hedge themselves
against risk. However, even the best run firms make mistakes and
complexity may render these mistakes large and dangerous. Moreover, it offers an ideal smoke screen behind which fraudulent participants can hide the illegality of their operations, deprive others of
their funds, and cause crises.

Fourth, growing interdependency, particularly in the international
markets, increases the risks of spillover from a crisis occurring at one
institution to the whole financial system.

Thus, these four factors contribute to both the risk of insolvency
for individual institutions and to the systemic risk that a single bank
failure or crisis will be swiftly transmitted through the financial sector and to the economy as a whole. While each of the factors will be
individually examined in some detail in the sections that follow, it
should be noted that they all are interrelated. Indeed, it is possible
that a need for lender-of-last-resort assistance could result from a
combination of these factors.

SIZE AND CONCENTRATION

The sheer magnitude of economic activity and the growing concentration of specific forms of financial risk among a limited group of
industry participants has led to an increased risk that major lender-
of-last-resort assistance will be necessary in order to prevent or contain a financial crisis. The large dollar payments system and large
banks' exposure to managed liabilities, international debt defaults,
and off-balance sheet risk are examples of the ways in which increases
in size and concentration may impact the lender of last resort. Greater
detail is available in the Appendices.

Large-Dollar Payments Systems

The growth in electronic funds transfer and the concentration of
payment activity among a small number of financial institutions can
lead to an increased need for lender-of-last-resort assistance as well

as the need for substantial assistance. During 1986, the average daily dollar volume of payments transferred across the two large wire transfer systems for the dollar totaled nearly $1 trillion, equal to 129.7 percent of the basic money supply (M1). This compares to only $368.4 billion or 81.5 percent of M1 in 1981, and the trend seems to be continuing upward. Almost 55 percent of the value of wire transfers is being transferred through the Federal Reserve (Fed-Wire) with the remaining 45 percent across the Clearing House Interbank Payments System (CHIPS).[1]

The concentration of payment activity also rests with the largest banks. For example, only 138 of the country's more than 14,000 banks use CHIPS, and these banks all use one of thirteen "settlement banks" for final payment. The concentration of payments flows through this relatively small number of banks increases the probability that a failure to settle by any one of these settlement banks will have a serious effect on the clearing of payments. The Federal Reserve would then have to decide whether to step in and provide emergency assistance in order to prevent settlement failure from then becoming a much larger, systemwide problem.

Risks. The credit and operational risks involved in the private networks are significant. Credit risk refers to the individual risk of default, the inability of a single participant to cover its overdraft position with the system, as well as the systemic risk that an individual default would prevent the system as a whole from settling. Operational risk refers to the potential for a disruption in the payments mechanism due to computer failure, fraud, or other operational problems at one of the participants or by the system as a whole. A failure in one of the wire transfer networks could significantly disrupt normal domestic and international payment flows.

The payments system provides four important services that are essential to the economy. Their essentiality must be considered in evaluating lender of last resort responsibilities. First, most transactions in the U.S. economy are conducted either electronically or by check.[2] These exchanges are primarily funneled through the banking system. The direct role of providing a low-cost, efficient mechanism for rapidly transferring funds between financial institutions is the obvious impetus behind the development of the private payments systems. Second, it is through the payments system that credit is supplied to a national market. Third, the U.S. Treasury uses the payments system and the related Treasury bond market to fund the operating needs of the U.S. government. Fourth and finally, the ability of the Federal Reserve to implement monetary policy is dependent upon an effective payments transmittal system.

An unresolved crisis in the present, Fed-dominated, domestic payment system would not only delay or disrupt payments between banks, corporations, and individuals, but could also disrupt the credit intermediation process, produce a crisis in the ability of the government to fund itself, and could even prevent the Federal Reserve from taking measures to offset these situations. Rather than face such a situation, the Federal Reserve could be expected to provide liquidity assistance to one of the private payment networks and its participant banks in order to maintain overall economic stability.[3]

The Federal Reserve has traditionally used its support of the banking system as its primary tool for providing liquidity to the real sector. It relies on the information gathering and analytical expertise of commercial banks to efficiently provide credit flows to the rest of the economy. Federal Reserve support of the payments system is part of this strategy. Nevertheless, the legal and operational distinction between commercial banks and other financial institutions is rapidly disappearing under deregulation. Non-depository financial institutions (NDFIs) now carry out some of the same functions of commercial banks. NDFIs originate transfers on the payments networks. A liquidity crisis at one of the NDFIs could conceivably spread through the payments system to commercial banks and the real sector, or alternatively, a crisis in the payments system could overtake the banks, and rapidly spread to the real sector.

The BONY Disruption

An example of Federal Reserve assistance to the payments system occurred on November 20, 1985, when the Bank of New York (BONY), one of the major bank participants in the U.S. government securities market, experienced a computer failure in its government securities processing system.[4]

This resulted in the Bank of New York being unable to receive payment for its securities transactions. Consequently, during the day BONY accumulated a large daylight overdraft at the Federal Reserve. The Federal Reserve Bank of New York became so concerned about the repercussions of BONY's incapacitation on the financial markets and the failure of its own attempt to insulate the rest of the market from BONY's problems that it made an unprecedentedly large discount window loan of $23.6 billion to the troubled bank.

As E. Gerald Corrigan, president of the Federal Reserve Bank of New York testified:

> Fortunately for all concerned, the Bank of New York was able to restore normal operations within a short time after the stoppage was put in place. So we did not have to confront a general stoppage in market activity or clearings that day. [...] So what I conclude from this experience is that, at least as things now exist and without potentially major changes in market practices and clearing techniques, it is unrealistic to think of "disconnecting" a major participant except in circumstances which, in the end, might require closing the market as a whole. (Corrigan 1985)

Fed critics have complained, however, that the Fed congratulates itself without specifying the costs and benefits of its actions (Kane 1987a).

International Debt

Since 1982, the ability of less developed countries (LDCs) to service their bank debt has been in question. A series of "debt crises" erupted, the most recent beginning in 1986, casting doubt on whether U.S. commercial banks will receive payment on their LDC debt portfolios.

The liquidity and solvency risks stemming from the international debt problems are not different in type from other financial difficulties which can arise in operating a depository institution. They are however, vastly different in degree due to the magnitude of the debt problem. As of December 1986, the 206 banks reporting exposure to the Federal Financial Institutions Examination Council (FFIEC) had outstanding loans to the major LDC debtors totalling $88.8 billion, or 81 percent of capital. The nine largest banks have the highest LDC debt exposure-$57.8 billion, or 132.66 percent of capital.

A key question is whether the Federal Reserve and the other bank regulators have the ability to control the massive financial crisis which would arise if all or several large LDC debtors simultaneously defaulted on their debt. It is, however, unlikely that all troubled debtors would default at once or that all of the debt of one country would be uncollectible.

One method for estimating the effect of the international debt situation on the solvency of commercial banks is to look at the discounts offered in the secondary market for loans to major debtor nations. There are problems with this method because the market is small. While some argue that the market is growing. (See Kane 1986b), market volume data are not available publicly to accurately determine market size. The prices in the secondary market are a more accurate reflection of the price which market participants, mainly European banks and regional or small U.S. banks, are willing to sell part of their LDC debt portfolio than a reflection of the probability of debtor repayment. Nonetheless, this procedure provides some information on the potential size of the problem. If the full discounts offered in March 1986 for the debt traded in the secondary markets are applied to the reporting banks, 27.3 percent of their capital would be compromised. This percentage rises to 43.9 percent for the nine largest banks.

Several U.S. commercial banks, beginning with Citibank, have significantly boosted loan-loss reserves to reflect the reduced probability of debtor repayment. The market has responded favorably to this action by bidding up the banks' stock prices despite the fact that some of these banks will post large losses for 1987.

Further complicating problems associated with LDC debt are the international and political aspects of any potential crisis. Although virtually all the LDC debt is denominated in dollars, European and Japanese banks are major lenders to LDCs.[5] Therefore, unilateral commercial bank, regulatory, and central bank responses to the LDC debt crisis raise competitive issues. If, for example, U.S. bank regulators require additional reserves for LDC debt exposure (a measure being considered), U.S. banks might be placed at a competitive disadvantage to those banks which do not have a similar regulatory requirement.

Finally, unlike other potential trigger areas for a financial crisis, an LDC debt crisis could erupt from the political arena. Several debtor nations, including Peru, Bolivia, and Brazil have curtailed debt repayments. These actions are politically, not financially, motivated. Additional debtors may motivate partial or full repayment moratoriums in response to growing popular pressure. Therefore, any measures designed to ease the LDC debt crisis, including continued economic austerity, must consider how the local population will fare. Otherwise, the proposed solution could backfire and exacerbate the crisis.

An international debt default that increases the probability of bank failure would reduce the willingness of large depositors to renew their CDs (certificates of deposit) at banks with large international exposures. A "flight to quality" could develop, in which uninsured depositors attempt to switch funds to those banks with lower exposure. In the short term, this flight would result in a liquidity squeeze and increased borrowing rates for the institutions with greater exposure. Without lender-of-last-resort support, or a private recycling of deposits from strong to weak banks, these institutions might be forced to sell assets at a heavy discount and face certain and/or deeper insolvency.[6]

The insolvency of several of the largest financial institutions could have serious consequences for the rest of the economy. For example, in the long run, reduced funding and higher risk premiums on deposits would lead to reduced lending opportunities for the institutions involved and a serious credit intermediation gap stretching beyond the financial sector.

The Dangers of a Flight To Quality

A redistribution of funds in reaction to changing perceptions of riskiness among financial institutions is both normal and healthy for the financial system. However, when such a redistribution happens on a massive scale, a disruption in the banking system can result. Kaufman (1987) argues that money is unable to flee the banking system (it is simply shifted from one bank to another) and the crisis should therefore not affect the money supply.[7] Nevertheless, credit flows can be disrupted. The banks receiving deposits might not have the capital, managerial ability, and/or inclination to provide for the credit needs of the customers of the banks losing deposits.

There are three factors that have to be considered with respect to the credit markets' efficient functioning. First, in the 1930s, there was no national loan market. Failure of their bank left many firms and individuals without access to credit. Bernanke (1983) has argued that a reduction in credit intermediation contributed to the severity of the Great Depression. A question arises whether a similar situation could arise today.

Since borrowers are more concentrated geographically than depositors, large banks have developed the expertise to handle the sophisticated financial needs of the large borrowers. Could the failure of one or more of these large banks leave some large, regional, or middle market borrowers without bank access? While today access could probably be reestablished, there is a certain amount of time and expense which is required in developing a banking relationship. This does not imply that banking markets are inefficient, but simply that information gathering and other transactions costs are sizable. Thus, the failure of several large banks would hamper borrowers who needed to reestablish banking relationships with other sound banks. Finally, the smaller domestic banks are likely net providers of funds to the larger banks and would lose their safe outlets for funds. Avoiding the disruption of existing large and important credit relationships is possibly the most important role of the lender of last resort.

What everyone ultimately fears is a repetition of the experiences of the Great Depression where massive bank failures disrupted the money supply, credit flows, and overall economic activities.[8] But even in the Great Depression, the largest banks did not fail, in general. The simultaneous failure of a number of the largest banks is unprecedented in the United States.[9] Even the high cost of containing the failure of Continental Illinois would be small in comparison to the cost of providing massive lender of last resort assistance to contain a widespread international debt crisis. The liquidity and solvency risks stemming from the international debt problems are not different in type from the normal financial difficulties which can arise in operating a depository institution. They are, however, vastly different in degree due to the magnitude of the debt problem. A key question is whether the Federal Reserve, and the other federal banking regulators, have the ability to manage a massive solvency problem at the major banks with the same ease with which the Federal Reserve can handle the liquidity problems arising from the international debt or some other crisis.

Off-Balance Sheet Liabilities

The changing nature of bank risk, with an increased concentration on contingent or off-balance sheet risk, is of concern as it may increase the frequency of the need for lender-of-last-resort assistance. A tendency has developed among financial institutions, particularly large banks, to increase revenues and add exposure without adding assets as they are measured by federal regulators, under regulatory accounting principles (RAP) or even under generally accepted accounting principles (GAAP).[10] This process has been accomplished by the addition of free-generating transactions which result in off-balance sheet liabilities. Where these activities result in contingent liabilities, they are recognized on the economists' notion of an expanded, all-inclusive balance sheet. Where known, these contingent liabilities can reduce the value of stockholders' net worth. Thus, while, in fact, supported by the economic capital of the bank, these contingent liabilities do not currently enter into the regulatory calculation of capital adequacy. Since most of risk is borne by bank capital, the effective capital cushion is being reduced by the growth of off-balance sheet activities. However, early in 1987 the Bank of England and the Federal Reserve issued a joint proposal on capital adequacy, which takes some first steps toward including off-balance sheet exposures. As the year progressed the risk-based capital proposal was referred to and adopted by other western countries.

There are many different types of off-balance sheet risk that can be undertaken by commercial banks. The revised, 1986 call reports provide data on sixteen off-balance sheet items. The resulting data, disaggregated by size category of bank, are presented in Table 4-1. The total value of commitments comprised 8,051.7 percent of capital and 157.0 percent of assets in December 1986 at banks having over $10 billion in assets. On average, at the banks in the next largest size category ($1–10 billion in assets), commitments were almost 500 percent of capital and almost 30 percent of assets. Commitments were also important in relation to capital at the remaining three categories of banks.

For the largest banks, investments to buy foreign exchange forward were the largest item; commitments to make or buy loans, the second largest component; and standby letters of credit, the third. These items were also the most important at the next category of banks, although their rankings were different. While these data are noteworthy, they are not fully comprehensive. Data on interest rate swaps, an important new off-balance sheet involvement, for example, were omitted from the call reports until 1985 and are also omitted from Table 4-1. The data items that are being collected by the regulators represent only a portion of the off-balance sheet transactions and adequate measures of risk exposure do not exist. Additionally, many of the data had not been collected until recently, making intertemporal comparisons difficult.

Table 4-1. Off-Balance Sheet Commitments: December 1986 ($ Billion).

Bank Size	Above $10	$1–10	$0.3–1	$0.1–0.3	$.025–.01	Total
Consolidated Assets	1055.4	899.2	276.7	305.0	333.6	2,869.9
Consolidated Capital	54.3	53.5	18.7	22.2	27.2	175.9
Commitments						
Standby Letters of Credit	128.1	33.2	4.6	2.0	0.0	167.9
Commercial Letters Credit	19.0	7.4	1.1	0.5	0.5	28.5
Commitments to Make/Buy Loans	357.9	168.6	22.7	13.5	8.0	570.7
Commitments to Buy Fut/Forwards	89.1	9.7	0.2	0.3	0.0	99.3
Commitments to Sell Fut/Forwards	72.3	7.0	0.2	0.1	0.0	79.6
Obligations to Buy Under Option Contracts	25.5	1.9	0.2	0.0	0.0	27.6
Obligations to Sell Under Option Contracts	9.5	2.0	0.1	0.1	0.0	11.7
Participation in Acceptances Conveyed to Others	4.4	1.1	0.0	0.0	0.0	5.5
Participation in Acceptances Acquired	0.0	0.3	0.0	0.0	0.0	0.3
Commitments to Buy When-Issued Securities	7.3	2.3	0.2	0.0	0.0	9.8
Commitments to Sell When-Issued Securities	4.5	1.6	0.1	0.0	0.0	6.2
Commitments to Buy Forward Exchange	869.0	23.4	0.1	0.0	0.0	892.5
Securities Borrowed	2.9	1.3	0.8	0.4	0.0	5.4
Securities Lent	1.7	1.4	0.4	0.3	0.2	4.0
Other Significant Commitments	65.9	4.7	0.1	0.2	0.0	70.9
Total Commitments[a]	1,657.1	265.9	30.8	17.4	8.7	1,979.9
As a Percentage of:						
Consolidated Capital	8,051.7	497.0	164.7	78.4	32.0	
Consolidated Assets	157.0	29.6	11.1	5.7	2.6	

Source: Data calculated by the authors from Federal Deposit Insurance Corporation (1986).
a. Excludes Data on interest rate swaps, valued at $367 billion industry-wide in 1986.

Thus, during 1986 and 1987, the regulators took some preliminary steps to come to grips with these problems. New contingent liability items were added to the call reports as regulators came to appreciate both the substantial risk and increased usage of off-balance sheet items. The call report revision results in recognizing additional liabilities explicitly on the balance sheet without adding any new assets. The fee changed for the line of credit, for example, has already appeared on the income statement and balance sheet. Thus, the process of recognizing contingent liabilities serves to reduce the reported, book value, of new worth. It brings the reported value more in line with the economist's concept of capital and the markets' estimation of the value of equity. If the regulators retain the stated levels of capital adequacy, the banking industry will need to raise new capital.

Moreover, the risk-based capital proposal divides assets into several categories according to their perceived riskiness and requires more capital to be held to back risky asset portfolios. In general, the Federal Reserve and the Bank of England are moving toward raising capital requirements. Thus, capital ratios appear likely to rise in the banking industry, but this favorable trend is not yet evident in the thrift industry.

Standby Letters of Credit

One often-used measurement of the growth in off-balance sheet risk is the increased use of standby letters of credit (SLC).[11] The risk of these transactions is similar to that of a commercial loan. Although many bankers would claim that these transactions are less risky than most commercial loans since they are intended to be made available for only their best, "blue chip" customers, the risk of loss to the bank is, nonetheless, somewhat equivalent to a loan of similar duration to these same customers.[12]

Data on standby letters of credit are provided in Koppenhaver (1987) and are reproduced in Table 4–2. The table shows that SLCs at all commercial banks grew from $5.0 billion at year-end 1973 to $169.5 in 1986. In 1973 only 7.7 percent of banks had reported holding this off-balance sheet item. By December 1986, the percentage had risen to 55.6. SLCs are particularly important to large banks. At the end of 1986, all thirty-three commercial banks with assets

Table 4-2. Gross Standby Letters of Credit Issued by U.S. Commercial Banks: 1973-86.

Year End	Outstanding (in Billions $)	All Banks		Assets > $500 Million			Assets > $10 Billion		
		Percent Reporting	Ratio to Equity[a]	Percent Reporting	Ratio to Equity	Market Share[b]	Percent Reporting	Ratio to Equity	Market Share
1973	5.0	7.7%[c] (1,095)	8.4%	80.0% (155)	15.9%	91%	72.7% (8)	23.8%	38%
1974	10.6	12.8 (1,851)	6.8	92.6 (200)	13.8	94	100 (12)	39.2	68
1975	11.7	14.3 (2,092)	6.4	91.4 (201)	13.4	94	100 (12)	41.9	69
1976	15.1	20.1 (2,942)	6.5	95.8 (226)	13.5	93	100 (13)	48.2	73
1977	19.7	24.1 (3,529)	6.9	95.6 (258)	15.7	94	100 (15)	54.6	74
1978	25.7	29.3 (4,286)	7.8	96.1 (297)	20.4	94	100 (17)	61.2	76
1979	34.7	33.7 (4,891)	7.9	96.1 (317)	23.0	94	100 (17)	79.5	76
1980	46.9	37.6 (5,507)	8.9	96.6 (344)	27.9	94	100 (19)	92.4	75
1981	71.5	43.3 (6,297)	10.4	96.7 (385)	33.9	95	100 (22)	125.5	77

1982	100.3	48.1 (7,011)	12.6	97.6 (403)	63.1	95	100 (23)	166.8	77
1983	119.6	54.3 (7,849)	11.8	98.7 (444)	43.9	96	100 (23)	183.1	77
1984	145.6	47.8 (6,920)	12.9	92.8 (450)	48.1	96	100 (24)	194.1	76
1985	175.0	52.5 (7,656)	12.7	91.5 (483)	52.1	97	100 (28)	191.2	76
1986	169.5	55.6 (7,859)	11.7	93.9 (523)	46.2	97	100 (33)	155.9	76

Source: Koppenhaver (1987, 30).
a. Average ratio for issuing banks only.
b. Standbys issued relative to total amount outstanding.
c. Numbers in parentheses are the numbers of banks reporting SLCs.

over $10 billion held SLCs, which comprised 155.9 percent of their equity and 76 percent of the total SCL market. The 523 largest banks with assets over $500 million commanded 97 percent of the market. Of these large banks, 93.9 percent held SLCs and their ratio to equity was 46.2 percent.

Off-Balance Sheet Risk

Many of the off-balance sheet transactions are highly complex, and risk may be high for smaller institutions who do not completely understand and/or are unable to control all aspects of risk. Regulators are just beginning to study off-balance sheet risk closely, as they examine the data the call reports provide.

In addition to the effective reduction of capital adequacy (and therefore the increased probability of insolvency), one of the major problems with the off-balance sheet liabilities is the fact that overall bank liquidity may be reduced significantly through the use of off-balance sheet financing. Banks may move their best, more liquid assets such as loans to prime borrowers, off their balance sheets. They may replace them with riskier illiquid assets such as loans to customers who are in difficulties and have taken down their contingent credit line. Then a small liquidity crunch could result in funding problems. Moreover, if the bank were perceived to be jeopardy as a result of off-balance sheet losses, funding problems could deteriorate rapidly.

Illiquidity could be further complicated by the off-balance sheet commitments to lend at set rates. Fixed rate commitments expose banks to interest rate risk which can make them unprofitable if funding costs rise. Moreover, if the banks facing takedowns of loan commitments made at below market rates are unable to attract funds to meet these demands at any price, they will have to turn to the lender of last resort for liquidity assistance on a more regular basis. If the liquidity crisis is severe, all (or many) banks may have to turn to the lender of last resort simultaneously. Finally, the lender of last resort would not have access to the highest quality assets (which are now off-balance sheet) as collateral for liquidity support.

Banks have increased off-balance sheet activities in response to competitive changes in the financial services industry. Syndicated lending, the backbone of traditional international banking, has fallen dramatically.[13] This is largely because commercial firms are now able to obtain cheaper funding directly in the capital markets (Federal Reserve Bank of New York 1986). Consequently, the commercial banks' total share of the direct credit market has been reduced. To compete with cheaper alternative funding sources, commercial banks have reduced spreads on new loans, thus reducing profit margins. As will be discussed later in this chapter, this trend reduces the effectiveness in the Fed's traditional way of handling crises through the banking system.

THE SPEED OF TRANSMISSION AND URGENCY OF REGULATORY RESPONSE

Bank technology has increased the speed by which funds flow through the financial sector. Together with an increased availability of information and rapid worldwide communications, financial markets have become more efficient and responsive to market opportunities. However, this same technology has also increased the speed by which a crisis can encompass a single institution or be transmitted throughout the financial system. Therefore, the potential need for urgent regulatory (including lender of last resort) response has similarly increased.

As the analyses by Sinkey (1986) of the crisis at Continental Illinois and by Garcia (1987a), Kane (1987b), and McCullough (1987) of the problems in the privately insured thrifts in Ohio and Maryland demonstrate, the market reacts rapidly to negative information. The reaction is especially strong when there is bad news that confirms insolvency where previously there was uncertainty regarding the quality of bank assets, as was the case at Continental as well as some of the savings and loans associations in Ohio and Maryland.

Continental. Continental Illinois' liquidity troubles first appeared in its inability to retain large institutional deposits. In this case the "run" was electronic. Major institutional depositors in effect "lined up" in Continental's wire room by declining to renew short-term uninsured deposits. Because of Continental's dependence on short-term purchased funds, federal regulators had only a couple of weeks to agree on a course of action to prevent the collapse of the nation's seventh largest bank (in terms of assets) and prevent any possible contagion or spillover effects. This contrasted sharply with previous assistance packages such as the one at Franklin National Bank, where assistance was increased in 1974 over a period of months while the regulators attempted to devise a plan to deal with the situation.

Dependence on Managed Liabilities. The banking system's dependence on managed liabilities, which consist of large CDs and purchased funds, has risen from less than 10 percent in 1962, just after Citicorp invented the large CD, to 30 percent of bank assets in December 1986. At the same time, the share of core deposits (which include demand deposits, savings and small time deposits, and since the beginning of 1983, money market deposits) has fallen correspondingly from 87.3 percent of non-equity liabilities to 60.4 percent. These data are shown in Table 4–3. Over the period, checkable deposits declined from 54.4 percent to 22.2 percent of bank liabilities, while small time and savings deposits remained at a relatively constant percentage until the introduction of the money market deposit account and reached 38.2 percent of bank liabilities at the end of 1986.

Moreover, it is the large banks that are particularly dependent on managed liabilities. As Table 4–4 shows, at the end of 1986, 47.1 percent of large bank assets were funded by managed liabilities, while only 10.5 percent of small bank liabilities were obtained from this source.

S & L Crises. Likewise, the deposit insurance crises of Ohio and Maryland deteriorated very rapidly. The underlying problems had developed over a period of years. Informed depositors withdrew their funds before the bad news became public and made the individual S & L insolvencies evident to all. Then, individual depositors lined up at the banks and attempted to withdraw their funds when it was realized that the solvency of the state-sponsored (private) deposit insurance funds was in jeopardy.[14] The states (with logistical support from the federal regulators) were forced by circumstance to respond within days, possibly before they understood the full implications of the problems.

BONY. More recently, the Federal Reserve Bank of New York considered that it had no real choice other than to advance an overnight loan of $23.6 billion dollars to the Bank of New York in order to

Table 4-3. Core Deposits and Managed Deposits at Commercial Banks: 1962–86.

| | Total Liabilities ($ billion) | Checkable Deposits | Small Time and Savings Deposits | Percentage | | |
				Core Deposits[a]	Large Time Deposits[b]	Federal Funds and RPs[c]
1962	247.4	54.4	32.9	87.3	6.6	0.0
1965	317.7	46.8	36.4	83.2	9.8	0.5
1970	496.3	38.2	36.1	74.3	10.9	0.9
1975	877.2	27.7	34.6	62.2	17.3	3.4
1980	1,469.1	23.3	32.2	55.5	18.5	7.8
1985	2,295.3	20.4	39.1	59.5	14.4	7.9
1986	2,535.7	22.2	38.2	60.4	13.2	7.7

Sources: Authors' calculations from data in Board of Governors of the Federal Reserve (1986b, 17, 18); Revised Quarterly Levels 85/QIV–87/QI, Sector Statements, Commercial Banking.

a. Core deposits are checkable deposits plus small time and savings deposits.
b. Deposits over $100,000.
c. Federal funds purchased and security repurchase agreements.

Table 4-4. Core Deposits and Managed Liabilities by Bank Size, December 1986.

Asset Size	Number of Banks	Liability Composition (percentage)		
		Core Deposits[a]	Managed Liabilities	Other Liabilities
$10B or more	33	35.48	47.07	12.31
$1B to $10B	307	59.74	27.99	6.31
$300M to $1B	550	70.55	18.91	3.80
$100M to $300M	1,902	76.53	12.21	2.99
$100M or less	11,406	78.72	10.46	2.43
All Banks	14,198	56.40	30.04	7.35

Source: Authors' calculations from data in FDIC (1986).
a. Weighted mean.

avoid a disruption in the Treasury bond market resulting from a computer failure. Only hours were available to make this multibillion dollar decision (Volcker 1985, Corrigan 1985).[15]

COMPLEXITY

The increasing complexity and sophistication of financial transactions also tends to augment the potential need for frequent lender-of-last-resort assistance. In the past two decades there have been some basic changes in the competitive structure of banking. Traditionally, banks would borrow from local depositors and lend to local businesses and individuals. If excess funds were available, these would be invested in other banks or in government securities. Today, some banks no longer depend on the intermediation of local demand and time deposits.

An increased sophistication and a sensitivity to interest rates among corporate cash managers and individual depositors have lead to the virtual elimination of core deposits (demand deposits, consumer transactions, and savings deposits) at some institutions (Corrigan 1982). Liability management, the careful matching of the volume of loans and other assets with the multitude of liability and capital sources available, is becoming the rule rather than the exception at financial institutions. At the same time, the maturities or the durations of assets and liabilities may not be matched, so that the bank is exposed to losses from interest rate risk. Innovative risk management techniques, including the use of options and financial futures, are being used at some financial institutions. As regulatory and accounting concerns are met, it is expected that the use of these innovative techniques will increase (Merrick and Figlewski 1984; Booth, Smith, and Stoltz, 1984).

On the asset side, transactions are also tending towards greater complexity. A number of financial intermediaries may be involved in the same transaction (as lenders, guarantors, or agents), each with different risks, legal rights, and obligations. Securitization, the process of bundling a portfolio of assets (for example, auto loans, mortgages, or credit card receivables and even commercial loans) and selling them to Wall Street investors has gained in popularity. This increased intermediation has resulted in a reduction of the transparency of financial transactions. It is often not clear to participants and regulators, let alone outsiders, who actually bears the risk when several layers of financial intermediaries are involved in a single transaction.[16] Existing systems of information gathering may be inadequate to enable the Federal Reserve and other bank regulators to properly evaluate some transactions. This situation may make it difficult for them to measure the solvency of financial institutions and could prevent or seriously delay the provision of collateralized discount window support in a crisis.

Complexity and Risk

There are two contradictory explanations of how risk can be affected by adding layers to the transaction. On the other hand, *overall* risk may be increased if this lack of transparency prevents market participants and their regulators from properly analyzing complex transactions, or causes them to assume that other participants have properly evaluated the risk. On the other hand, it can be argued that adding layers of underwriting to the transactions will only serve to increase diversification and so reduce risk. Diversification can add more capital to protect against a given level of risk, and underwriting the transactions will only serve to increase overall diversification and provide for a more efficient allocation of risk through the economy.

Several problems have arisen from transaction "opaquences" sur-rounding mortgage guarantees provided by insurance companies. The losses incurred by TICOR and the Bank of America illustrate the dangers of transaction complexity used by dishonest people to de-fraud financial institutions of various kinds. In 1985, TICOR (as insurer of mortgages in default and written on overvalued energy and real estate partnerships) lost two-thirds of its capital in making good its guarantees. In the same year, Bank of America lost $133 million as a result of acting as escrow agent for numerous small banks and thrifts that wrote insured mortgages on real estate partnerships formed by Equity Program Investments Corporation (EPIC)—an affiliate of Community Savings and Loan Association which failed during the Maryland S & L crisis. The mortgage insurance proved worthless. In both of these cases, the parties to the contacts had (wrongly) trusted that someone else had conducted a careful and honest credit analysis of the borrowers.[17]

While the evidence on the effects of greater complexity on the direction of overall riskiness is inconclusive, increased complexity can lead to increased difficulty in the execution of lender-of-last-resort assistance when it is required. Regulators will have a more dif-ficult time identifying potential losses and contingent liabilities. The line between illiquidity and insolvency will be even harder to distin-guish than it has been in the past, when it was already acknowledged to be a problem.[18]

One final consideration is that the more sophisticated and com-plex transactions are also more likely to be accompanied by signifi-cant externalities (costs which are not borne by the institution in-volved, but rather by a third party or by society as a whole). For example, an economically insolvent commercial bank might be more willing to engage in speculative foreign exchange transactions know-ing that its deposits were backed by federal deposit insurance. With federal insurance it would not have to pay higher rates to attract deposits to support its risky activities. If successful, the bank might overcome its solvency problems, while the deposit insurer would underwrite any losses. This problem has existed since the creation of deposit insurance in 1934, but has become much more important as transactions have become more complex and subject to new types of risk.

A private sector participant may only be looking at internal prof-itability and ignore costs which it will not bear directly. When part of the costs and/or risk can be passed on to other market participants such as the federal deposit insurers or the lender of last resort, total risk is likely to increase (Kane 1986b). If a significant portion of these costs will be borne by society in the event of a failure, the probability that the lender of last resort will have to step in will also increase.

INTERDEPENDENCY

The final aspect which must be considered in evaluating potential lender-of-last-resort assistance is the growing interdependency between financial institutions (and to a lesser extent between financial and nonfinancial institutions) that could affect both the frequency and size of lender-of-last-resort assistance.[19]

Interbank Markets (Domestic and International)

The interdependency is most obvious when examining the relationship between depository institutions.[20] Banks and other depository institutions, participate in the interbank market in order to "move towards their preferred position with respect to required reserves, loans and deposits . . . and their capital accounts" (Aliber 1985, 90). The interbank market provides a low cost method for attaining this preferred position. In the domestic financial system, the federal funds market developed as a method for banks in a surplus reserve position to sell funds to banks in a deficit reserve position.[21] The fed funds market also enables banks to arbitrage (profit from while equalizing) interest rate differentials produced by geographic and demographic variation.[22] The international interbank market has these same characteristics but has added political and foreign exchange rate risks.

Interbank chains, both domestically and internationally, can be used to diversify and reduce risks, but if mishandled, they can expose the uses to contagion. Intermediary banks may be willing to share the spread they obtain between the rate received by depositors at the beginning of the chain and that paid by risky non-bank borrowers at the end of the chain. The least risky banks (called upstream banks) funnel the deposits they receive through a spectrum of increasingly risky banks to the downstream banks that finally lend to the real sector borrowers. Intermediary banks feel that sharing the risk with other institutions more than compensates them for the reduction in return. That is, they perceive that the shared return is higher than the risk-adjusted rate of return they would obtain if they funded the loan directly from their own deposits.

Furthermore, participants may also believe that some of the banks in the chain have additional information regarding the risk of the final customers. The uninformed bank uses the interbank market to utilize this superior information. These factors result in the observed "risk tiering" of banks.[23] Each bank views the capital of the other banks in the interbank chain as a buffer against losses from the risky non-banks; in this way spreads are kept low and the interbank chain grows.

While the interbank chains are designed to spread risk, they also provide a mechanism for the swift transmission of financial crises. In this analysis, Aliber demonstrates how financial and economic shocks among the non-bank borrowers can spread through the inter-bank chain. Minor disturbances can easily be contained, however. Credit may be rationed and spreads increase, but the banks closest to the problem have capital that is strong enough to absorb the losses:

> As long as the solvency of the downstream banks [net users of funds from the interbank market] is not threatened by the shock, these banks act as a buffer between the losses of particular borrowers and the stability of the upstream banks [net providers of funds to the interbank market]. The upstream banks benefit from international diversification effected through the interbank deposit chain. If in contrast, the solvency of the downstream bank appears threatened by the shock, the upstream bank may seek to reduce its exposure to the downstream banks. And in this case, the downstream banks are squeezed between an increase in loan losses and a reduction in their ability to sell deposits to other banks (Aliber 1985, 102)

For more serious disturbances, where there is concern regarding the liquidity and solvency of some of the banks in the chain, the interbank market may prove incapable of containing a crisis. The up-stream banks, fearful of potential losses, will reduce their lending as existing debt comes due for repayment. In the international area, since the loans needing to be repaid are often not denominated in the currency of the downstream bank, the borrowing country will face a transfer problem—difficulty in obtaining necessary foreign exchange at acceptable prices:

The traditional domestic lender-of-last-resort arrangements are not especially helpful, in that the currency of the interbank market is a "foreign currency" from the viewpoint of the downstream bank and its central bank. (Aliber 1985, 104)

The forced reduction in the loan portfolios of the downstream banks and the transfer problems of their host governments will heighten the liquidity and solvency problems facing all banks in the interbank chain. The net effect may be to amplify the crisis as it moves from bank to bank along the chain. The problem is further exacerbated when several different nationalities and currencies are involved and where there is no lender of last resort (with unlimited access to the currency in question) that is ready to assist the troubled banks.

While Aliber's analysis deals specifically with international banks and the international interbank deposit chains, the model can easily be extended to domestic banks. Thompson and Todd (1987) discuss contagion risk in general and take some first steps to measure inter-bank exposure from, for example, correspondent relationships among banks in the Fourth Federal Reserve District. The authors point out the inadequacy of call report data for assessing interbank exposure and propose regulations that would reduce this exposure.

Contagion can also spread to banks from the real sector and from other financial institutions. Corrigan (1982) and others consider that the role of the lender of last resort is to support the banking sector (that is, depository institutions) which in turn, will support other troubled financial firms and the real sector borrowers who are sol-vent but need liquidity assistance. This scenario may be appropriate during normal times, but when financial or economic shocks arise, private banks may be unwilling or unable to supply the necessary funds to those who need them. A gap in lender-of-last-resort availa-bility could then arise.

SUMMARY

Thus it appears that increased size and concentration, speed, com-plexity, and interdependency in the financial markets have increased the potential for a crisis to occur.

Inappropriate laws and regulations have contributed to these de-velopments. For example, Kane (1986a) argues that the system of deposit insurance encouraged banks to overexpose themselves in the international debt arena and that Federal Reserve subsidies have encourages the growth and concentration of the domestic system of electronic transfers. A lasting solution to these problems can best be achieved by changing the incentive structure to discourage the markets from building on quicksand. However, no lasting solution is in sight. Proposals to achieve one are ignored because the transition problems of moving from the present inappropriate system to a more optimal one are substantial. Congress shows no willingness to make the changes that farsighted visionaries recommend. In the meantime, a crisis might arise. The lender of last resort and the rest of the financial safety net would be expected to handle it. The question whether they could adequately handle it remains pertinent.

Thus the increased size, concentration, complexity, and interdependence of financial transactions has increased the likelihood that a serious crisis will occur and escalate if left unattended. Unfortunately, at the same time that the probability of a serious crisis is increasing, the Federal Reserve's arrangements for handling a crisis are becoming less adequate.

The Declining Role of Banks in the Economy

Increasing attention is being paid to the attrition in the commercial bank's role in the economy (Federal Reserve Bank of New York 1986). The data on Table 4–5 show that commercial banks have lost market share to non-bank financial institutions during the past forty years. Much of the loss occurred between 1946 and 1965, but the trend has continued since then. During the same period, thrifts increased their market share in comparison to banks. Nevertheless, the share taken by banks and thrifts together has declined from almost 70 percent in 1946 to a little over 50 percent in 1985.

The data presented in Table 4–6 show another dimension of the problem that confronts commercial banks and the Federal Reserve. The commercial bank share of short-term business credit declined from 94.8 percent in 1973 to 86.8 percent in 1984. Domestic banks, the large weekly reporting banks, both inside and outside New York City, lost market share. Foreign banks increased their share from 7.6 percent of the market in 1973 to 17.8 percent in 1984. The volume of commercial paper loans that banks cannot offer also rose from 5.2 percent in 1973 to 13.2 percent in 1984.

Table 4-5. Assets of Private Domestic Financial Institutions: 1946-85.

	Commercial Banks[a]	Assets Held By Non-bank Financial Institutions[b]	Thrifts[c]	Depository Institutions[d]
1946				
$ Billion	134.2	100.0	18.9	153.1
Percentage	57.3	42.7	12.4	69.7
1965				
$ Billion	340.7	586.2	186.5	527.2
Percentage	36.8	63.2	20.1	56.9
1970				
$ Billion	504.9	882.9	152.4	657.3
Percentage	38.0	62.0	21.2	57.0
1975				
$ Billion	834.6	1,317.5	454.2	1,288.8
Percentage	38.8	61.2	21.2	60.0
1980				
$ Billion	1,389.5	2,482.8	793.4	2,182.9
Percentage	35.9	64.1	20.5	56.4
1985				
$ Billion	2,202.3	4,562.8	1,291.7	3,494.0
Percentage	32.5	67.5	19.1	51.6

Source: McCall and Saulsbury (1986).
   a. Commercial banks include U.S. banks and their domestic affiliates, foreign bank offices in the U.S. and banks in U.S. possessions, but exclude affiliates of bank holding companies and U.S. bank branches abroad.
   b. Includes S & Ls, savings banks, credit unions, life and other insurance companies, private pension funds, finance companies, open-end investment companies, security brokers and dealers, REITs (real estate investment trusts), and money market mutual funds.
   c. Data are included in those referring to non-bank financial institutions.
   d. Data are also for commercial banks and thrifts combined.

In short, the Fed's preference for giving direct assistance to commercial banks gives coverage to a smaller percentage of private assets today than it did four decades ago. Moreover, more business credit is covered by foreign banks than fifteen years ago. There is less certainty that LLR assistance will be provided to all foreign banks, because not all foreign banks are supported by a central bank that is as adept and willing to act as a lender of last resort as is the Federal Reserve.

Table 4-6. Commercial and Industrial (C & I) Loans: Dollar Volume and Percent of Short-Term Business Credit, December Average.

	1973		1977		1981		1984	
	$ Billion	Percent	$ Billion	Percent	$ Billion	Percent	$ Billion	Percent
C & I loans at all commercial banks	160.3	94.8	204.5	93.0	344.7	86.6	469.4	86.6
Domestic banks	147.5	87.2	182.5	83.0	271.1	68.1	373.2	69.0
Weekly reporting banks	107.4	63.5	121.4	55.2	198.8	49.9	252.6	46.7
New York City	32.4	19.2	35.3	16.0	54.9	13.8	63.5	11.7
Outside New York City	75.0	44.4	86.2	39.2	143.9	36.1	189.1	35.0
Other domestic	40.1	23.7	61.1	27.8	72.3	18.5	120.6	22.3
Foreign banks[a]	12.8	7.6	22.0	10.0	73.6	18.5	96.2	17.8
Commercial paper	8.8	5.2	15.5	7.0	53.3	13.4	71.3	13.2
Total short-term credit	169.1	100.0	220.0	100.0	398.0	100.0	540.7	100.0

Source: Federal Reserve Bank of New York (1986).
a. U.S. agencies, branches and subsidiaries of foreign banks.

Implications for the Lender of Last Resort

The trend away from bank financing raises an important concern for the ability of the lender of last resort to provide assistance to the financial sector during a crisis. As discussed in Chapter 3, the Fed uses the banking system as a conduit for liquidity assistance to NDFIs and IPCs. If the commercial banks provide a smaller share of the credit granted to the financial, commercial, and consumer sectors they will have reduced access to information about those in need of assistance in these sectors. In the past, it has been the commercial banks' unique knowledge about their customers that has made the Fed's preferred indirect approach to aiding troubled firms and individuals viable. In the new environment, the effectiveness of such an indirect approach to aid might be seriously impaired.

The following chapter lays out the criteria utilized in Chapters 6 and 7 for assessing the performance of the Fed in handling domestic and international crises.

NOTES

1. There were originally three private networks in existence, CHIPS (New York–Clearing Association), CHESS (Chicago Clearing House Association) and CashWire (Payments Administration Institute). CashWire was disbanded in 1985. CHESS ceased operating in 1986.
2. Avery et al. (1986) show that even among households, the sector of the economy still likely to be the most dependent on cash, 64 percent of all transactions are made by check or credit card.
3. Protecting the payments systems would be an appropriate response by the lender of last resort, but steps must also be taken to control the credit and operational risks of the private payment systems. In order to lessen the need for such assistance, the Federal Reserve and Office of the Comptroller of the Currency (OCC) have been studying the risks and recently, new regulations have been implemented to decrease systemic risk in the payments system.
4. On an average day in 1986, $230 billion changed hands across the Federal Reserve's book entry system which electronically records the ownership of Treasury instruments. The Bank of New York was the largest clearing agent in the market, processing $60 billion during a typical day.
5. Currency conversion, exchanging dollar obligations for either local or another foreign currency obligation, was an important component in the

1982 rescheduling process. It was believed that currency diversification would improve repayment probability by reducing the LDCs' dependency on the value of a single currency. A majority of the debt, however, remains dominated in dollars.

6. Even with central bank support, there is no guarantee that the problems will not result in technical insolvency at some institutions if a significant portion of the LDC debts cannot be paid. In May 1987, Citicorp voluntarily made large loan-loss provisions for its LDC debt. Other banks, including large banks with low capital, followed suit. By September 1987, no insolvencies had been declared because the loan-loss reserves are included in both the regulators' primary and total capital measures.

7. If the banks receiving the funds kept higher reserves (due to conservative management or the funds being switched into more liquid accounts which have higher reserve requirements) there could be a reduction in the money supply for a given quantity of reserves. This could, however, be counteracted by Federal Reserve actions.

8. See Bernanke (1983) and Friedman and Schwartz (1963).

9. It is not, however, unprecedented in other countries. See Kindleberger (1985). In other countries the failure of Creditsbank of Austria in 1928, believed by many to have precipitated the events leading to the Great Depression; the German hyperinflation following World War I; and the recent collapse of some of the financial systems in the developing nations, provide rare examples of simultaneous problems among the largest banks.

10. Koehn and Santomero (1980) demonstrate how (given the existence of deposit insurance) riskier banks may decide to increase the overall riskiness of their portfolio in order to earn an acceptable return on capital. An alternative to increasing the risk of the funded portfolio is to avoid the capital adequacy guidelines by adding off-balance sheet liabilities.

11. A standby letter of credit is a recent variant of the commercial letter of credit which is widely used in international trade. In a commercial letter of credit, for example, a line of credit is established by a bank for the importer. The importer uses the credit line to speedily pay the exporter before the imported goods are sold to the final consumer. A standby letter of credit, on the other hand, can be used to guarantee performance on a contract. The credit line is taken down only when the provider of the good or service fails to perform according to contract.

12. See Bennett (1986) for an earlier discussion of the growth and significance of SLCs.

13. Syndicated Eurobank loans have fallen from $96.5 billion in 1981 to $21.6 billion in 1985 (BIS 1986).

14. The *Washington Post* (17 May 1985) reports that out of state depositors began withdrawing their deposits by mail from privately insured S & Ls in Maryland five weeks before depositors lined up to withdraw their funds in person.

15. Fed critics argue that the Fed merely followed the path of bureaucratic least resistance. Giving aid was simpler, say the critics, than refusing it, because the Fed is not held accountable for the costs of the aid it provides.

16. The earlier proposed relationship between Citicorp and Chatsworth Corporation is an example of a complex, opaque financial transaction. Citicorp planned to "sell" blue chip loans to Chatsworth, an independent company. Citibank would guarantee the first 10 percent of portfolio losses and Chatsworth would obtain a guarantee from an insurance company for the remaining 90 percent. Since Citibank was only responsible for 10 percent of the risk, the bank wanted to reflect the 10 percent as a contingent liability and remove the assets entirely from its balance sheet. Because the 10 percent guarantee was larger than any expected loss on the blue chip portfolio, the OCC ruled that Citibank had not actually reduced its risk exposure and could not, therefore remove the exposure from its balance sheet and would have to show the "sale" as "other borrowings." Following this ruling, Citibank declined to use Chatsworth Corporation for further "asset sales."

17. These issues are discussed further in GAO (1987c). The EPIC and TICOR cases are also discussed in Anderson (1987) and Garcia (1987a).

18. When the Penn Square Bank was liquidated instead of being purchased and assumed, one of the reasons for closure cited by the regulators was the existence of a large quantity of loans sold with recourse to Penn Square. This contingent liability could have been transferred to the FDIC if the bank had been kept open in a purchase and assumption agreement.

19. Longstreth (1983), a commissioner of the Securities and Exchange Commission (SEC), maintained that the links between financial service intermediaries (depository, insurance, and investment institutions) "are too extensive (and growing stronger and more numerous) to prevent one failure from triggering others" and that "the collateral consequences of failures often pose unacceptable costs to our financial system." He therefore argues that a new system of regulation, encompassing all financial intermediaries and combining the forces of disclosure and market discipline, is required.

20. The following analysis of interbank chains is drawn largely from Aliber (1985).

21. As long as the Federal Reserve does not pay interest on reserve positions, a commercial bank maintaining excess reserves is inefficiently using its surplus resources. Interest which can be earned, even at low rates, should be preferred to maintaining reserves above optimal levels (including required reserves, working reserves, and some level of precautionary reserves). The Fed funds market provides an inexpensive low risk method of matching banks with excess reserves with banks with reserve shortages.

22. Both depositors and borrowers prefer dealing with local banks. Borrowers tend to be more geographically concentrated (at least by dollar volumes)

than depositors. Therefore, in the absence of the federal funds and international interbank markets, loan rates would be lower in those areas which have a higher concentration of lenders. Through arbitrage this differential can be reduced, and financial markets are able to function more efficiently. See Aliber (1985) for a more complete discussion.

23. The expected rate of return for the riskier banks is higher than that of those banks perceived to be less risky. "These banks maintain their lower cost of capital by being selective and cautious about the loans they wish to acquire . . . [Banks that are net borrowers in the interbank market] have a higher cost of capital because they are perceived to be riskier. Given their higher capital costs, they must limit themselves to the riskier subset of available loans, because the interest rates on the less risky loans may be too low given the bank's cost of capital." (Aliber 1985, 97)

5 EVALUATION CRITERIA

As described in the Preface, an eclectic approach was adopted to establish the criteria presented in this chapter. These criteria will be used in the following chapters to assess Federal Reserve performance in its domestic and international lender-of-last-resort roles. Experience was gained from expert writings and from the research team's examination of the case studies that are presented in the appendices. The criteria were also discussed with leading academics and with other interested parties, particularly Federal Reserve officials and the staffs of the U.S. Congress, House and Senate Banking Committees.

ESTABLISHING THE CRITERIA OF EFFECTIVENESS AND EQUITY

A discussion of the lender of last resort's role is typically approached from a practical rather than theoretical perspective. Shafer (1982) points out that there is no formal theory of liquidity assistance in the literature based on a mathematical framework, which is often the preferred approach among academic economists—the people who usually talk and write about lender-of-last-resort operations.[1] Even knowledgeable academics have chosen a practical, intuitive, rather than a theoretical, approach.

The criteria are applicable to a world in which the U.S. central bank is operating independently of, or in cooperation with, the federal financial safety net. They are set to allow the Federal Reserve to prevent and contain crises in the present, imperfect world where inappropriate laws and regulations have provided incentives to undue risk taking which, in the less inflationary world of the mid 1980s, has revealed the financial system to be exposed to insolvencies and crises. The criteria apply to a Federal Reserve that will be expected to contain these instances as they occur. In a more perfect world that would follow deposit insurance and other financial sector reforms, the Fed would have a smaller role to play.

Effectiveness and equity are the principal criteria used to evaluate the Federal Reserve's performance as lender of last resort.[2] Effectiveness is chosen as the first criterion to facilitate a judgment as to how well the Federal Reserve—the principal agency responsible for lender-of-last-resort operations—in cooperation with the rest of the safety net, achieves its goals of ensuring the safety, soundness, and efficiency of the financial system. The ultimate test of effective central bank performance is how well it preserves the strength of the overall financial economic system and public confidence in it. Effectiveness is used to measure how well the Federal Reserve mitigates the adverse effects of external shocks on the banking system, the financial system, and the rest of the economy.

Equity is the second criterion, since the Federal Reserve can be judged against its success in protecting the equalitarian ideals of the U.S. society embodied in its political, legal, and moral traditions. The ultimate equity goal of the lender of last resort should be to provide fair and impartial access to, and treatment of, those similar institutions that have legal access to its liquidity facilities. Equity is used to judge whether the terms and conditions of liquidity assistance ensure certain access for all solvent market participants, do not subsidize the losses of a few large institutions, and equally treat the similar customers, depositors, creditors, and shareholders of different institutions. LLR actions should also be fair to society by not imposing undue costs, explicit and behavioral, in relation to their benefits. Where the lender of last resort's potential clienteles are dissimilar for some reason, the new economic theory of "super-fairness" (Baumol 1986) is applied to evaluate the equity of Federal Reserve actions and policies. The ultimate goal of equitable lender of last resort and financial safety net performance is to act in the interests of society and the entire financial system, not of particular institutions.

There are trade-offs between effectiveness and equity. Trade-offs are common in the economy. For the Federal Reserve, the pursuit of effectiveness may create inequities. Alternatively, efforts to promote equity might interfere with the efficient functioning of the financial markets (Okun 1975). The central bank needs to strike an acceptable balance between these two objectives when necessary. It also needs to balance the societal costs of its actions to their social benefits. These points are elaborated later in this chapter. Specific examples are given when the Federal Reserve's performance is described in the following chapter.

ASPECTS OF EFFECTIVENESS

The effectiveness of the lender of last resort within the financial safety net in the event of a domestic financial crisis is broken down into several components. Assistance is effective when it achieves its goals for the safety, soundness, and efficiency of the financial system. This goal requires that the Federal Reserve act speedily, comprehensively, over a sufficiently flexible and long time span, with appropriate frequency, and in sufficient size to contain a crisis and prevent spillover to other institutions. To perform in this manner, the central bank needs to act vigorously to maintain or restore public confidence. It is also necessary that it refrain from encouraging undue risk taking by potential recipients. These aspects of effectiveness are discussed individually below.

Speed of Assistance

For liquidity assistance to be effective, it must be rendered swiftly during a financial crisis. This was true in Bagehot's day and has become even more relevant today. An urgent response is critical in coping with modern technology which has increased the speed with which most financial transactions are settled. With increased speed comes the potential for the rapid deterioration of an individual institution and the transmission of the crisis from one institution to others and ultimately to all of the financial sector and the economy in general. The rapid market reaction to negative information—which can increase the speed by which a crisis can encompass a single institution and spread throughout the financial system—was discussed earlier in Chapter 4 and also appears in the Appendix.

A case study (described in Chapter 4) illustrates the paramount need for speed. There, Chairman of the Federal Reserve Board Paul Volcker vividly described in testimony the concern at the Federal Reserve Bank of New York and the Board in Washington over the incipient effects on the Treasury securities markets of the sudden, unexpected and massive computer snafu in November 1985 at the Bank of New York (BONY) which left it unable to process its widespread security transactions and threatened to completely disrupt the government securities markets.

A second illustration, also introduced in Chapter 4, describes tiering in the international interbank markets, which can lead to the very rapid transmission of a crisis. The strongest, safest, and soundest international banks lend money through a succession of increasingly risky banks to risky, private, Third World borrowers. The failure of one of these borrowers can be transmitted upstream from the smallest and riskiest to the largest and most sound lenders such as the U.S. international banks. A similar exposure to interbank indebtedness exists in the domestic markets, and was one of the reasons given by the regulators for the bailout of Continental National Bank in 1984.

Thus, speedy and decisive LLR action is necessary to prevent liquidity crunch from escalating to a solvency crisis. As described in Chapter 2, liquidity strains can develop when institutions are feared to be insolvent. Loss of liquidity can quickly deteriorate into insolvency at marginally solvent depository institutions which incur losses when they are forced to sell illiquid assets at "fire sale" prices during the liquidity crisis. Moreover, hidden extant insolvencies are made apparent when depositors run. Runs can cause an institution's degree of insolvency to deteriorate rapidly. Then speedy and decisive action is necessary if damage to specific financial institutions is to be mitigated, and adverse repercussions on the financial system and the economy avoided.[3]

Safety net action can also preclude the insolvency of one bank from bringing down other banks. The action taken may be to inject capital or to postpone recognizing losses that have occurred. In either case a subsidy, explicit or implicit, is being conferred (Garcia and Polakoff 1987). The appropriateness of these actions is discussed later.

Comprehensiveness of Coverage

A question arises concerning the scope of lender-of-last-resort activities for effectiveness to be maintained. The classical writers argued that assistance should be available to "all sound borrows with good collateral to offer," (Bagehot 1921, 69). The "all" referred to both financial and non-financial firms. As discussed in Chapter 3, the Federal Reserve Act initially gave, or was interpreted to have given, the Fed responsibility to make discount window loans only to member banks. As described in Chapter 3, in the fifty years following the Great Depression, the Federal Reserve also gave aid indirectly to non-member banks, and thrifts, on occasion. In 1980, the MCA extended Federal Reserve direct responsibility to all depository institutions. With the exception of Section 13b cases, IPCs have not been assisted since the 1930s. Yet liquidity assistance needs to be available to all solvent institutions, financial or non-financial, whose rapid deterioration into insolvency could seriously disrupt the economy. Consequently, direct assistance may need to be provided to some NDFIs in the future. The efficacy and equity of the Fed's dual system of direct and indirect aid to solvent institutions are discussed in Chapters 6 and 7.

The issue whether lender-of-last-resort assistance should be extended to insolvent institutions is a separate one. The classic view was that it should *not* be so available. Many modern authorities adhere to this position, because of its encouragement to risk taking. Recent writings disagree, however, and argue that there may be occasions when lender-of-last-resort assistance should be granted to insolvent institutions. For example, Benston et al. (1986) favor giving aid to insolvent institutions, but only when it can be shown to be cost effective. The Federal Reserve has stated that it will give assistance to insolvent institutions to facilitate their orderly disposition by other participants in the financial safety net (Federal Reserve Bank of Cleveland 1986). Further study of this issue is warranted. Congress may wish to have the Federal Reserve investigate the issue and report on its findings.

The Duration of Assistance

Lender-of-last-resort assistance needs to be provided over a flexible time span. Common sense suggests that it must be provided over a sufficiently long time span to overcome the public's incentives to run and normal funding patterns to resume. Early writers on the subject, such as Thornton and Bagehot, support this common sense assessment. As Humphrey (1975) points out, Thornton and Bagehot agree that lender-of-last-resort assistance must be supplied until the threat of a widespread crisis is averted.[4]

On the other hand, the classic writers argue that liquidity assistance is designed to be temporary so as not to interfere with the central bank's monetary policy responsibilities. Moreover, if assistance is provided with sufficient authority and visible determination on the part of the responsible agent, the public should be quickly reassured and the crisis should as quickly abate. The need for assistance should, therefore, be short-term, as long as the recipient is solvent and known to be so. At present, there is no consensus on the provision of long-term discount window assistance to insolvent institutions, but its disadvantages are discussed in the following two chapters. But it has been made in the past and, as is shown in discussions of the crises in Ohio and Maryland, at S & Ls nationwide between 1985 and 1987, and at Continental, Illinois, it may be unable to stem runs when they occur.

Frequency of Assistance

In order to maintain financial stability the LLR needs to be prepared to take action each time a crisis occurs. That means that it needs to decide whether to act and what actions to take each time a financial institution gets into difficulties.

As LLR action is confidential, unless Congress holds hearings on the case, it is difficult to know how often the Fed has granted aid to a specific institution. However, the increasing frequency of problems and insolvencies at banks and thrifts and the number of bank failures since 1973, suggests that Fed actions have also probably become frequent. The very frequency of problems and implied LLR actions, suggests that the federal financial safety net is malfunctioning. Moreover, inappropriate LLR actions in the safety net and monetary policy by the Federal Reserve can contribute to this malfunctioning in ways discussed in Chapters 6 and 7 (Kane 1987a).

Size of Assistance

It seems clear that lender-of-last-resort assistance can be required in very large amounts. The lender of last resort needs to maintain the position that, regardless of the extent of the funds necessary to quell a run or to subdue some other form of financial crisis, it can and will provide whatever funds are necessary. Bagehot made this point clearly, as discussed earlier in Chapter 2. Among modern writers this point is universally made, but is stated most forcibly perhaps, by Meltzer (1986) and Barth and Keheler (1984): "To function as a lender of last resort . . . an organization must have authority to create money, i.e., provide unlimited liquidity on demand" (Barth and Keleher 1984, 16).

A case study provides an example of the need for large-scale assistance. The Bank of New York received a discount window loan of $23.6 billion in November 1985 (while long-term discount window assistance is estimated to have reached $7.5 billion in the case of Continental Illinois during 1984). It is doubtful that any other regulatory agency could have immediately provided assistance in such large amounts.

The potential need for large scale assistance means that there is ultimately only one agency equipped to handle the LLR role in any country. That agent is the one maintaining the ability to create money—the country's central bank. In the United States that is the Federal Reserve. It also means that it can best provide assistance in its own currency.

While Congress and the administration have the power to provide assistance in large amounts as a result of their ability to tax, such assistance requires legislation and is not, therefore, immediately available or suppliable with certainty. In the case of municipal governments and non-financial firms, the demise to illiquidity and insolvency usually occurs slowly enough to permit Congressional intervention.[5] However, the coincident requirements of speedy and large scale assistance makes the monetary authority the ultimate lender of last resort for financial firms whose deterioration can be more precipitous. As discussed further in Appendix A, this need presents an important impediment to the provision of liquidity assistance in the international financial markets. There is no international central bank with unlimited power to create money.

Information Needs

Lender-of-last-resort assistance can be effective only if enough information about problems relating to the troubled institution is available. Two sets of people—the regulators and the public—have information requirements that need to be met. First, the regulators and the provider of liquidity assistance, in particular, need detailed and timely information on the troubled institution's assets and liabilities in order to be able to effectively evaluate its collateral and judge its solvency. To achieve these objectives the LLR needs information on the values of net worth and profits. For legal questions concerning failure, the accounting book values of net worth are relevant. For practical decisions of when and how to deal with a troubled institution the market values assets, liabilities and net worth are needed. The LLR also needs data on the risk exposures (that is, credit, interest rate, off-balance sheet, liquidity risk exposures) of the firm. It also needs to know who would be willing to acquire the troubled institution in a cost-effective resolution.

Typically, the Federal Reserve leaves the formal determination of solvency to the chartering authority; however, any information that allows the Fed to form its own opinion as to the solvency of the institution is valuable. However, information on both the pre-crisis and current market value of collateral is a *sine qua non* for LLR assistance.

The importance of information on the delicate balance between illiquidity and insolvency is well illustrated by Zweig in his book *Belly Up*. There, he describes the interplay among the three regulators involved in the failure of the Penn Square National Bank. The Federal Reserve's position during the crisis was that it would continue to provide liquidity assistance to the bank as long as it was solvent and had adequate collateral. The Office of the Comptroller of the Currency (OCC), as the chartering agency, held the power to declare the bank insolvent and then hand the bank to the FDIC as receiver. The FDIC's interest lay in declaring the bank to be insolvent sooner rather than later, because delaying allows uninsured depositors to withdraw their funds from the bank. Runs by uninsured depositors leave the FDIC with a greater share of the bank's losses. The OCC, on the other hand, was reluctant to close the bank before insolvency was indisputable, because it feared lawsuits if it closed the bank prematurely. Accurate information is particularly important as delaying closure often does not enable a firm to recover but does serve to increase the losses suffered by the insurer (GAO 1987d).

Second, the public needs information that will enable it to act appropriately. It needs data on the financial condition of the institutions to which it may entrust its funds. Information is particularly important to uninsured depositors and unsecured creditors who are at risk in a bank or thrift failure.[6] The markets, in fact, need access to the same data that the regulators have, if they are to manage their interests safely. The protective actions of those at risk can provide useful market discipline to DI owners and managers who might otherwise take excessive risks. In the past regulators, particularly those in Maryland where the publication of information on privately insured thrifts was severely limited, preferred to keep many DI data confidential in the belief that its release would weaken public confidence. The Federal Home Loan Bank Board and its staff took a similar position in 1985 and early 1986 in reaction to the General Accounting Office's (GAO) public discussion of the number (but not the identities) of S & L insolvencies (Gray in GAO 1986a).

Congress and the public also need information about the benefits and costs of each specific LLR action. At present Congress freely delegates LLR responsibility to the Federal Reserve and rarely holds it accountable for its actions. It prefers to trust the Fed to act appropriately. However, the recent spate of bank and thrift insolvencies and bailouts needs an explanation. Arguments are being made that the safety net, of which the LLR is a part, is promoting risky behavior and so contributing to the number of failures. Finally the public needs to know that the authorities will act appropriately in dealing with the crisis. Above all they need to know the rules of the game they are playing.

Preventing Spillover

The classical position is that "the best way to prevent the derivative failures is to arrest the primary failure that causes them" (Bagehot 1873, 25). What is involved in the "arrest" is at issue today. The classical position was that the lender of last resort should not bail out an insolvent bank to prevent a liquidity crisis from occurring, but should contain a run as it happened. The modern Bank of England has given capital assistance in emergencies but prefers to sell of an insolvent bank to new owners who recapitalize it (Reid 1982). Modern U.S. writers allow Federal Reserve both to forestall liquidity and solvency crises at depository institutions to aid individual DIs and to prevent problems from spreading to other financial firms and the rest of the economy. Aid, in many instances, has included capital infusions from the FDIC or the FSLIC. Moreover, the LLR has a general responsibility not to mismanage monetary policy so as to cause unnecessary bankruptcies in the real sector that are often the cause of bank and thrift failures.

Aliber (1987b) believes that contagion from one bank to another is more of a problem today than it was earlier because "a larger share of deposits have now been concentrated in a smaller number of large institutions, which means that the contagion issue is more important." Table 5-1 confirms that the top ten banks in 1986 did hold a disproportionately large share of deposits.

The evidence on bank concentration and its changes over time is somewhat complex. Table 5-1 presents concentration data for the nation's superbanks. The information in the table disagrees with Aliber's thesis. The percentage of bank assets held by the top ten banks has declined since 1976 from 29 to 24 percent. These are the banks that the Comptroller of the Currency characterized as "too big to

Table 5-1. Concentration Among the Nation's Superbanks.

Top Banks	1976 Percentage		1982 Percentage		1986 Percentage	
	of Banks	of Bank Assets	of Banks	of Bank Assets	of Banks	of Bank Assets
10	0.07	29	0.07	28	0.07	24
50	0.35	45	0.35	46	0.35	41
100	0.69	52	0.69	53	0.70	51
Number of banks	14,411		14,452		14,198	

Source: Data derived by the authors from FDIC Reports of Income and Condition.

liquidate" in 1984. Similarly, the proportions of assets held by the top fifty and 100 banks have declined since 1976 and 1982.

However, the picture of concentration amongst the next largest layers of the nation's banks is different and agrees with Aliber's hypothesis. Table 5-2 shows that each strata of the nation's largest

Table 5-2. Comparative Statistics on Commercial Bank Concentration (*sample includes all FDIC insured commercial banks for a given year*).

	Percent of Industry Assets		
Percent of Banks	1976	1982	1986
Top 0.1%	33%	32%	27%
Top 0.25%	42	42	37
Top 0.5%	49	50	46
Top 1%	56	57	55
Top 1.5%	60	62	61
Top 2%	63	65	64
Top 3%	67	69	69
Top 4%	70	71	72
Top 5%	72	73	74
Top 10%	78	79	80
Top 15%	82	83	84
Top 20%	85	86	86
Top 25%	87	88	89
Top 30%	89	90	90
Top 35%	91	91	92
Top 40%	92	93	93
Top 45%	94	94	94
Top 50%	95	95	95
Top 55%	96	96	96
Top 60%	96	97	97
Top 65%	97	97	97
Top 70%	98	98	98
Top 75%	98	98	99
Top 80%	99	99	99
Top 85%	99	99	99
Top 90%	100	100	100
Top 95%	100	100	100
Top 100%	100	100	100

There were 14,411 banks in 1976; 14,452 banks in 1982, and 14,198 banks in 1986.
Source: Data derived by the authors from FDIC Reports of Income and Condition.

commercial banks, measured at 5 percentage point intervals, from the top 5 percent through the top 40 percent, each held a higher share of commercial bank assets in 1986 than ten years earlier. In 1986, for example, the top 5 percent of banks held 74 percent of all U.S. bank assets. The comparable figure in 1976 was 72 percent. Figure 5-1 summarizes the information on bank concentration in three Lorenz curves, which report the cumulative percentage of bank assets held by banks ranked according to their size in each of the years 1976, 1982, and 1986.

There is no general agreement on how far the Fed should go to prevent bank insolvencies, which occur in a crisis environment. In particular, there is no agreement on whether or how to deal with spillover derived from insolvencies that originate from widespread, sectoral problems in the real sector but which spread to banks. This is the problem that regulators confront in the late 1980s among banks and thrifts in agricultural and energy states. Nor is it agreed whether and how the Fed and the rest of the federal safety net should aid insolvent institutions so that their demise can occur in a calmer-than-crisis atmosphere. However, after viewing the evidence presented in the next chapter, the authors conclude that the regulators should be less willing to aid insolvent banks and thrifts than they have been of late.

That spillover from insolvencies can run from NDFIs to banks and thrifts is evidenced by the experience of Bank of America, which lost money on worthless mortgage guarantees written by two insolvent insurance company subsidiaries (GAO 1987c). Home State in Ohio and other S & Ls suffered serious losses on repurchase agreements made with ESM, a small government securities dealer that failed early in 1985. (The firm was based in Fort Lauderdale, Florida, and was named for its owners Ronnie R. Ewtor, Robert C. Seneca, and George C. Mead.) The demise of EPIC, a real estate affiliate of Community Savings, contributed to the Maryland S & L crisis of 1985. Moreover, Old Court and Merritt, two of the most seriously troubled S & Ls in the Maryland crisis, lost substantial amounts of money when Brevill, Bresler and Schulman, another securities dealer, failed in 1985.

Spillover to DIs also occurs when large numbers of real sector firms fail, as in the energy and agricultural industries in the mid 1980s. For example, the problems associated with the failure of Penn Square National Bank in 1982 illustrate this process.[7] Penn Square's

Figure 5-1. Concentration in Commercial Banking.

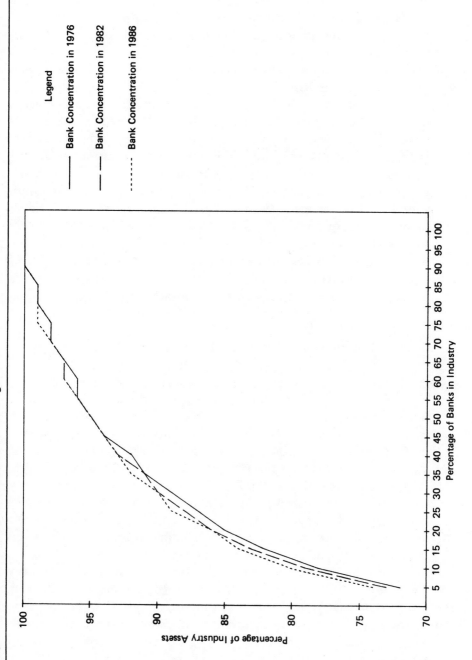

problems with bad loans accumulated over a long period of time. The regulators delayed closing the bank until well after its economic insolvency. The resulting large losses to uninsured depositors and loan participants were passed upstream to Continental Illinois, Seafirst, Michigan National, Manufacturers, Hanover, and to other small and medium-sized U.S. banks.

In summary, the regulators' emphasis with respect to contagion has shifted in the past 100 years. Bagehot emphasized preventing and containing contagion, but not bailing out insolvent firms. Regulators today are so concerned about the possible repercussions of a crisis that they act to hide the problems at and/or prevent the closing of a larger insolvent, or potentially insolvent, institution such as Continental Illinois, Financial Corporation of America, or a larger number of smaller institutions such as S & Ls during the 1981-2, 1985, and 1987 crises. The emphasis has shifted to delaying individual declarations of failure rather than containing their consequences. Staff of the Federal Reserve Bank of New York expressed particular concern about contagion in interviews with the authors of this text.

Maintaining and/or Restoring Public Confidence

It is clear that, for the lender of last resort to operate effectively, it must be able to sustain public confidence in the financial system to prevent crisis escalation. For this reason, the Federal Reserve publicly announced that it was providing liquidity to the banking system on October 20, 1987, the day following "Black Monday" when the stock market crashed, losing 508 points from the Dow Jones Index. It was later revealed that this liquidity was provided by open market operations rather than discount window assistance. The commercial banks were encouraged by the Fed to exercise their traditional role as lenders of next to last resort, by lending to brokerage firms and others short of cash as a result of the crash.

Public confidence is more secure if the financial system is healthy (see Chapter 2). Whether a healthy financial system can result from a free, deregulated market with an improved system of examination and supervision, or whether it requires a system of strict regulation is a matter of ideological debate among political economists and not pursued here. However, the public will be confident when the financial system functions smoothly. In the event of a crisis, confidence will be restored by effective lender-of-last-resort action.

A steady hand at the monetary helm is conducive of health and stability. Rapid inflation followed by serious deflation, as occurred during the Great Depression and the 1980s, sets the stage for real and financial sector insolvencies and liquidity crises.

Bagehot argued that the central bank needs to do two things to sustain public confidence. First, it needs to assure the markets during non-crisis periods that it can and will act decisively whenever necessary. Second, it needs to state in advance and adhere to principles for granting assistance. The authors also believe that the Fed should provide evidence after a crisis that the Fed has adhered to the principles it announced. It should be held accountable for deviations from its stated rules, particularly when assisting insolvent DIs, to ensure equity and the provision of appropriate incentives. The Fed should also be accountable to Congress for the cost effectiveness, from society's perspective, of its actions.

A question arises whether lender-of-last-resort assistance needs to be visible in order to be effective. Certainly, today the Federal Reserve does not make a "fetish" of visibility. The modern Fed prefers a behind-the-scenes role such as that of Chairman Volker during the silver crisis and the Ohio and Maryland crises. The Fed prefers to operate without publicity because obscurity allows greater flexibiloty and self-determination. The Federal Reserve's position is that it would like the public to be certain that it can trust its judgment to act when it is necessary and to refrain from action when it is not. Such complete delegation of responsibility to, and trust in, the Fed would make immediate visibility during a crisis unnecessary. Moreover, it would retain maximum flexibility for the central bank. The declaration of conditions under which banks and others have guaranteed access to aid would create property rights among institutions that meet the criteria for aid. Their lawyers might be able to sue the Fed if aid were denied.

Flexibility makes it easier for the Federal Reserve to function and it renders it the sole judge of the appropriateness of its actions. It makes it harder for the markets to operate. As pointed out in Chapter 4, the financial markets have been changing rapidly during the past decade. These changes create uncertainty about how the Federal Reserve would respond to a crisis that might develop in some of the new financial arenas. The markets may not have any relevant precedents that indicate how a crisis would be handled. As the classic writers pointed out, uncertainty inhibits public confidence and should be contained at socially acceptable levels, if not avoided entirely. Some modern analysts, however, regard uncertainty as a good thing because it may serve to make participants more cautious. The authors agree that it may make some more cautious, but are concerned that it may make others—the risk takers—less cautious.

Then, a clearly enunciated policy regarding who is eligible for assistance, under what circumstances, what collateral is acceptable and what price schedules will be imposed on assistance would "assure the markets beforehand" and serve to maintain public confidence. The need for a clearly stated policy should take precedence over the Fed's preference for flexibility.

Providing Incentives for Appropriate Risk Taking

Government intervention in the economy can change incentives which affect behavior. For example, placing a tax that raises the price of a certain product almost always causes consumers to favor some alternative in preference to the taxed product. Conversely, subsidizing a product encourages its use. Lender-of-last-resort assistance can be viewed as a form of subsidized government intervention. If potential recipients interpret such assistance to mean that the central bank would step in to bail out any institution in difficulty, the availability of assistance could encourage (even subsidize) additional risk-taking among institutions with lender-of-last-resort access. Such extra risk taking may not be good for the economy in general, and could give unfair advantage to those with access to liquidity assistance over those without it.

Classical writers stress that the central bank needs to take account of this eventuality. Such considerations account for Bagehot's and Thornton's insistence that lender of last resort assistance be given only to solvent borrowers at penalty interest rates. To provide assistance at rates below those being paid by competitors gives the borrower an advantage over those competitors. Rewarding risk taking in this way can result in more risks being taken than society is comfortable with. As Thorton pointed out, it would not "become the Bank of England to relieve every distress which the rashness of country banks may bring upon them: The bank, by doing this, might encourage their improvidence." (Thornton 1939, 188) The same view was espoused in the United States in 1825 by Nicholas Biddle, President of the Second Bank of the United States: "It is the order of nature that if men or nations live extravagantly, they must suffer till they repair their losses by prudence and that neither man nor banks should impose on the community by promises to pay what they cannot pay. (Lanier 1922)

Modern academic writers (Meltzer 1986; Guttentag and Herring 1983) have also expressed similar concerns.[8] One social cost of offering liquidity assistance is that "there may be substantial indirect costs to the extent that the availability of lender of last resort facilities leads some banks to assume riskier positions than are socially optimal and thereby make the whole banking system more vulnerable." (Guttentag and Herring 1983, 9)

In the prolific literature on this subject, this trade-off between providing confidence-sustaining commitment of assistance to the market and encouraging risk taking has received widespread attention. To maintain confidence, Bagehot recommended clearly stating in advance the conditions under which liquidity assistance would be available. By confining loans to solvent borrowers and imposing a penalty rate, moral hazard would be avoided. The success of the Federal Reserve in appropriately discouraging risk taking is considered in Chapters 6 and 7.[9]

It should be noted, however, that the determination of failure is complicated by the different definitions of insolvency that may be applied. Where accounting book-value insolvency is used as the yardstick for failure, there is a large margin for error in determining the appropriate write-downs for bad loans and so some doubt about when failure has occurred. Some economists, particularly Benston and Kaufman (1987), argue that market value should be used to determine insolvency. But when interest rates change rapidly, market values are volatile. Moreover, they are not readily available for some (but a decreasing proportion of) depository institution assets. Finally, the regulators currently use regulatory capital which typically imposes more lenient standards than either GAAP or market-value accounting and whose definition changes as expediency demands, often to avoid facing the reality of insolvency. In these circumstances, the declaration and timing of insolvency become regulatory judgments.

In this situation, no meaningful, operational distinction can be made between insolvency and illiquidity during a run. Deposits are withdrawn when their owners doubt the solvency of their institution and the worth of any guarantees. If a run occurs, the LLR needs to provide liquidity to meet the public's needs until the institution can *quickly* be closed or sold.

ASPECTS OF EQUITY

Lender-of-last-resort assistance is considered equitable when all potential borrowers are treated impartially by the lender of last resort and the safety net. Impartiality implies that the needs of all classes of borrowers are treated similarly and that no class of borrower receives special subsidies or favorable treatment. Equity is divided into two sub-criteria: equal access and fairness in treatment. Equal access refers to the right to seek and receive lender-of-last-resort assistance. Fairness in treatment refers to the terms and conditions under which such assistance is evaluated and given.

Equal Access

To be equitable, access to lender-of-last-resort facilities must be assured for all potentially solvent borrowers experiencing temporary liquidity shortages when funding is unavailable from other market sources. Equal access may be considered from a number of perspectives: access by size of institution, by type of business, by geographic location, by portfolio composition, and by market or organizational structure.

The classical argument for effectiveness also supports the goal of equity in access to the lender of last resort. It decrees that the responsibility of the lender of last resort is to the entire financial system and not to any particular institution. Therefore, the central bank should lend to "any and all sound" borrowers (financial or real) regardless of size or type of business. Modern writers, notably Meltzer (1986), also argue that equal access is necessary for effectiveness. They reiterate Bagehot's point that the overriding concern of the lender of last resort is to stay alarm and that to discriminate against specific classes of borrowers would only increase market anxieties.

Therefore, what is justified as promoting effectiveness turns out also to promote the equitable principle of equal access.

Discrimination by Type of Business and Size. The classic and modern lender-of-last-resort concepts both argue against discrimination among borrowers based on their line of business. Bagehot (1873, 25) stated this point clearly: "Lender of last resort loans should be available to markets, to minor banks, to this man and that man." Furthermore, equity dictates that lender-of-last-resort facilities must be available to larger and small institutions alike.

Discrimination by Portfolio Composition. For the lender of last resort to act equitably, it should make no distinction with regard to eligibility in response to the kind of business, that is, the portfolio composition of a troubled institution. The classic writers believed that all types of solvent borrowers should be equally eligible, as long as they could offer good collateral. The objective of the lender of last resort is to satisfy the market's demand for liquidity in times of crisis. Therefore, according to Humphrey (1975) and Meltzer (1986), as long as there is good collateral and a penalty rate is imposed to discourage unwarranted borrowing, the central bank should not discriminate between different types of borrowers.

Discrimination by Region or Organizational Structure. Also, the geographical location of a borrower should not be the basis for unequal treatment. Potential borrowers should be given equal access to liquidity assistance regardless of their state or community of residence. Similarly, the market or organizational structure of a borrower should not be an issue. That is, to be equitable, access to the lender of last resort should not be based upon whether or not the borrower is a single branch bank, statewide branching bank, local bank in a small community, large bank in a big city, a farm bank, an energy bank, a multinational bank, thrift institution, NDFI, or other IPC.

Fairness in Treatment

The second component of equity in liquidity assistance is fairness. Neither the classical nor the modern writers discuss the issue of fairness in treatment. Instead, for both groups, fairness is implied through the provision of assistance to any and all sound borrowers and through the uniform application of a penalty rate on borrowings. However, fairness is more far-reaching. It demands that all firms seeking and receiving assistance do so on a "level playing field." That is, the terms and conditions under which aid is granted should not penalize one group of borrowers while subsidizing others. By offering assistance fairly, the central bank can treat similar depositors, customers, creditors, and shareholders of different institutions impartially in similar crisis situations. Finally, society needs to be treated fairly by having only cost-effective incidence of LLR action.

Fairness in treatment can be broken down into three subcomponents: fairness in collateral requirements, fairness in pricing among recipients, and fairness to society as a whole. In the present case, fairness in treatment may not necessarily imply equality in treatment. That distinction arises because of the configuration of the Federal Reserve system which requires depository institutions to maintain non-interest bearing reserves. If DIs are forced by the Fed to hold more reserves than they would voluntarily hold, the requirement imposes a cost on these institutions. In return for the cost imposed on them, the Federal Reserve treats DIs as a special class of institutions that has immediate access to the discount window. No fee is imposed for access, and the charge for any funds borrowed there is calculated at a below-market rate. Other businesses and individuals that do not maintain reserves at the Fed would, therefore, be given an unearned advantage if they were given exactly the same terms and conditions when receiving liquidity assistance. This issue is evaluated in the following two chapters.

Fairness in Collateral Requirements.   The common man would argue that the type of collateral accepted should not favor a specific class of institution. Ideally, similar guidelines for accepting and valuing collateral presented for liquidity assistance should apply for all firms receiving it. For example, one firm should not have an asset rejected as collateral when another firm has that asset (of the same type and quality) accepted.[10] Failure to provide similar standards of collateral could alter market perceptions, resulting in a misallocation of resources to those favored institutions.

Collateral availability and adequacy become a vital determinant for aid when the Federal Reserve functions as part of the safety net aiding insolvent institutions.

Fairness in Pricing.   The pricing of lender-of-last-resort loans should also not unduly penalize one class of borrowers. Ideally, other things being equal, if assistance is to be offered at a penalty rate, as dictated by classic writers, the same penalty should apply to all borrowings of a similar duration. Any unfair rate structure on loans which subsidizes (or fails to penalize) one class of borrowers may result in an increase in moral hazard in that subgroup of the financial sector.

Fairness to the Interests of Society

A final aspect of fairness which must be considered in providing lender-of-last-resort assistance is fairness to the society as a whole. To be fair to the taxpayer, the lender of last resort should not normally subsidize risk taking by over-valuing collateral or by charging below-market interest rates because these actions can cause charges to be passed on to the taxpayer. The central bank should be most reluctant to provide funds to potentially insolvent institutions in order to postpone bankruptcy. The delay allows uninsured depositors to flee and increases the cost to the federal deposit insurers. Ultimately, the taxpayer and healthy firms in the industry stand behind the insurance funds. When the Federal Reserve determines that it is necessary to take actions which assist insolvent institutions, subsidize individual institutions or a subgroup of depositors, it should justify the decision to Congress.

Explicit consideration should be given by the Fed, and the Congress, to which it is accountable, to balancing the costs and benefits of LLR action. LLR actions have societal costs. They grant subsidies, change the balance of competitive advantage among firms, and direct behavior toward riskier activities. LLR actions also have social benefits. As the Fed emphasizes, its actions can promote financial stability and maintain growth in the real sector of the economy. Central bank wisdom lies in distinguishing between short-term crisis suppression and long-term financial stability. An inappropriately frequent use of LLR actions to suppress crisis can increase long-term instability. This subject is revisited in Chapter 7.

TRADE-OFFS BETWEEN EFFECTIVENESS
AND EQUITY

Often the goals of effectiveness and equity are mutually exclusive. While considerations for effectiveness may point to one type of policy, equity considerations may point to another. Arthur Okun considers that this situation is endemic in a free market system:

> The contrast among American families in living standards and in material wealth reflect a system of rewards and penalties that is intended to encourage effort and channel it into socially productive activity. To the extent that the system succeeds, it generates an efficient economy. But that pursuit of efficiency necessarily creates inequalities. And hence society faces a tradeoff between equality and efficiency. (Okun 1975, 1)

The same need for trade-off between effectiveness and equity applies to the provision of lender-of-last-resort assistance. Three such possible trade-offs are identifiable: (1) the desire to limit moral hazard versus declaring intentions in advance to assure public confidence; (2) favoring support for institutions that are "too large to fail" versus equal support to all institutions regardless of size; and (3) equal direct access to the lender of last resort regardless of type of business versus channeling assistance to NDFIs through the depository institution sector. The Federal Reserve's handling of these trade-offs is discussed in the following chapters.

Professor Aliber, in commenting on this book, observed:

> In a period of systematic crisis, fairness should receive virtually no weight by the lender-of-last-resort relative to effectiveness. The major group at interest in the event of a bank crisis is the public—the objective is to avoid any likelihood that a run at one institution will spread to other institutions. (This means that at most the authorities can allow only one large institution to close before they announce that they will support other large institutions. (Aliber 1987b)

Kenneth A. McLean, staff director of the Senate Banking Committee strongly expressed a similar point of view—in a crisis, effectiveness would and should take precedence over equity. He also observed that Congress prefers that the independent Federal Reserve deal with questions of fairness. Delegating this responsibility to the Federal Reserve has taken decisions out of the realm of politics, which had, for example, bedeviled the Reconstruction Finance Corporation (RFC) after the Depression.

Assurance versus Flexibility

The classic writers believed that in order to maintain public confidence, the lender of last resort should "state its principles in advance and adhere to them" (Humphrey 1975, 6). The Federal Reserve, however, maintains that in order to execute its support function effectively, it requires flexibility in designing the assistance it gives during any given crisis. That is, the Federal Reserve would rather handle each crisis on a case-by-case basis. Flexibility, however, implies that all situations will *not* be dealt with in a similar fashion. Consequently, reacting to each crisis individually might result in an inequitable response. On the other hand, equitable assistance might impinge on effectiveness since it might limit the Federal Reserve's ability to tailor its response to individual circumstances. Therefore, the Federal Reserve must strike a balance between pursuing the dual goals of equity (which would simply be a more uniform set of reactions to financial crisis) and effectiveness (which, it believes, could require a more varied approach to individual crisis).

The classic writers felt very strongly that a formal policy was necessary in order to stem financial panics. As long as the policy was to assist only solvent institutions which possessed acceptable collateral, they felt that the absence of a policy would only lead to increased instability and eventually require a greater intervention. The modern situation is more complex. The presence of deposit insurance has reduced the probability of bank runs, but at the same time the changing composition of bank portfolios has increased the difficulty in distinguishing between solvent and illiquid institutions, in that insolvent or marginally solvent institutions will attempt to increase risk (at the expense of the lender of last resort, and/or the deposit insurer) hoping to stay open long enough to gamble their way back to solvency.[11]

Thus the lender of last resort faces a dual problem. If it announces that it will act, especially to aid insolvent institutions, it invites moral hazard problems. If it makes no announcements, financial sector instability may increase. Not announcing a policy can also lead to an additional problem. The market, relying on its interpretation that the

Federal Reserve's actions show great concern to avoid crises, may assume a certain level of lender-of-last-resort assistance will be available. These expectations of support, if not actively disavowed by the lender of last resort, would tend to become self-fulfilling. By leading to higher levels of risk taking, the expectations may result in the need for even greater assistance to avoid instability.

If a situation were to arise where the Fed felt it necessary to violate its stated broad policies, a potential remedy for the conflict between the two principles would be for the Federal Reserve to announce that it will deviate from these policies only in the presence of serious overriding concern about financial stability in general. Each time that the policy is violated, the Federal Reserve should then announce the particular reason for the violation. Then the Fed would need to state whether the departure was to become standard operating procedure in the future or whether it planned to return to the old principles.

Thus, if flexibility were essential to effective action, there would be a trade-off between effectiveness and equity. However, the flexibility argument was rejected earlier in this chapter, in the section on maintaining or restoring public confidence. In the event that a conflict between the two principles should arise, a policy of clear enunciation was preferred there in order to assure the markets and maintain public confidence. Moreover, a broadly stated set of LLR policies would still leave the Fed some room to tailor responses to individual situations.

In these circumstances, the authors believe that there is *no* trade-off between effectiveness and equity on this issue. Both are enhanced by a clearly stated policy.

Large Institutions Versus All Institutions

Regulators currently fear the spillover potential from the failure of large DIs, which hold a disproportionately large share of nation's bank assets. Large banks, in particular, are often the recipients of uninsured deposits from other financial institutions and from abroad. These other lenders could be brought down by losses incurred on their deposits following the failure of the large borrowers. Thus, to be effective in preventing spillover, the regulators work particularly hard to support a large troubled bank. However, equity demands that banks of different sizes be treated equally.

Professor Aliber, in commenting on this book observed:

[L]arge banks, and especially money center banks, are very different from small banks. One of the major differences is that large banks have a much larger volume of large uninsured deposits, and the owners of these deposits are extremely sensitive to the possibility of loss. Hence it is extremely important to provide liquidity assistance to these larger banks. The externalities of the failure of a large bank are very different from those of the failure of a small bank. Indeed, in many cases a small bank may fail without any externalities, at least externalities in the sense of triggering runs on other institutions. (Aliber 1987b)

Table 4-4 in the previous chapter, confirmed that large banks fund proportionately more of their assets with uninsured, managed liabilities than does the industry as a whole. For example, in December 1986, banks with assets above $10 billion had 47.1 percent of their total liabilities in the form of managed liabilities. Only 35.5 percent of their assets were funded by core deposits. In contrast, 78.7 percent of the smallest banks' (assets below $100 million) assets were funded by core deposits and only 10.5 percent by managed liabilities. While the banking system, including the large banks, had virtually no managed liabilities before Citicorp introduced the large CD in 1960, large banks had become highly dependent on them twenty years later. Nevertheless, this dependence declined during the middle years of the 1980s. The top banks were even more dependent on managed liabilities ten years ago and four years ago than they were at the end of 1986. For example, as shown in Figure 5-2, a smaller 32.9 percent of the largest banks' assets were funded by core deposits in 1976 and only 23.3 percent in 1982.

Although there are over 14,000 commercial banks in the United States today, as was seen above, the banking system is highly concentrated. While concentration has declined somewhat among the top 1 percent of banks, it has increased among the next largest banks— those ranked among the top 40 percent in the country over the past ten years.

Direct Versus Indirect Assistance

The Federal Reserve's policy is to provide aid indirectly to NDFIs and IPCs to effectively use the confidential information that commercial bankers possess about the aid recipients. Equity would de-

Figure 5-2. Core Deposits as a Percent of Assets.

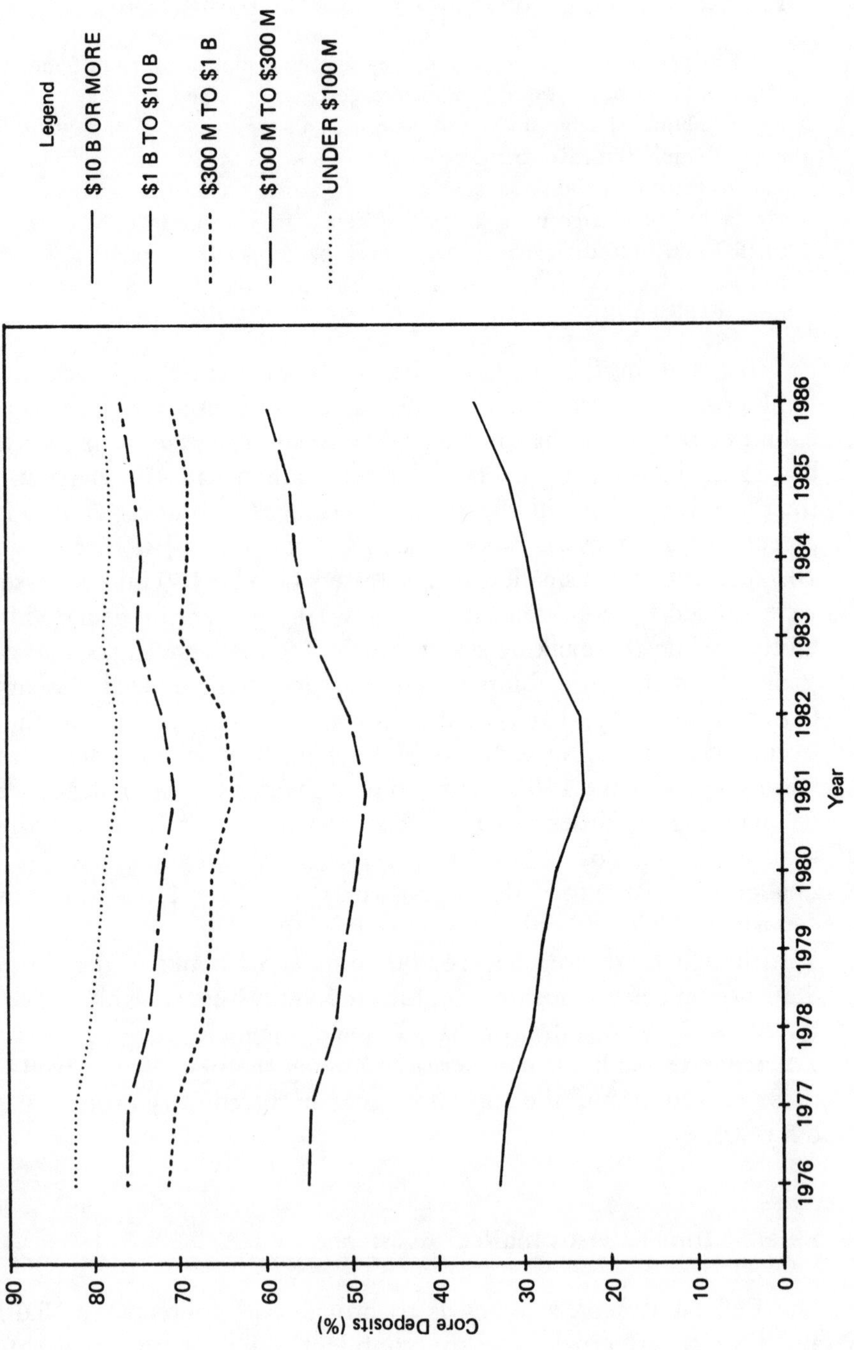

Legend

— $10 B OR MORE

— $1 B TO $10 B

···· $300 M TO $1 B

— · $100 M TO $300 M

···· UNDER $100 M

mand, in the absence of offsetting factors such as reserve requirements, that access be equal for all. Given the offsetting costs, fairness would be gained by allowing institutions a choice between (1)
offering transactions deposits and undertaking the reserve cost of
access together with the benefit of eligibility for LLR assistance, and
(2) not offering transactions deposits and foregoing both the cost
and the benefit of access.

SUMMARY—THE RELATIONSHIP BETWEEN
THE MODERN AND CLASSIC CRITERIA

Table 5-3 summarizes the criteria and sub-criteria that have been
established in this chapter for evaluating Federal Reserve performance
in its domestic LLR role. It also compares these criteria with those
propounded by the classic writers which were described in Chapter 2,
and points out unresolved issues that will be discussed further later
on in the text.

In almost all cases, the evaluation criteria mesh well with Bagehot's classical prescriptions, but there are some differences and some
unresolved issues. For example, the classic model would grant LLR
assistance to all solvent individuals and firms. The modern approach
singles out DIs for special attention but foresees aid being given to
some NDFIs under certain conditions. The modern LLR will also aid
insolvent institutions in emergencies. The modern concept recognizes
information needs that were not of paramount importance to classic
writers. The classic model stressed run prevention through aid to
individual institutions and the whole financial system. Currently, the
federal safety net interprets preventing a crisis to mean refusing to
admit that a failure has occurred and being reluctant to resolve it.
The classicists stressed taking actions that would ensure system stability in the long term. The modern LLR emphasizes short-run problems. Finally, the modern criteria explicitly addressed considerations
of equity; the classic criteria did not.

These issues of effectiveness and equity are discussed further in
the following two chapters which evaluate whether the Federal Reserve in recent years has successfully met these criteria for providing
domestic LLR assistance.

Table 5-3. Relationship Between the Modern and Classic LLR Criteria.

	Modern Criteria for LLR Assistance	Relationship to Classic Criteria	Unresolved Issues
Speed	Should be speedy.	Analogous.	Should LLR wait for determination of solvency?
Comprehensiveness	(a) Available to all DIs (and some NDFIs in the future).	Not as broad—any eligible borrower.	Which NDFIs should have direct LLR access?
	(b) Sometimes given to insolvent DIs	Contrasts-aid not given bankrupt firms.	When should insolvent firms be aided?
Size	Unlimited.	Agrees with directive to lend freely.	International assistance may be limited in some situations.
Duration	Long enough to deal with panics.	Not aiding insolvent firms makes need for short-term aid.	Aid can become indefinitely long.
Frequency	Whenever necessary—but that should be rarely.	Not addressed.	When is LLR action appropriate? Is it currently occurring too frequently?
Information	(a) LLR needs information to judge solvency and value collateral.	Not specifically addressed.	Data access when the Fed is not the regulator.
	(b) Public requires information to assess the viability of separate institutions and the whole systems.	Not explicitly addressed.	Conflict between regulator penchant for secrecy and the public's needs.
	(c) The public needs to know that and how the LLR will act to deal with the crises.	Agrees.	Overcoming the Fed's penchant for secrecy.

	Prevent by aiding:	Agrees with responsibility to entire system *and* individual firms.	How far should LLR go in aiding individual institutions?
Spillover	(a) Individual instructions. (b) The system at large.		
Prevention	(a) Central bank should not initiate crises through inappropriate monetary policy. (b) LLR should prevent crises, individual and systemwide.	(a) Consistent with stable long-term money growth. (b) Agrees in favoring prevention—which does not extend to bailing out failure.	Finding correct balance between short-term crisis suppression and long-term stability. Prevention misinterpreted to mean masking failure.
Public Confidence	Needs to be sustained: before, during, and after a crisis.	Agrees, but emphasis placed on "the before" and "during" a crisis.	Reluctance to preannounce conditions, sometimes omission of reassurance during a crisis.
Incentives	Should encourage an appropriate degree of risk-taking.	Equivalent to "lend freely at a high rate."	What is an appropriate penalty?
Equity	Not discriminate in access on the basis of size, type, location, or portfolio composition.	Implied by LLR availability to any and all solvent borrowers.	Weighing costs and benefits of letting a large firm fail. Political pressures. Balancing the costs and benefits of access.
Fairness	Assistance should be given fairly.	Not explicitly addressed, but implied.	Lack of case histories and *ex post* accountability.

NOTES

1. There is literature on the genesis of bank runs and on their repercussions. See, respectively, Diamond and Dybvig (1983) and ensuing papers, and Kaufman (1987).

2. Benston et al. (1986) also use equity and efficiency as criteria, but the present discussion contains greater detail.

3. Two reviewers consider the study's emphasis on speed to be misplaced. "What is required is the confidence of private agents that they can rely on the authorities' competence to prevent transmission." (Schwartz 1987a).

4. Early U.S. tradition emphasized that Federal Reserve loans should be of short maturity in conformity with the real bills doctrine, which was in vogue at that time.

5. See U.S. GAO (1984d).

6. Giving assistance to an insolvent firm gives uninsured depositors a chance to run. Their running can increase the bank's degree of insolvency. It places all burdens of loss in a liquidation; for example, on those uninsured depositors and unsecured creditors who do not, or cannot, run and finally on the insurance agency and the taxpayer.

7. See Singer (1985) and Zweig (1985). The problems were passed on immediately when Penn Square failed, although the full extent of the problems only became apparent during the following years.

8. Other writers such as Kane (1986a) have argued that mispriced deposit insurance also encourages undue risk taking.

9. The success of the special industry lender to S & Ls is discussed in Chapter 7. The liquidity facility for credit unions is not considered in this study.

10. Assets of similar type but of different quality would have a higher collateral ratio imposed by the Fed.

11. This problem, an "agency problem," for the lender of last resort is identical to that faced by the deposit insurers. See Kane (1986a) for an analysis of moral hazard and deposit insurance and Garcia (1987b) for evidence that potentially risky direct investments and acquisition and development loans are held in greater proportions by insolvent S & Ls than by solvent thrifts.

6 HANDLING DOMESTIC CRISES

The purpose of this chapter is to describe the ways in which the Federal Reserve has handled various types of crises in its role as domestic lender of last resort. This description will serve as an aid to the next chapter's evaluation of Federal Reserve domestic LLR performance. In the evaluation, the major criteria will be the effectiveness and equity of the assistance given as they were discussed in Chapter 5.

Since the Great Depression, the Federal Reserve and the other financial regulators have not allowed potential individual crises in the federally regulated financial sector to escalate.[1] However, there are concerns about the present execution of the Federal Reserve's role. Some of the problems the Federal Reserve encounters arise from its adherence to tradition at a time when the financial sector is changing rapidly. Others derive from its interactions with the rest of the federal financial safety net. The escalating numbers of bank and thrift insolvencies and failures, presented in Chapter 1, call into question the appropriateness of the policies adopted by the safety net, of which the modern LLR is a part. Moreover, there are also questions whether Fed LLR policies and procedures that have preserved financial stability in the past will continue to prove adequate in the future. These judgmental issues are discussed in Chapter 7.

HAS THE FEDERAL RESERVE'S
ASSISTANCE BEEN EFFECTIVE?

As discussed in Chapter 5, lender-of-last-resort assistance is considered effective when it maintains stability in the financial sector without impeding the efficiency of the economy in general.[2] The following sections present an evaluation of the speed, comprehensiveness, duration, frequency, and size of lender-of-last-resort assistance, as well as an examination of the Federal Reserve's ability to acquire needed information, maintain or restore public confidence, contain spillover, and provide incentives to guide risk taking in directions which best serve the public interest.

Speed of Assistance

An effective lender of last resort must be able to render assistance swiftly at the onset of a financial crisis. There may have been only one occasion since the Great Depression where assistance was provided to solvent depository institutions too slowly to be effective. That recent occasion concerned Home State Savings Bank in Ohio.

Home State Savings Bank. Meltzer (1986) considers that the Federal Reserve was slow to assist Home State Savings Bank in Ohio in 1985. The written evidence suggests that the Federal Reserve Bank of Cleveland was reluctant to lend (even against collateral) to an institution which on examination would most probably be found to be insolvent.[3] In writing about the crisis in its annual report, the Bank appears to have leaned towards the classic admonition not to lend to unsound firms but that, after some hesitation, it did open the discount window to Home State. Nevertheless, the crisis spread. The Cleveland Fed's 1985 annual report states that the Federal Reserve will provide LLR assistance to aid the disposition of an insolvent depository firm where resolution is guaranteed. Senior Fed staff at the Board, when asked about the Ohio crisis, denied that there was any delay in giving liquidity support to Home State. They point out that deliveries of cash were made as requested by Home State's management. Cash deliveries began on March 5, immediately after the failure announcement of ESM, an obscure broker-dealer in Florida.

It appears that there was a disagreement between the Board and at least some of the regional Reserve bank's staff on the advisability of aiding Home State. The Board in Washington appears to have been more ready to aid Home State than were the regional bank personnel or personnel in the Federal Home Loan Bank System. Moreover, the Fed chairman intervened personally in another (the Maryland) crisis to encourage aid. During the Ohio crisis, the Chairman of the Federal Home Loan Bank, Edwin Gray, was initially unsympathetic to the problem S & Ls in Ohio which, because they were privately insured, did not fall under his jurisdiction. He later revised his position and cooperated in the joint federal–state rescue.

While emergency cash deliveries to Home State began on March 5, the Fed gave formal, LLR-collateralized assistance on March 8, 1985. The state guaranteed resolution of the thrift's problems on March 9, 1985. There is room for disagreement whether a greater readiness by the Cleveland bank to lend to Home State would have made LLR action more effective. Quicker action might have prevented the run at Home State and avoided its escalation to other privately insured S & Ls in Ohio and Maryland. This might have allowed DIs in these states to continue with business as usual. But events have revealed that "business as usual" at some S & Ls in Ohio and Maryland was flawed business that needed to be changed. It is a matter of debate whether the runs that occurred served a cathartic purpose by revealing previously obscured weaknesses, and forcing them to be resolved.

If the state's regulators had more closely monitored Home State and had closed it promptly when it became insolvent, depositors need not have feared losses, runs would have been avoided, and the Ohio Deposit Guarantee Fund (ODGF) need not have become insolvent. The Fed, knowing Home State was exposed to ESM loans, could also have obtained information about it and other Ohio S & Ls before the crisis. In fact, lack of information about Home State and other S & Ls in Ohio delayed Federal Reserve action.

Other Incidents.   The Federal Reserve has often proven its ability to provide speedy assistance to other banks when needed. In recent years it has responded quickly and agilely to a number of potential bank and non-bank crises. The more well-known, recent instances of liquidity assistance include forestalling the collapse of Continental Illinois in 1984; providing liquidity support to assist privately insured savings and loans (other than Home State) in Ohio and Maryland in early 1985; and stabilizing the government securities markets following the temporary failure of the Bank of New York's computer system in November 1985.

The Federal Reserve, facing a major disruption in the government securities market, immediately advanced $23.6 billion to the Bank of New York (BONY), a commercial bank that is also a major dealer and clearing agent, to cover the shortfall in its receipts from government securities transactions which could not be completed due to a computer software failure.[4] The Federal Reserve was informed of the software "glitch" early in the day, but it was not until late afternoon that it became aware of the magnitude of the problem and of BONY's inability to resolve the situation. The Federal Reserve, nevertheless, orchestrated a solution in a matter of hours after some (not irreparable) disruptions to the government securities market.[5]

Speed of assistance appears to have been adequate in the past in most cases. However, lack of information hampered LLR actions in Ohio. Whether the Fed can and should continue to be so quickly responsive in the future is discussed in Chapter 7.

Comprehensiveness

The scope of Federal Reserve assistance differs among the four classes of institutions: member banks, other depository institutions, non-depository financial institutions and non-financial firms. The way in which the Federal Reserve has handled crises in these four sectors is described below. Two issues that arise will be discussed in Chapter 7. First, does the Federal Reserve extend its support far enough afield, or is its preference for dealing directly with and through banks counterproductive? Second, when dealing with banks, does its assistance go too far?

Assistance to Member Banks.   Between the Great Depression and the Monetary Control Act in 1980, the Federal Reserve provided discount window assistance directly to member banks only.[6] Until the early 1970s, the Federal Reserve was criticized for aiding large member banks more readily than small ones. In response to these criticisms, the Fed instituted reforms in 1972 to enable it to provide assistance comprehensively to both large and small member banks.

Thereafter, it speedily and directly met the liquidity needs of individual member banks in isolated cases, and also when adverse economic conditions affected large numbers of institutions.

Assistance to Nonmember Depository Institutions. Before 1980, nonmember banks and thrifts were not expected to receive any liquidity assistance from the Federal Reserve directly or indirectly.[7] Even *indirect assistance* was forbidden without the express permission of the Board:

> No member bank shall act as the medium or agent of a nonmember bank in applying for or receiving discounts from a Federal reserve bank under the provisions of this Act except by permission of the Federal Reserve Board. (Federal Reserve Act 1913, Section 19)

During periods of financial stress (1921, 1933, 1966, 1969, and 1972) the Board gave general approval for members to indirectly provide LLR assistance to nonmembers (Hackley 1973). No information is available about nonmember banks' experience after 1972.

In 1932, Section 13.3 was added to the Federal Reserve Act. For the first time Federal Reserve banks could provide, with Board approval, *direct aid* to IPCs in the form of discounts of eligible paper. Hackley (writing in 1973) reports that it was never used by nonmember banks. In 1933, Section 13.13 was added to allow advances at a penalty rate to be made for no more than ninety days on Treasury collateral. In 1968, the authority was broadened to allow advances to be made on agency securities. Uses of Section 13.13 by nonmember banks "have been few and far between" (Hackley 1973, 123).

Where the crisis was more widespread, the Federal Reserve would use open-market operations to buy government securities to provide more generalized liquidity. Between the Great Depression and the mid 1960s financial crises were rare. In 1966, however, a serious credit crunch occurred as a result of a sudden shift in Federal Reserve macroeconomic policy that slowed the growth of credit. The resulting illiquidity affected both banks and thrifts. For example, S & Ls experienced a loss of deposits when the interest rate ceiling, Regulation Q, was applied to them for the first time in 1966. Commercial banks also experienced a shortage of funds and in response, they significantly reduced their holdings of U.S. government and municipal securities. The tax exempt market was seriously disrupted in consequence.

In August 1966, the Federal Reserve became concerned about the developing credit crunch and took actions to forestall it.[8] First, it reversed its tight money policy to one that supplied reserves "consistent with the maintenance of orderly money market conditions and the moderation of unusual liquidity pressures," (Board of Governors of the Federal Reserve 1966, 174). Second, the Fed sent a letter to each member bank to explain that discount window assistance would be available to member banks that stopped liquidating municipal securities but continued to reduce business loan growth (Board of Governors of the Federal Reserve 1966, 103). Third, the Board gave general, but unused, approval for aid to be granted directly to non-member banks (but not thrifts). These actions ended the crisis at the commercial banks. Thrift problems were resolved through the general easing of credit in the markets. According to Board staff, no thrift was given direct aid prior to the 1980 act. Borrowing authority had been put in place on more than one occasion, but it had not been used.

Since the MCA of 1980, direct LLR coverage has extended to all depository institutions. Federal Reserve regulations require the resources of the FSLIC and NCUA special industry lenders to have been exhausted before a federally insured thrift approaches the Fed. As discussed in Chapter 3, an exchange of letters between Federal Reserve Chairman Volcker and Federal Home Loan Bank Board Chairman Richard Pratt in August 1981 allowed the Federal Reserve and Home Loan Bank System to share in principal responsibility for providing adjustment and extended credit to FSLIC-insured thrifts. Since the MCA, the Fed has given LLR assistance to FDIC-insured savings banks and non-federally insured thrifts.

The Fed has also provided both adjustment and extended credit to FSLIC-insured S & Ls since 1980, despite the Fed regulation that they first access their FHLBank. For example, Fed staff confirm that in one week during the first quarter of 1982, twenty-one FSLIC-insured S & Ls were receiving extended credit from the discount window. The numbers of recipients diminished rapidly later in the year. (The Garn–St Germain Act eased thrift funding problems by authorizing the money market deposit account and nationwide SuperNOW account.) Moreover, some privately insured S & Ls in Ohio and Maryland continued to receive Federal Reserve extended credit after they obtained FSLIC insurance.

In short, the Federal Reserve has typically used open market operations, occasionally employed indirect aid, and rarely granted direct assistance to meet the liquidity needs of nonmember banks and thrifts in isolated cases and also when adverse economic conditions affected large numbers of institutions.

Aid to NDFIs. The Fed's position with regard its legal obligation to lend to NDFIs is explained most clearly by Chairman Volcker's response to a question during the hearings on BONY's discount loan. Mr. Volcker stated that the Fed would *not* have made the discount loan, had a securities dealer rather than a commercial bank experienced a similar problem. Fed Chief of Staff Axilrod again expressed the Fed's unwillingness to provide direct aid to an NDFI when testifying on potential assistance to the Farm Credit System.[9] Furthermore, the Federal Reserve did not lend directly to the Bache Group Inc., the holding company, or to Bache Halsey Stuart Shields Inc., the broker dealer during the silver crises of 1980. Neither did it lend to Drysdale, a government securities dealer, when it collapsed in 1982. Instead, in the latter case, it opened the discount window for member banks that were most affected by Drysdale's failure and lent securities to dealers affected by Drysdale's failure.

During the disruptions in the government securities markets in 1982 (following the failure of Drysdale Government Securities), the Fed provided assistance to several dealers without giving them discount window assistance. Because several dealers were short of securities and would have been unable to meet their commitments, the Fed lent securities to these dealers (Federal Reserve Bank of New York 1985, 45).

The Federal Reserve Bank of New York also lent securities to dealers during the stock market crash of October 1987. Gerald Corrigan, the Reserve bank's president, explained in conversations with this text's authors that such lending had been Reserve bank practice for several years. To facilitate the operations of the forty dealer-brokers with whom the Fed regularly does business, the Fed will lend government securities from its portfolio that are temporarily in short supply in the markets. Any securities lent must be fully collateralized by other government securities. Consequently, such Fed actions do not constitute a bailout of troubled NDFIs (Federal Reserve Bank of New York, 1985).

Thus, the Federal Reserve has authority under the Federal Reserve Act to lend to NDFIs (and IPCs), but it deliberately chooses not to do so. A June 1987 interview with senior Fed staff members confirmed that agency's continued reluctance to lend to non-banks. It has been, and remains, hesitant to expand discount window assistance to NDFIs and IPCs, for four reasons.

The first reason is practical. The Federal Reserve may not possess the information to evaluate non-bank collateral and assess solvency.[10] In this situation, Federal Reserve effectiveness is enhanced by utilizing the commercial banks' specialized, non-public knowledge. In the course of making loans to customers, commercial banks obtain specialized, confidential information about loan applicants' health. As the loan relationship matures, the banker acquires a repayment history for its borrowers. Even the deposit relationship with a bank provides the banker with information on average, minimum, and maximum deposit flows over time. Thus, the commercial banks will have data concerning their troubled customers' financial health and the value of their collateral, data that are not available to the Federal Reserve.

The second reason concerns equity. Depository institutions are required to maintain non-interest earning reserves. Access to the discount window is used as a way to compensate DIs for the interest income they forego when holding reserves. The third reason is conceptual. There is an opinion, widely held by the Federal Reserve and others, that banks and only banks are special. They should, therefore, receive special LLR treatment. The fourth and final reason is that open-market operations have been in the past and still are today the Fed's preferred way to deal with liquidity strains in the economy. When strains appear, the Fed typically relaxes its monetary policy stance as it did in 1966 and in periods of disintermediation during the 1970s (Wolfson 1986; Melton 1985) and during the stock market break of October 1987. In 1982, the monetary reins were again loosened in response to difficulties being experienced by banks, thrifts, and lesser developed countries. For example, in discussing its discount rate reduction at the end of August 1982, the Federal Open Market Committee (FOMC) referred in its policy directive to the New York Federal Reserve Bank, to "some well-publicized problems in recent months of a few banks here and abroad and the financing difficulties of Mexico. . . ." (Board of Governors of the Federal Reserve 1982, 126.)

The validity of these reasons and the appropriateness of continuing the Federal Reserve's policy of indirect assistance to NDFIs is discussed in Chapter 7.

Aid to IPCs.   Discount window support has been given only indirectly to non-financial firms since 1959.[11] Nevertheless, to date, the indirect approach appears to have been adequate.

Indirect aid was adequate, for example, during the Penn Central crisis of 1970. Brimmer (1984, 36-7) reports that the concern in that year for Penn Central's plight was so great that the Nixon Administration asked Congress to pass legislation that would enable it to provide financial assistance to Penn Central. After six weeks of debate the measure failed to obtain Congressional approval. Seeing the legislation stalled in Congress, the Administration then asked the Federal Reserve Board to permit the Federal Reserve Bank of New York to lend directly to Penn Central. The Bank could have provided discount window assistance if the borrower was creditworthy, had adequate collateral, and if five members of the Board of Governors had approved the loan.

In response to the Administration's request, the Federal Reserve staff appraised Penn Central's creditworthiness and advised that the railroad company would probably not be able to repay any credit extended to it. Despite lack of creditworthiness, Penn Central could still have been assisted if all seven members of the Board of Governors had voted unanimously in favor of aid. However, Federal Reserve staff advised, and the Board agreed, that aid should not be granted. Penn Central's bankruptcy then became inevitable.

Instead of lending directly to the railroad, the Federal Reserve tackled the incipient financial crisis at the stage when it touched the commercial banks. The Federal Reserve used both open-market operations and discount window assistance to aid involved member banks to prevent the situation from deteriorating (Melton 1985; Wolfson 1986).[12] The bankruptcy of the Penn Central Railroad threatened the disruption of the commercial paper market because Penn Central had $82 million of commercial paper outstanding when it filed for bankruptcy on June 21, 1970. The failure of the railroad, which had previously been thought to be sound, made it more difficult for some other firms to raise funds in the commercial paper market. Firms experiencing difficulties turned to the commercial banking system by drawing down the lines of credit that typically accompany commercial paper issuance. This put pressure on the liquidity of the commercial banks involved.

In its 1970 Annual Report, the Board of Governors described the directive given to the Federal Open Market Committee. Open market operations were to be "conducted with a view of moderating pressures on financial markets" (p. 137). These pressures included "market uncertainties and liquidity strains." Moreover:

> The authorities supplemented their efforts to ameliorate market strains through open market policy with other policy measures. It was made clear that the Federal Reserve discount window would be available to assist banks in meeting the needs of businesses unable to roll over their maturing commercial paper. Also the Board of Governors moved promptly to suspend maximum rate ceilings on large denomination CDs with maturities of 30 to 89 days. (Board of Governors of the Federal Reserve 1970, 18)

The Penn Central crisis was resolved traditionally—at the point where the crises that originated in the real sector affected the commercial banking system. That is, the Fed gave discount window assistance to member banks involved with Penn Central and eased monetary policy through open-market purchases of securities.

Furthermore, the Federal Reserve did not provide assistance to other non-financial entities such as New York City, Lockheed, or the Chrysler Corporation whose problems disturbed the financial markets in the 1970s. In these instances, time was available for Congress to resolve the crises. Furthermore, the Federal Reserve did not lend to the Hunt Brothers or Bache Securities during the silver crisis of 1980. Instead, as shown in Appendix B, the Federal Reserve stayed behind the scenes and allowed a consortium of large commercial banks to provide a secured loan to the Hunt family in order to contain the crisis, despite the credit restraint program that was in operation at that time as well as Fed and administration admonitions against making loans for "speculative" purposes.

During the international debt crises, the Fed and the other U.S. banking regulators choose to downplay the severity of the implications of LDC payment problems' on the solvency of commercial banks, by not forcing the banks to write down the loans to their market or net present value. Perhaps the federal agencies feared that runs would occur if the real net worth picture was formally acknowledged. If so, they failed to recognize that the insurance guarantee for the small depositors avoided runs, and the trust on the part of large depositors that the regulators would not take any action to resolve the market-value insolvencies that would impose any losses on depositors. Bank stock values below book values in the mid 1980s suggest that the markets were not deceived by the net worth fiction.

Working Capital. While non-discount window aid today is the approved means of support for IPCs, it has not always been the only means of support. In June 1934, Section 13b was added to the Federal Reserve Act. Uncharacteristically, it authorized Federal Reserve banks, in exceptional circumstances, to provide working capital for periods up to five years to established industrial or commercial businesses (Todd 1986). The Reserve banks were also permitted to cofinance commercial banks' working capital loans to businesses.

Section 13b was heavily used during the 1930s (Hackley 1973). Moreover, working capital loans were also made under the Reconstruction Finance Corporation (RFC) Act both to financial institutions and other businesses. After World War II, Section 13b was again used frequently.[13] It was repealed in August 1958, when Federal Reserve Chairman William McChesney Martin told the Senate Banking Committee that the primary duty of the Federal Reserve system was to guide monetary and credit policy, and that it was "undesirable for the Federal Reserve to provide capital and participate in management functions" (Hackley 1973, 145).

In summary, with regard to comprehensiveness, the dual approach of direct and indirect assistance has proved adequate in the past. However, the Board's present policy of indirect aid to IPCs and NDFIs, and its earlier experience of direct support to IPCs, raise issues of effectiveness and equity that will be discussed in the following chapter. Moreover, given the increasing speed and complexity of financial transactions, discussed in Chapter 4, the question arises whether the present dual system will remain adequate in the future. Comprehensiveness is closely related to speed. There is a particular concern that if a crisis were to arise outside the banking sector, indirect aid through the banking system would not be provided quickly enough to all sectors of the economy. This question, also discussed in the following chapter, would be especially important in the case of non-depository financial institutions which may face liquidity pressures similar to those of depository institutions.

Duration of Support

There are two issues here. First, does the Federal Reserve provide liquidity support over a period long enough to allow solvent institutions to recover from their liquidity crises? There is no evidence of any occasion since the Great Depression where assistance has been curtailed prematurely. A discount window loan was given to BONY, which recovered. Assistance may also have been provided to other institutions, which later recovered. However, the Federal Reserve is unwilling to confirm that institutions have recovered, or to reveal either the names of institutions aided in the past or the extent and conditions of the assistance given.

The second issue is whether the Federal Reserve has provided assistance over too long a period so as to constitute a bailout of an insolvent institution. Under the classic criteria, lender-of-last-resort assistance should only be provided to solvent institutions and for limited periods of time.[14] In modern times, however, the banking and thrift regulators have on occasion deemed it to be in the public interest to provide lender-of-last-resort assistance to specific insolvent institutions for prolonged periods. The staff of the Federal Reserve Bank of New York clearly stated their views in interviews with the GAO on the importance of these "public interest" aspects of lender-of-last-resort policy. The Federal Reserve Bank of Cleveland (1986), clearly enunciated the conditions under which the Cleveland Federal Reserve Bank is currently willing to lend to insolvent institutions.[15] The regional Reserve bank's position is that aid will be provided where resolution to an insolvency has been assured. However, finding and implementing a resolution can take a long time. In the interim, presumably, discount window assistance would remain available.

For example, in some cases infusions of cash were considered necessary in order for the institution to remain open until a more permanent resolution of the problem could be found. Franklin National Bank was given lender-of-last-resort assistance between May and October 1974 before being sold. Continental Illinois was granted liquidity assistance for five months in the Spring and Summer of 1984 before receiving a capital infusion from the FDIC, and it continued to benefit from extended discount window credit afterwards. In fact, senior Fed officials revealed to the GAO in June 1987 that Continental Illinois was then still receiving assistance. S & Ls in

Maryland, however, were then no longer being aided. Penn Square National Bank received assistance for several months before being liquidated. The Federal Reserve Bank of Cleveland aided some insolvent institutions in Ohio over an unknown period to facilitate their disposition. The Federal Reserve Bank of Richmond readily assisted insolvent thrifts in Maryland in 1985 and continued that support for a prolonged period.

Thus, the Fed, operating as part of the financial safety net, has provided assistance for long periods of time to seemingly (but undeclared) insolvent institutions as part of an effort by others in the financial safety net to achieve a more orderly solution to problems experienced by certain financial institutions. Notwithstanding the objectives of prolonged LLR assistance, there are problems with extended lending to institutions that ultimately prove to be nonviable, and also even to those that ultimately recover.[16] These problems will be described in Chapter 7.

Frequency

The Federal Reserve does not publicly release information on its LLR assistance. Therefore, it is currently impossible to know whether LLR action has been granted too frequently. (It is easier to judge whether action has not been given frequently enough, because the resulting strains are likely to cause institutions to fail, and failure is public acknowledge.)

Nevertheless, the frequency with which banks and S & Ls are becoming insolvent raises the question whether LLR action is being taken too often. Is LLR action given sometimes, often, or nearly always before a DI is declared to have failed? Such information is entirely lacking.

Size of Lender-of-Last-Resort Assistance

The Federal Reserve has been willing and able to lend freely to U.S. banking institutions during a crisis. As already discussed, the $1.7 billion loan to Franklin National and the more than $7 billion loan to Continental Illinois were drawn down over a period of months. The Federal Reserve had no difficulty in supplying the necessary funding. Even the most recent case of major individualized lender-of-last-resort support, the $23.6 billion overnight loan to the Bank of New York, was accomplished with relative ease. Thus, past experience indicates that the Federal Reserve is willing and able to provide dollars in any amount needed during a crisis.

While emphasis is most often placed on the answers to the question when LLR assistance can be provided in sufficiently large quantities, it is also pertinent to ask whether too much assistance is sometimes provided. This certainly seems to be the case among S & Ls. In 1987 nine insolvent thrifts had more than 50 percent of their assets funded by advances provided by the Federal Home Loan Bank System and one had over 100 percent.

Despite past experience, some have expressed doubts about the ability of the Federal Reserve to provide unlimited liquidity support on short notice without disrupting the execution of monetary policy. Proponents argue that Federal Reserve assistance could not be made in a quantity larger than the existing stock of depository institution reserves without disrupting monetary policy objectives.[17] The argument is that the Federal Reserve would not be able to counterbalance a discount window loan of $50 billion because this sum is larger than the stock of reserves that could be withdrawn from the banking system by open-market sales of securities.

This argument is rejected on two grounds. First, the discount window loan made to the troubled institution would not stay at that institution but would be fed into the banking system. In this way, the systemwide supply of reserves would be raised as a result of the discount window assistance. The Fed, therefore, could conduct open-market operations to any appropriate amount up to the limit of the sum of initial total reserves plus discount window loans. In short, the stock of reserves initially available provides no upper boundary on the extent of contractionary open-market operations in the long run. Moreover, in the very short run, an abundance of reserves might be appropriate to alleviate any liquidity problems elsewhere in the system. That is, long-term monetary policy objectives could be temporarily overridden during a crisis, without prejudicing their ultimate achievement. Monetary policy was eased, for example, for a period of almost two months following "Black Monday" and "Terrible Tuesday" of October 1987.

A second argument is made that the Federal Reserve can conduct open-market sales (which would reduce any unwanted excess reserves and money) only to the extent that it has Treasury or federal agency securities in its portfolio, excluding those necessary to back Federal Reserve notes in circulation. At the end of May 1987, the Federal Reserve's stock of such securities was $207.3 billion. Of this amount, $180.6 billion was held as collateral to back Federal Reserve notes in circulation. Nevertheless, the difference between these two amounts ($26.7 billion) need not place a boundary on the extent of open-market sales conducted to counteract any excess systemwide reserves produced as a result of lender-of-last-resort assistance. The Federal Reserve could, no doubt, borrow and sell additional securities from the U.S. Treasury. Alternatively, it could raise reserve requirements to immobilize surplus reserves. In sum, there is no basis for concern over the Federal Reserve's ability to provide and control any dollar assistance it needs to make.

It should be noted, however, that such complete command extends only to the ability to create and control the quantity of dollars in existence. The Fed does not have similar authority to create money denominated in foreign currencies. Any assistance given in a non-dollar currency could be limited by the Fed's existing stock of the foreign currency or its ability to borrow, swap, or otherwise acquire that currency in the foreign exchange markets. Thus, the Federal Reserve could provide liquidity assistance to meet a run in dollars that occurs in a domestic U.S. bank, in any subsidiary of a foreign bank that accepts dollar deposits in the United States, or in any subsidiary of a U.S. bank that accepts dollar deposits abroad. The Fed has only limited power to assist subsidiaries of U.S. banks that operate abroad and accept deposits in foreign currencies, however. Nevertheless, Aliber (1987a) does not consider this foreign currency limitation to be of any practical significance at present, because he judged that the dollar amounts likely to be needed in a crisis would be small enough for the Fed to handle.

Access to Information

For the lender of last resort to operate effectively, it requires two kinds of sufficient, timely information. First, it needs to be able to evaluate discount window applicants' collateral. Second, it needs information about their solvency. Before 1972, the Federal Reserve dealt with its information need by lending to institutions it knew best—typically large member banks, especially those in holding companies. The Federal Reserve has more information about large banks because they have to report their money supply and portfolio composition data to the Fed more frequently than other banks. The Federal Reserve is also the examiner, supervisor, and regulator of bank holding companies, so that it has access to the best available information on their solvency.[18] The Fed, therefore, is particularly knowledgeable about large banks that are part of a holding company and can readily evaluate their collateral.

The 1971 *Reappraisal of Federal Reserve Discount Procedures*, which made discount window assistance more widely available to all member banks regardless of size, increased the Fed's information needs and forced it to look beyond its own data to information from other agencies. The Federal Reserve supplies liquidity assistance to banks based on assurances of solvency provided by the chartering agencies (OCC or state banking authorities) as well as its own and FDIC examinations.

Today the Federal Reserve is prepared to lend to all depository institutions. The Monetary Control Act, by giving all depository institutions access to the discount window, again increased the Federal Reserve's need for information to a wider set of institutions. With these data needs in mind, the Federal Reserve's discount window booklet advised eligible banks and thrifts to make advance arrangements to borrow at the window should the need arise.[19] Such arrangements include providing information about the potential borrower.

The Fed's acute need for information about institutions it had not previously encountered is illustrated by its examination of Penn Central and the S & L crises in Ohio and Maryland. In 1985 the Fed sent a small army of examiners to each state to evaluate collateral and examine the books of illiquid thrifts.[20] These operational difficulties, reported by the Fed as occurring in both Ohio and Maryland, make it clear that advance preparations that would facilitate assistance should a crisis occur were not made in these cases.

In cases where the Federal Reserve needs to rely on information provided by other agencies, the call report data may not be adequate to determine solvency. The Federal Financial Institutions Examination Council has made an effort to establish identical procedures regarding call report data or minimally acceptable data, but has not been totally successful.[21] Additionally, efforts to make banks release additional data are resisted on the grounds that they would place additional, burdensome demands on banks.[22] A further problem is that call report data provide book values, which will depart substantially from market values when interest rates change. As discussed in Chapter 1, accountants, lawyers, and economists disagree about the relative merits of using book, regulatory, or market values to determine solvency.

Moreover, making lender-of-last-resort loans to non-depository financial institutions probably would require that a wider range of collateral be accepted in emergency situations. The S & L crises have already forced the Fed to take one step in that direction. Thus, the potential inability to gain rapid access to available information is a barrier to the Federal Reserve's extension of direct lender-of-last-resort responsibility to non-depository financial institutions. For example, it is not clear to what extent examination techniques for valuing bank assets are applicable to thrift institutions or to other segments of the financial services industry.

In short, the Fed often has insufficient access to information. While the Fed hesitates to impose additional costs of information reporting on depository institutions, its lack of information is ultimately of its own choosing. The Fed could make efforts to have all DIs that have legal access to discount window assistance, make preliminary filings with it. Moreover, those institutions that the Fed knows may need aid could be required to provide information to the Board in advance of a crisis.

The markets, particularly uninsured depositors, creditors, stockholders, and loan customers also need information in order to protect their own interests. Typically, relevant data are not readily accessible.

Containing Spillover

Between the 1930s and the 1980s the Federal Reserve was successful in restraining contagion. Today, the system has two separate containment procedures. On the one hand, institution-specific crises originating among banks, thrifts, or non-depository financial institutions are prevented from spreading through the rest of the financial sector and affecting the real sector. For example, the Federal Reserve allowed the crisis at Home State in Ohio to spread to other ODGF-insured institutions in the state but acted quickly enough to prevent it from escalating to federally insured institutions.[23] In fact, the decision by the federal regulators to intervene in Ohio and Maryland was based on assessment of the social costs attendant on escalation of the crisis. Similar concerns existed when the Federal Reserve opened the discount window to Continental Illinois.

On the other hand, crises that begin outside depository institutions are contained as and when they reach the banking system. For example, during the crisis associated with the Penn Central bankruptcy, the Federal Reserve (1) provided discount window resources to banks to lend to creditworthy firms unable to roll over their maturing commercial paper issues and (2) it lifted Regulation Q ceilings on large short-term certificates of deposit to ease funding difficulties. At the same time, it gave assurances to the financial markets that needed liquidity would be provided through the banking system (Brimmer 1984; Melton 1985; Wolfson 1986).

During the silver crisis in 1980, containment occurred through commercial bank loans channeled to the Hunt family through Placid Oil—a Hunt controlled firm. When the Hunt brothers defaulted on margin calls made on their silver futures positions, the Chairman of the Federal Reserve Board was apprised of the situation when Bache requested that the COMEX (Commodity Exchange Inc.) be closed until the developing crisis was resolved. At that point Volcker quietly arranged a meeting of all the relevant regulatory authorities, to determine strategy—which was, apparently, not to intervene. Thereafter, he was kept closely informed of developments. He permitted creditor banks to join together to resolve the crisis despite the fact that the resulting loan agreement violated the credit control program in operation at that time. The concurrence of the chairman indirectly led to an agreement by the banks to lend $1.1 billion to Placid Oil Company. This firm, in turn, made a loan to the Hunt family, which was used to pay off existing Hunt obligations at Bache Securities.

In the silver crisis, the commercial banking system had been used as the instrument for providing liquidity to troubled firms and individuals. But this crisis resolution was particularly shrouded in mystery.[24] It violated the classical prescription to publicly announce policy in advance of a crisis and reassure the markets during the crisis.

Moral "suasion" is another technique for preventing spillover. It has been used heavily by the Bank of England, but also by the Fed to get others to cooperate in an assistance effort. For example, Chairman Volcker placed a telephone call to the Governor of Maryland to urge him *not* to declare a bank holiday during the state's 1985 S & L crisis. The governor complied. Federal Reserve Bank presidents in Chicago and New York placed calls to bankers in their districts to reassure them that the Fed would provide generalized liquidity, so that bankers would overcome any reluctance to lend to securities firms during the crash of October 1987.

Thus, the Federal Reserve, through indirect discount window assistance, open-market operations, and moral suasion has been able to contain recent crises originating outside the banking system as they pass through the banking system. But it has not always assured the markets before the crisis, nor reassured them during and after the crisis. Moreover, there are concerns, discussed in next chapter, about the continued efficacy of this ambiguous approach. Moreover, as discussed at the end of the Appendix, the Federal Home Loan banks, as special industry lenders to S & Ls, have imposed no penalty on LLR lending even when made to insolvent institutions.

Maintaining and/or Restoring Public Confidence

As pointed out in Chapter 3, to maintain public confidence the Federal Reserve prefers to prevent crises rather than neutralize their impact. Not only is this position stated in the Board's 1914 annual report, it is reiterated when the Board wrote, in 1971: "sophisticated open market operations enable the system to head off general liquidity crises" (Board of Governors of the Federal Reserve 1971, 19).

The policy of preventing rather than neutralizing crises is acceptable today, as discussed in Chapter 5. The preference for prevention stems from the multiple roles of the Federal Reserve. In addition to its lender-of-last-resort responsibility, the Federal Reserve is the financial regulator of bank holding companies and implements monetary policy. It may, therefore, be advantageous for the Federal Reserve to actively minimize the probability of financial crises when it performs these roles. For example, open-market operations were used to head off an impending, or contain an existing crisis in 1966, 1982, 1984, 1986-7 and 1987.[25] The Federal Reserve's announcement of its willingness to provide liquidity before the markets opened on October 20, 1987, is regarded as the one event that stabilized the financial system and prevented the crash from becoming a catastrophe (Garcia 1988).

A policy of crisis prevention should cause no problems for the economy, as long as it does not generate inflation or extend aid to insolvent institutions in such a way as to disadvantage their competitors or encourage financial firms to undertake undue risks. The presence of these dangers, however, is discussed further in the following chapter.

The Federal Reserve departs substantially from a second policy prescription, made by Bagehot, to maintain public confidence. Classicists argue that the central bank should clearly state its lender-of-last-resort policies and procedures.

The departure is exemplified in the Ohio and Maryland crises. In those cases, the privately insured S & L depositors did not have any information—in the form of policy statements or past precedents—to determine what course of action would be undertaken by the Federal Reserve, the federal and state bank regulatory officials, and the state governments. The depositors in Maryland, who were affected after the Ohio crisis, could not rely on the Ohio resolution for information. Fed regulators made contradictory statements and no after-the-fact assessment was available until the Cleveland Reserve Bank published its annual report well after the crisis.[26] The uncertainty surrounding the policies for stemming the runs, coupled with the well-publicized lines of depositors waiting to withdraw their funds, undoubtably served to exacerbate the respective crisis.

Federal Reserve actions are shrouded in mystery. Data on lender-of-last-resort discount window loans are not made public. Researchers have to infer the volume from movements in the value of total extended credit, data published in the Federal Reserve *Bulletin.* Moreover, the Federal Reserve offers no comment on any researchers' estimates. Some modern commentators concur in that secrecy, as a way to inhibit moral hazard, but others oppose it. This argument is discussed further in the following chapter.

Provisions of Incentives For Apropriate Risk Taking

The provision of incentives to the market to discourage possible lender-of-last-resort abuse is best exemplified in the Federal Reserve's pricing policies on its loans. The classic prescription on this issue was to impose high interest rates to ensure that lender-of-last-resort assistance would be used only in emergency situations. However, historically, the Federal Reserve has kept the discount rate on every day adjustment credit below the federal funds rate and other market interest rates. That is, borrowing from the Fed was and still is subsidized. Moreover, until recently it did not impose a penalty rate on its (emergency) extended, credit discount window loans in order to prevent misuse of discount window privileges. It reserved the right to deny assistance rather than set a punitive interest rate [Melton 1985]. For example, as shown in Appendix A, Franklin National received a large subsidy on its assistance. Chapter 3 has shown that since 1983 this lenient policy has been changing toward imposing a more market-related, less-subsidizing rate. Nevertheless, Kaufman, in Benston et al. (1986), estimates that Continental was subsidized in 1984 on its discount window assistance despite the new rate structure.

Thus, in the case of large or long borrowing, the Federal Reserve is moving away from actually subsidizing an institution's discount window borrowing. But it has not yet completely eliminated the subsidy potential.

IS THE FEDERAL RESERVE'S ASSISTANCE EQUITABLE?

As discussed in Chapter 5, lender-of-last-resort assistance is considered equitable when all potential borrowers are treated impartially during a financial crisis. The factors taken into consideration when evaluating the equity of Federal Reserve's lender-of-last-resort assistance are equal access and fairness in treatment. Rendering an evaluation of how well the Federal Reserve has performed in providing equitable lender-of-last-resort assistance is difficult. It is not feasible here to survey all institutions which have had or have been denied lender-of-last-resort assistance to ascertain whether all institutions have been treated equitably. Nevertheless, past experience does provide general impressions. Overall, the Federal Reserve strives to be equitable when providing lender-of-last-resort assistance. However, there are some selected areas of concern which are specified in each section below.

Equal Access

As stated in Chapter 5, equal access means that lender-of-last-resort assistance is assured for all potentially solvent borrowers experiencing temporary liquidity shortages that cannot be satisfied elsewhere. The evaluation of equal access is separated into three subcategories: equal access by type of business, size of institution, and geographic region.

Type of Institution.   Lender-of-last-resort assistance is *not* provided equally for all types of institutions.[27] Direct assistance is not, in practice, available at present to NDFIs or IPCs. Since the Monetary Control Act of 1980, access to the discount window has been theoretically available for all depository institutions. There are, however, some distinctions between the degree of access within the subsets of depository institutions. Commercial banks and FDIC-insured savings banks have immediate access to the Federal Reserve's lender-of-last-resort facilities.[28]   Fed officials have confirmed that LLR assistance was given to one or more FDIC-insured mutual savings banks and some S & Ls during the 1981–2 crisis. FSLIC-insured thrifts and NCUA-insured credit unions, on the other hand, use the resources of their special industry lenders before resorting to the discount window. Whether this dual support system helps or hinders thrifts is discussed in the following chapter and the Appendices.[29]

The recent changes in regulatory and accounting standards designed to aid troubled agricultural and energy banks indicate that access to the lender of last resort may not be equal for all banks regardless of their portfolio composition and organizational structure. Potential problems with the capital forgiveness programs are discussed in Chapter 7.[30]

Size of the Institution

The Federal Reserve no longer admits to any distinction by size with regard to access to the discount window. Pages of the 1971 *Reappraisal of the Federal Reserve Discount Mechanism* referred to "the underlying principle of equal treatment for banks in equal circumstances [so that] standard operating procedures should develop in all discount offices." The report also recommended increases "in the level and frequency of communication among the discount officers of the 12 reserve banks" to promote equal treatment. The change in policy and procedures was implemented to end the perceived advantage of large banks over small ones in discount window access.

However, the Federal Reserve still retains flexibility in granting lender of last resort assistance on a case-by-case basis. As a consequence, uncertainty regarding access to lender-of-last-resort facilities may still provide an unfair advantage to large institutions because the federal safety net treats institutions of different size differently. The market tends to assume that lender-of-last-resort assistance will be granted sooner, longer, and/or on more generous terms to large institutions than to small ones (Guttentag and Herring 1983; Sprague 1986). This perception was heightened in the aftermath of the Continental Illinois situation, when Comptroller of the Currency Conover stated that the federal regulators would not allow any of the eleven largest banks to be liquidated.

Geographic Region

There is no indication that the Federal Reserve deliberately provides preferential treatment with respect to lender-of-last-resort access on the basis of geographic region. For example, both Continental Illinois in Chicago and Penn Square in Oklahoma, two frequently compared bank failures, received equal access to the discount window. In both cases, lending continued until some other regulatory action was taken, and probably after both institutions had become both book and market-value insolvent.

The Federal Reserve may, however, inadvertently favor institutions from specific geographic regions. The market perception of a two-tiered system of support that favors larger depository institutions implies that regions with money center banks may receive preferential treatment. Additionally, the recent changes in the regulators' use of accounting practices designed particularly to assist troubled farm and energy banks and S & Ls may, in practice, result in preferential treatment for midwestern and southwestern depository institutions.

FAIRNESS IN TREATMENT

As discussed in Chapter 5, fairness in treatment refers to the terms and conditions under which lender-of-last-resort assistance is granted. To be equitable, these provisions should not penalize one class of borrowers while subsidizing others. Moreover, the terms of assistance should be similar for the customers, depositors, creditors, or shareholders of different institutions in similar situations. Fairness in treatment involves fairness in collateral provisions and in pricing, and fairness to the taxpayer (that is, to society at large).

The Federal Reserve's desire to retain flexibility in formulating its lender-of-last-resort response in individual situations and the lack of information concerning the terms and conditions of lender-of-last-resort support make it difficult to determine whether the Federal Reserve fairly provides lender-of-last-resort assistance. The somewhat differing collateral valuation guidelines in operation at the twelve Federal Reserve banks suggest that problem institutions may receive treatment that differs according to the region in which they are situated.

However, it is clear that providing lender-of-last-resort assistance to insolvent institutions violates the principle of equal treatment of depositors in similar circumstances. As Benston et al. (1986) point out, when an institution becomes insolvent and closure is delayed, uninsured depositors who withdraw their funds quickly will be paid in full. Those who delay may not be so fortunate.

Fairness in Collateral Provisions

As indicated in Chapter 3, the types of collateral acceptable to the Federal Reserve differ according to the type of institution. For example, depository institutions may receive advances secured by "United States Government and Federal agency securities, and, if of acceptable quality, mortgage notes covering 1–4 family residences, state and local government securities, and business, consumer and other notes," [Federal Reserve Regulation A, 1980, CFR 201.4(B)]. Moreover, Federal Reserve officials report that there is wide latitude in what is judged acceptable. Under 12 USC Section 317c and 12 CFR 201.3(c) non-depository financial institutions and IPCs, on the other hand, can receive advances only in exchange for limited collateral—"any obligation which is a direct obligation of, or fully guaranteed as to principal and interest by, any agency of the United States." However, under 12 USC Section 343 and 12 CFR 201.3(c), on the approval of five or more members of the Board of Governors, aid can be granted to NDFIs and IPCs by discounting a broader range of negotiable paper.

Therefore, the Federal Reserve treats NDFIs and IPCs differently from depository institutions with respect to the collateral provisions of lender-of-last-resort support. At first sight this may appear unfair. It may, however, represent a trade-off of equity in favor of effectiveness. As mentioned earlier, the Federal Reserve has limited access to information about the assets of non-depository financial institutions and IPCs. Also, the type of assets in the portfolios of non-depository financial institutions and IPCs vary considerably. Gathering information on and assessing the quality of non-depository financial institution and IPC assets that do not have secondary markets could prove costly and time consuming for the Federal Reserve. Restricting (in the absence of an exception created by Board vote) eligible collateral of the NDFIs and IPCs to government or government guaranteed securities, therefore, may represent an attempt by the Federal Reserve to limit its information costs and to speed up the process of providing assistance should it decide to lend directly to non-depository financial institutions and IPCs.

Nevertheless, secondary markets already exist for the securities acceptable to the Federal Reserve. Therefore, it is unlikely that NDFIs and IPCs would choose to discount their U.S. and agency securities with the Federal Reserve. Instead, they would probably prefer to sell them or borrow against them via repurchase agreements made in the secondary markets. While the Federal Reserve obviously needs to limit collateral for informational purposes, in the interest of fairness, quality loans or other bank-type collateral should be acceptable regardless of whether the owner is a depository institution, NDFI, or IPC whenever the Federal Reserve decides that direct aid is necessary. At present this outcome is only possible by a vote of the Board.

The Federal Reserve also retains flexibility in the valuation of the posted collateral. Conversations of the authors with Federal Reserve officials revealed differing guidelines in the twelve regional Federal Reserve Banks. Moreover, the guidelines are applied principally to decisions concerning day-to-day adjustment credit. The rules tend to be jettisoned when a crisis arises and emergency credit is requested. Then valuation decisions are made on a case-by-case basis. Therefore, it appears likely that valuation principles are not applied consistently over time or across Federal Reserve districts. Clearly such a decentralized, ad hoc policy can lead to, at least, the appearance of inequity.

There are some fairness issues with regard to the FHLBanks' and FSLIC's handling of collateral requirements for S & Ls. Appendix C shows that the FHLBanks have been lending regularly to insolvent institutions and that collateral has sometimes been inadequate. These events are departures from Federal Reserve practice and involve significant breaches of the classic needs for LLR assistance.

Fairness in Pricing

The pricing structure of lender-of-last-resort assistance penalizes NDFIs and IPCs as compared to depository institutions (see Chapter 3).[31] The appropriateness of the penalty is considered in Chapter 7.

Again, the Federal Reserve's reluctance to provide information regarding lender-of-last-resort assistance to individual institutions makes it difficult to derive any conclusion regarding fairness in the pricing of LLR aid among depository institutions. However, it is unlikely that the assessment of a constant basis point penalty over the basic discount rate will prove to be fair over time. For example, a 100 basis point penalty over the discount rate is proportionately more severe when the discount rate is 5 percent than when it is 10 percent. This observation also applies to the 200 basis point penalty for short-term large borrowings introduced in May 1986.

The March 1985 adoption of "a flexible market rate structure" on extended borrowing represents an attempt by the Federal Reserve to limit any moral hazard inherent in subsidizing lender-of-last-resort loans. However, there is no public information on how such a rate is determined or examples of what rates have been applied under this new structure. Therefore, the fairness of the new rate structure cannot be determined.

The FHLBanks impose no penalty for LLR assistance. Advances are priced equivalently at any time by each FHLBank for each maturity of advance, regardless of the status of the bank or of its collateral. This structure, evidently unfair to competitors and society, is discussed further in Chapter 7 and Appendix C.

Fairness to the Interests of Society

Determining the costs to society of lender-of-last-resort support is difficult, particularly when the Federal Reserve and other regulatory agencies are not forthcoming with information concerning the details of the support given to troubled institutions. However, there is some evidence that because of the way lender-of-last-resort assistance is currently granted, society may be bearing some unnecessary costs. The very frequency of bank and thrift insolvencies in the 1980s suggests that the financial safety net has been producing incentives that encourage risk taking by financial institutions that impose cost on competitors, the insurance agencies, and the taxpayer.

Unnecessary costs are incurred for three reasons. First, any policy of offering lender-of-last-resort loans at below-market rates reduces Federal Reserve net earnings which are rebated to the Treasury. Second, the provision of lender-of-last-resort support by the Federal Reserve, FHLB, or NCUA to potentially insolvent institutions allows uninsured depositors to withdraw their funds from the institution and increases the contingent liabilities of the deposit insurance funds. The FDIC, FSLIC, healthy firms in the industry, or the taxpayer typically bear this increased risk and cost. The GAO (1987d) shows that relatively few (11.3 percent of S & Ls) that were insolvent at the end of 1982 had fully recovered to required capital levels and profitability four years later. Garcia and Polakoff (1987) show that the book value of FSLIC's liability to this set of S & Ls increased substantially over the same period.[32]

Third, LLR subsidies encourage risk taking by failing firms. Managers of insolvent institutions have incentives to gamble in the hopes of returning their firms to solvency (Kane 1986a; Garcia 1987b). Where the gambles are unsuccessful, the insurance funds, the healthy institutions in the industry, or the taxpayer inherit the expanded losses. Moreover, aid delays problem resolution and even without gambling, insolvent firms are prone to make losses and become more insolvent (GAO 1986a). Consequently, leaving national resources in the hands of managers who have demonstrated their lack of skill, by failing, reduces the value of national output.

Thus, extended lending to problem institutions may well prove unfair to healthy firms, society in general, and the taxpayer in particular. This and other present and potential future problems with the system of LLR assistance, together with some suggested resolutions, are discussed in the following chapter.

NOTES

1. However, the crisis originating at Home State Savings spread to other privately insured S & Ls in Ohio and also in Maryland.

2. This perspective on effectiveness does not consider the cost-efficiency nor fairness of Fed aid. These issues are considered later in the discussion of the equity of LLR aid.

3. See Garcia (1987a).

4. The Government securities market is used by the Federal Reserve to implement monetary policy and by the U.S. Treasury to fund the shortfall between revenues and expenses of the federal government.

5. See U.S. General Accounting Office (1986d) and U.S. Congress, House of Representatives 1985.

6. The case study in Appendix A on the failure of Franklin National Bank illustrates the way in which the Federal Reserve handled a crisis at a large member bank. The Fed aided the bank, even though it was insolvent and its crisis had been caused by bank mismanagement.

7. Kane (1987a) considers that nonmember banks were given short shrift by the Fed, especially during the 1930s.

8. Kane (1987a) complains that in this analysis, "(T)he Fed is given credit for acting to forestall a slowly developing crisis caused by deposit rate ceilings it was first pleased to see in place."

9. Axilrod's testimony was given to the Subcommittee on Economic Stabilization of the Committee on Banking Finance and Urban Affairs, November 21, 1985. The Federal Reserve Act has empowered the Fed to lend to the Farm Credit system's intermediate credit banks since 1923 (Todd 1986). In 1985 and 1986 the Farm Credit system did not formally request aid, and the Fed did not volunteer to provide it.

10. Kane (1987a) comments, "The Fed should long ago have set up an adequate flow of information."

11. Section 13b of the Federal Reserve Act (discussed below) was introduced during the Great Depression to allow the central bank to aid distressed industrial and commercial firms. Its use ran counter to the Federal Reserve

tradition of dealing directly only with member banks and it was repealed in 1958.

12. Carron (1982) does not consider the 1969–70 period to have been a serious crisis because only a few (large) firms had trouble placing their commercial paper and spreads rose no more than fifty basis points. The crisis may, however, have been more pronounced if the Fed had not taken action.

13. Todd (1986, 20) describes its use as "something of a political boondoggle."

14. As pointed out in Chapter 1, there are several definitions of insolvency which could indicate different solvency determinations.

15. The Cleveland statement, although that of one individual Reserve Bank, may or may not represent systemwide policy. All Federal Reserve publications are reviewed carefully by Board staff. The Bank statement, on a sensitive issue, would not have been approved by Board staff if it departed from Federal Reserve policy. Nevertheless, regional banks occasionally defy the Board and overrule Board staff objections to the publication of their views.

16. Kane (1987a) in commenting on an early draft of this study, pointed out that LLR action provides free government equity to those that recover. Garcia and Polakoff (1987) show that allowing a firm to continue in business without capital reduces a capital-constrained firm's costs and gives it an advantage as compared to its competitors.

17. Depository institution reserves averaged $54.62 billion during October 1986.

18. The Fed also examines state-chartered member banks.

19. See Board of Governors of the Federal Reserve (1980, 8).

20. The crisis was made more difficult for the Fed to handle because the collateral that the thrifts had to offer was principally one to four family mortgages. Residential mortgages comprise only a small percentage of the assets of large commercial banks. Nevertheless, the development of the secondary mortgage markets has established techniques for the accurate assessment of mortgage values, so the valuation task was manageable.

21. See U.S. General Accounting Office (1984a).

22. In the early 1980s, the Fed undertook a "zero-based budget" approach to data collection and jettisoned some of its earlier requests for information in response to complaints that its reporting requirements were unduly onerous.

23. See Horne (1985).

24. The long studies by CFTC (Commodity Futures Trading Commission) and the SEC of the silver crisis say almost nothing about the Fed's role in the resolution.

25. Use of open-market operations in two of these periods is discussed in Federal Reserve Bank of New York (1983, 51; 1985, 32).

26. Understandably, Fed staff and Board members refrain from discussing lender-of-last-resort actions while they are employed by the system, but there seems to be gentleman's agreement to reserve comment even after they have left the agency. Few governors have written about their experience; Brimmer (1984) and Maisel (1973) are among the exceptions.

27. Before 1980, nonmember banks also lacked access to the discount window except in exceptional circumstances needing Board sanction.

28. Thus, there is some disparity of treatment even among savings banks. Those insured by the FSLIC have access to the FHLBanks before resorting to Federal Reserve help. Those insured by the FDIC do not have a special industry lender and, therefore, access the Federal Reserve either directly or indirectly.

29. Some in the S & L industry initially opposed the requirement that federally insured institutions first turn to their special industry lender. Some S & Ls wanted to regularly access to the Fed for assistance. The Fed feared that the S & Ls would attempt to use the window as a cheap source of funds. The shared responsibility, referred to above, was the resulting compromise.

30. Banks and thrifts that become capital-impaired in these regions can apply for capital forbearance. LLR assistance may then be needed to keep them in operation.

31. In the period before 1980, the system of discount window assistance penalized nonmember institutions. S & Ls were at less of a disadvantage because they could access their Federal Home Loan Bank for an advance and credit unions could use the NCUA's Central Liquidity Facility.

32. The 1987 Treasury–Bank Board plan to recapitalize FSLIC, embodied in H.R. 27, places the burden of industry cleanup on S & Ls. Monies are to be taken from the surpluses of the Federal Home Loan Banks (which belong to industry members) and used to purchase zero coupon bonds which act as collateral for leveraged funds borrowed in the capital markets. The interest-costs of these borrowings are to be paid by regular and special assessment insurance premiums payable by FSLIC-insured thrifts. (See GAO 1987a.)

7 DOMESTIC CONCERNS AND RESOLUTIONS

Chapter 6 illustrated the ways in which the Federal Reserve satisfies, or does not satisfy, several criteria for effective and equitable performance as domestic lender of last resort in the context of the financial safety net. The present chapter discusses some general areas of concern that the item-by-item examination has revealed. First, there are concerns relating to the ways in which the Federal Reserve currently executes its LLR role. Moreover, the way in which the Federal Home Loan Bank System (FHLB system) has been handling the S & L crisis of 1987 has involved several escalations of LLR lending that the Federal Reserve may not want to follow. Second, there are problems with respect to LLR aid that have not yet surfaced but may arise in the future.

There are three criticisms of the way in which the Federal Reserve currently handles its LLR assistance. First, assistance may not always be granted and administered equitably. Second, the safety net and the terms and conditions of LLR assistance may not be effective in providing incentives that discourage undue risk taking and protect the interests of society. Third, the Federal Reserve's actions are conducted in secret. Secrecy makes it difficult to hold the Fed accountable and to assess how well—that is, how equitably, effectively, and economically—it accomplishes its task. Secrecy also serves to make access to and conditions of aid obscure and it fails to "assure the markets beforehand." Furthermore, the Federal Reserve, on occasion, has not reassured the markets during a crisis and the Fed is almost never held accountable for its actions after the crisis is over.

EQUITY

At present, the Federal Reserve, in practice, gives direct aid only to depository institutions, so the discussion of equity issues emphasizes but is not confined to, a discussion of access to and conditions of assistance for banks and thrifts. Four issues arise. First, member banks may still receive preferential treatment as compared to non-member banks and other DIs. Second, there is a dichotomy in treatment between large and small institutions. Third, there is a potential for disparity in collateral requirements at the different Federal Reserve banks and between banks and thrifts. Fourth, special arrangements exist for FSLIC- and NCAU-insured thrifts.

Federal Reserve Membership

The Monetary Control Act intended to end the Fed's preferential treatment for member banks. Secrecy surrounding the recipients and their terms and conditions of aid prevents an evaluation of the present system. It would seem possible, however, that those institutions (member banks or others) that hold their reserves directly at the Fed are in a better position to receive speedy assistance than other DIs.

Bank Size

Regulators are concerned about preserving the safety and soundness of the banking system. Failure of a large bank is more likely to threaten the system than a failure of a small bank. That disparity is particularly true where the problem institution holds a large volume of uninsured funds. In this situation, a delayed payoff that occurs when an institution is book-value insolvent and its economic net worth is seriously deficient, can impose heavy losses on uninsured depositors and unsecured creditors, many of whom may be other (often smaller) depository institutions. Thus, the delayed declaration of failure at a large institution can be contagious. It can bring down other banks and thrifts and their customers, as well as individuals plus commercial and industrial firms that are associated with the banks that fail.

However, if the institution is placed into receivership rapidly, as it becomes book-value insolvent, and if book value closely approximates economic value, only very small ("haircut") loss need be imposed on uninsured depositors, whose solvency should not normally be threatened.

For fear of contagion, assistance (including LLR aid) is much more likely to be given to large than to small banks. Equity, on the other hand, demands that large and small banks be treated similarly in similar circumstances. The staff director of the Senate Banking Committee, Ken McLean, has stated, in conversations on this issue, that equity would and should be jettisoned in favor of preventing contagion by aiding large institutions preferentially. Several commentators (and the regulators themselves) have, nevertheless, expressed distaste for the present system of disparities in aid between large and small institutions (Sprague 1986). The solution to this dilemma is to find ways (discussed further below) to resolve crises at large banks that avoid spillover yet equivalently treats the depositors, creditors, borrowers, management, and stockholders at large and small banks.

Collateral Provisions

As described in Chapter 3, the Federal Reserve banks have differing provisions that govern the collateralization ratio applicable to the different types of collateral. Consequently, it is possible that one bank may receive a higher ratio of loan-to-collateral value than some other bank merely because it is in a region whose Reserve bank uses higher loan-to-value ratios. These differences exist at present, but they will become less important as interstate banking progresses and allows banks in different regions to use whichever Reserve bank offers the most advantageous LLR access.

The Federal Home Loan Bank's collateral requirements also differ across districts. The FHLB system has been departing from Federal Reserve practice in providing advances in exchange for inadequate collateral. (See Appendix C.) This process discriminates unfairly between solvent and insolvent thrifts, between different segments of the financial services industry, and against society as a whole.

Special Industry Lenders

There are advantages and disadvantages to the use of special industry lenders. One advantage is that these special lenders are also the regulators for their industries. Thus, they should have ready access to the best information available on the "health" of any troubled institutions in their jurisdiction. Information is costly, so the use of special industry lenders may enable information to be efficiently utilized. The potentially bad news is that very little (even relative to Federal Reserve aid) is known about the policies and procedures adopted by these lenders. Consequently, their policies may be inequitable and also ineffective. Information presented in the Appendices now allows an examination of LLR assistance currently being provided by the Federal Home Loan Bank System. The NCUA's Central Liquidity Facility is not assessed, however.

The LLR Role of the FHLBanks

The Federal Home Loan Banks (FHLBanks) were created in 1932 to stabilize the S & L industry and provide funds for housing. The Office of Finance, with agency status, raises the funds in the capital markets that each FHLBank has requested individually. The proceeds are then allocated by the individual banks to their member thrifts in the form of advances. Several authors (Morrissey 1971; Silber 1973; Goldfeld, Jaffee, and Quandt 1980; and Kent 1983) have shown that advances have promoted industry growth and replaced deposits lost during cyclical periods of disintermediation. Before the Monetary Control Act of 1980, the FHLBanks carried the sole responsibility in practice for meeting their members' liquidity needs. Since 1980, however, this responsibility has been shared with the Federal Reserve system.[1]

The case study in Appendix C on the S & L crisis of 1985–87 shows that three major equity issues have arisen with respect to the FHLBanks' provision of LLR assistance to S & Ls. Two issues are new, and one is an escalation of a recurring problem. The first of the new issues involves granting LLR loans to insolvent institutions that have no guaranteed resolution. The Fed's latest pronouncement has been that it will aid insolvent DIs only where another agency is committed to resolving the problems. The second new issue involves LLR lending on the basis of collateral acknowledged to be inadequate. While the Federal Reserve has in the past stretched beyond the list of acceptable collateral items to attach bank buildings and foreign assets, its policy is *not* to lend when there is inadequate or nonexistent collateral.

The third issue, pricing assistance, is not new, but FHLBank crisis-assistance has recently exacerbated existing problems. As discussed elsewhere in this text, the Federal Reserve has subsidized LLR assistance in the past but is now moving to reduce the subsidies. In the present S & L crisis, the subsidies that insolvent S & Ls receive are particularly pervasive and are not being eliminated.

These problems involve significant departures by the FHLB system from both classic and modern precepts for LLR assistance. The present arrangements are unfair to healthy members of the S & L industry and to other competitor financial institutions. They are also unfair to society, because they delay the declaration of failure and typically increase total resolution costs (Garcia and Polakoff 1987).

These escalations of lending also detract from the effectiveness of LLR assistance, partly by providing the wrong incentives.

THE WRONG INCENTIVES

The regulators sometimes currently provide inappropriate incentives to banks and thrifts. Both by their words and actions, the federal regulators have postured themselves as prepared to assist (financially and in other ways) insolvent banks and thrifts. The sudden failure of a large, or numerous small, insolvent depository firms is viewed as a crisis whose transmission would be against the public interest. Hence, the emphasis has shifted in two stages. The first shift was from the classicists' view that failures without runs should be permitted and their repercussions contained, to an early Federal Reserve view that catastrophe should be prevented. The second shift was to a modern preference for postponing acknowledgement of failure so that the resulting crisis is pushed into the future.

Delay

Postponement of failure can exacerbate a crisis. DIs are required by their regulators to maintain a certain minimum ratio of book-value capital to bookable assets. Resolution of an unprofitable DI's problem as it crosses below a positive book-value capital threshold, but remains solvent, should be relatively easy to accomplish and costless to the insurance agency under certain circumstances. The institution's remaining capital should insulate the insurer in a liquidation or encourage a low-cost merger. Hence, the insurer should be able to affordably dispose of problem firms at an early phase of their deterioration.

This fortunate outcome will occur if the market value of assets equals or exceeds the book value.[2] Then, as the book value of liabilities usually approximates the market value, depositors' and creditors' claims can be met without cost to the insurer. If the market value of assets is temporarily depressed because of unexpectedly high interest rates, a liquidation or reorganization may involve the insurer in outlays which may, however, be recouped later if assets are successfully warehoused until rates fall. Where asset values are permanently depressed because of fraud, for example, the insurer will incur losses even if the institution is closed promptly as it becomes book-value insolvent. These losses are not likely to be reduced by their delayed recognition. Moreover, where the institution, such as Penn Square, has contingent, unbooked liabilities, the insurer will incur outlays in disposing of the failed firm.

For these reasons, Benston et al. (1986) argue that a DI should be closed or reorganized while it still has a small, positive market-value net worth. Regulatory and public access to information about DIs would need to improve substantially to make this recommendation feasible.

In many instances, however, the regulators delay action. They can do so because the nature of bank and thrift operations allows insured institutions to continue operating while at or near insolvency. Cash settlement of the costs of DI operations can be postponed in many cases. Interest due to depositors, for example, can be credited to their holders' accounts, rather than being paid out. Insured depositors typically are not concerned about the safety of either their principal or interest and do not withdraw them unless they lose faith in the insurer. Thus, insured firms can typically remain liquid despite their insolvency.

For uninsured depositors there is some risk of loss. Nevertheless, they may continue to keep their funds at a troubled firm because they do not have sufficient information to appreciate the seriousness of its condition, or because they are receiving a risk premium that compensates them for the chances they are taking, and/or because they expect the regulators to rescue or "forbear on" the troubled firm and allow depositors to withdraw their funds before the day of demise for their institution. DI managers have considerable discretion about the timing of the recognition of losses that have already occurred on problem loans. This discretion can obscure insolvency. Thus, an insolvent firm can continue to be liquid until its uninsured depositors learn of the problems and begin to run.[3]

Regulators can, therefore, delay taking action against insolvent firms that remain liquid. They may be forced to take action when a run occurs, however. In recent years there have been several examples of runs that have forced the regulators' hands. Penn Square, Continental Illinois, and the privately insured S & Ls in Maryland and Ohio all experienced runs where previously the regulators had delayed action.

"Catch 22"

The classic model points out that a successfully handled run at a solvent institution should be self-terminating. But theory and recent experience has shown that runs at insolvent institutions may continue, as they did at Penn Square, Continental Illinois, and the privately insured S & Ls. Yet once a run has occurred at an insolvent institution, the Fed may perceive (mistakenly, perhaps) that it is required by the immediate public interest to provide LLR assistance to prevent contagion and to help attain a resolution that is cost effective for the insuring agency. The perception can be mistaken because a run can be avoided or terminated by a timely reorganization of the failing firm. Reorganization has been the preferred approach adopted by the Bank of England in dealing with its insolvent banks. Many secondary banks in the crisis of 1973–4 in Britain were recapitalized by their owners or sold as soon as possible to insurance companies, pension funds or others (Reid 1982).[4]

The Fed has the unlimited resources to keep liquid an institution that is experiencing a run. A liquid institution can continue in operation despite insolvency.[5] Its failure need not be recognized as long as the LLR keeps on replacing lost funds. Yet delaying resolution may not prevent a crisis and it can be costly to the insurance agency and the taxpayer in the long run. Delaying resolution has made some insolvent S & Ls unduly dependent on FHLBank advances. For example, at the end of 1986, nine insolvent S & Ls had more than one-half of their assets funded by advances.

As Sprague (1986) points out, the public has become skeptical of the federal commitment to aid insolvent institutions. It has become skeptical because aid may be given—apparently, whimsically—at the regulators' discretion and because insufficient information is available to allow the public to judge for itself the viability of the troubled firm. The knowledge that the Fed is lending now does not appear to be sufficient to end a run in some cases. Private participation in the rescue packages became necessary to end the runs being experienced at First Pennsylvania in 1980 and Continental Illinois in 1984. Private participation was used to demonstrate that those with their own monies at risk were confident that the crises would be resolved without losses being incurred by uninsured depositors.

Resolution Cost

Delaying resolution of insolvent thrifts can exacerbate the cost of resolution, particularly as the recovery rate for troubled firms may be low, as demonstrated in GAO (1987d) for thrift institutions between 1982 and 1986.[6] It has been argued that delay may be cost effective where the problem is due to an interest rate mismatch during a period of abnormally high rates (as occurred for thrifts in the early years of the 1980s). As rates fall, the market value of the assets will rise and the cost of failure resolution by either liquidation or merger will fall. However, the receiver would similarly benefit from the rise in asset values if it had quickly taken over the failed firm and warehoused the assets until interest rates fell. Moreover, removing control from failed managers may avoid an exacerbation of losses caused by the propensity of weak firms to "bet the bank" and lose.

In other circumstances, particularly where credit risk is a problem, delay can be particularly costly. Whatever the cause, insolvent firms typically lose money, so that the degree of their insolvency is likely to increase with time. It is hard to make a profit when a firm is paying out interest on liabilities whose value is greater than that of its earning assets.[7] Thus, the cost to the insurance fund or the taxpayer of resolution is also likely to grow with time, even in the absence of adverse developments in the economy (GAO, 1986a).

Testimony by Williams J. Anderson before the U.S. House Committee on Banking, Finance and Urban Affairs, March 5, 1986, showed that earning assets of the average insolvent S & L were equal to only 90.7 percent of its total assets and 88.7 percent of its liabilities. Industrywide, earning assets were 94.7 percent of total assets and 97.7 percent of liabilities (excluding net worth). This discrepancy partly explains why 58.8 percent of insolvent S & Ls were also unprofitable in 1984 and 51.7 percent unprofitable in the first half of 1985. Those years should have been relatively good ones for the industry.

It should be noted, however, that some of these additional costs from insolvency may be unavoidable for society. When losses have already occurred, whether recognized on the books or not, it will be hard for the firm to earn enough money to cover the interest being incurred on its liabilities. Moreover, transferring these assets to the FDIC or FSLIC as receiver does not completely end the losses. Regardless of whether the institution or the receiver owns the assets, there may not be enough earnings from the assets to service the debt. Unless depositors, particularly uninsured depositors, are forced to suffer a loss of principal, the insurance agency will bear the responsibility to cover the earnings deficiency.

Regardless of whether or not delay is cost effective, whenever forbearance is granted the granter should obtain warrants that allow it and the taxpayer to benefit from the institution's recovery, and to receive some compensation for the burden it has undertaken and the valuable opportunity it has provided to owners and managers. Warrants were obtained in the rescue operations for Chrysler and Continental Illinois.

Change of Control

There is, however, some benefit to the insurance fund and the taxpayer from recognizing the losses and shifting the management of the assets and liabilities away from the original, losing hands. The advantage comes from reducing the size of the future losses. If the original managers retain control of the institution they can continue to exercise their demonstrated ability to either make mistakes and lose money or take risks and lose money. Some institutions get into difficulties because of managerial incompetence or fraud, others because the present incentive system induces managers to place long-shot bets that give the owners better than fair odds, but which nevertheless do not pay off.

Taking control away from incompetent management and giving it to those with a better track record should stem the hemorrhage that the institution and society will likely otherwise experience in the future. In short, economics teaches that society benefits when resources are trusted to the most capable hands.

But those capable hands are limited. The FHLBB's policy of placing failed S & Ls into receivership and replacing the old management by new executives borrowed from more successful firms (under the management consignment program or MCP) may have reduced the FSLIC's potential losses, but has *not* succeeded in the sense of returning participants to solvency or even to profitability. The GAO (1987) shows that most MCP participants suffered losses, both operating and non-operating, and were GAAP-insolvent in 1986. In these circumstances, it may be better to (1) retain the existing managers, who are honest and competent but misdirected, and (2) change the system of incentives that led them astray into taking bets that were better than fair for the institution owners, but unfair for society. Delayed resolution, therefore, is costly in many circumstances. Moreover, it provides the wrong incentives, that encourage activities threatening to solvency.

Thus, a major concern with past lender-of-last-resort actions is that the Federal Reserve has been signalling that it will go too far in supporting insolvent depository institutions in the short-term interest of maintaining public confidence. In this regard, five prominent economists argue that the lender of last resort today is too willing to prevent contagion:

> Public policy should not be directed at preventing bank runs or even failures from ever occurring. Given today's safeguards in the form of the FDIC and Federal Reserve and their ability to pursue stabilizing policies, the banking system is likely to operate most efficiently with some churning among individual institutions. This should be encouraged. However, some caution should

be exercised so that the number and magnitude of bank failures are not sufficiently large to ignite a substantial flight to quality or currency. At what point individual bank runs accumulate to set off such a flight is not known, but in light of the relatively minor economic harm that is likely to be done by flights on individual banks, even large banks, public policy need not err excessively on the side of caution. (Benston et al. 1986, 78)

These authors suggest that the FDIC, which has reasons to be concerned about the potential losses from end-of-game plays, should be required to approve LLR lending by the Federal Reserve.

Market Discipline and the Safety Net

Economists recognize that depository institutions provide services that enhance national output and social welfare. Moreover, there are externalities involved in the provision of these services. Consequently, the cessation of deposit or loan relationships reduces national income. So, the argument proceeds, frequent runs, contagion, and widespread bank and thrift closings should be avoided. The federal financial safety net was designed for this purpose. Kane (1986a), however, claims that regulators and politicians have abused the safety net to avoid the recognition of problems that have occurred "on their watch" which would harm their reputations and careers.

The safety net has other dangers—that it will interfere with the discipline that a market without guarantees (or with properly priced guarantees) exerts by rewarding the productive and punishing money-losing firms that use more resources than they produce. The threat of failure and the rewards of profitability serve to keep managers running their institutions efficiently and making the maximum possible contribution to national output and income.

Management of a failed firm is likely to be an obstacle to a manager's future career advancement. Among owners of ordinary, commercial firms, the fear that they will lose their contributed and accumulated equity induces a degree of caution about exposing their enterprises in risky undertakings. Creditors, usually uninsured at commercial firms, also monitor risky behavior, from which they can lose much but gain little.[8]

The financial safety net, however, has removed many of the anti-risk incentives at depository institutions. Many depositors are insured, while managers and owners are aware of the regulators' and politicians' reluctance to declare failure of a DI. Rather, they will "forbear on" it—allow it to continue in business with little or no capital. In these circumstances, owners and managers may realize that their wealth and their careers may benefit from those gambles that pay off, while suffering little from those that do not.

Market discipline will contain risky behavior at DIs only where owners have capital and managers have their careers truly at risk.[9] In the absence of market discipline, risk taking must be constrained by supervision and regulation by the authorities.

In other words, the safety net's emphasis on suppressing crises may bring short-term benefits of peace and prosperity at the long-term cost of encouraging risky behavior, whose price must be paid later, by which time it has become larger and unavoidable.

Unsecured creditors and uninsured depositors are aware of the deficiencies in the present system. Consequently, as long as large deposits are payable at par, or face value, and are immediately available on demand (or with the forfeit of a relatively small prepayment penalty), large depositors will retain incentives to run when the condition of their borrower deteriorates. They will be particularly inclined to run when the safety net appears incapable of providing a failure resolution that will protect them. Even when they do not run, large depositors can offset some of their exposure by taking out a loan at the DI carrying their deposit, so that their net position falls within the insurance guarantor's $100,000 limit. Moreover, if the credibility of both the institution and its guarantor is lost, even the small depositors will run, as they did in Ohio and Maryland in 1985 and in Texas in 1987.

Solutions Proposed

In this situation, five policy choices are available. All have proponents and opponents in political and academic circles.

Permitting Runs. First, isolated runs could be recognized as a form of market discipline and allowed to occur. The lender of last resort's role then would not be to prevent all runs but rather to contain isolated runs that occur against poorly managed DIs from spilling over to sound institutions and prejudicing the stability of the financial system. At the same time, the incidence of runs, which are unpleasant for all concerned, could be reduced if the chartering agency merged a deteriorating firm before, preferably well before, it becomes market-value insolvent. If an institution is reorganized or closed promptly while its economic net worth is positive, that is *before* it becomes book-value insolvent, all depositors and creditors can be paid in full and there is no need for them to run.

Ban Runs. The second choice is to prevent all runs from occurring. To prevent runs, all depositors could be guaranteed against loss. Then the task of protecting society's interests and maintaining economic efficiency would fall almost entirely on the regulators. Existing failed institutions would need to be dealt with during the transition from the old, inadequate regime to the new one. They could be allocated to a new Reconstruction Finance Corporation similar to the one set up on the 1930s, as would any firms that failed under the new system. The danger is that the system would approach nationalization of the banking and thrift industries unless market discipline can be created amongst owners and other creditors.

Eliminate Deposits. The third policy choice would allow unsecured creditors to continue to play a disciplinary role at DIs, but seek to prevent runs. Uninsured depositors would not be allowed to hold short-term, par value deposits from which they can run. Par value funds should be maintained only over extended terms, so that refinancing would become more similar to the situation facing commercial and industrial firms. The need to refinance would occur at irregular, but foreseeable intervals. In fact, deposits, uninsured, would be converted into subordinated debt.

Under this proposal, overnight and very short-term funds would continue to be available, although not in deposit form. Short-term accounts would be uninsured and not recoverable at par; instead, they would be repayable as from a mutual fund.

There are two problems with this proposal, however. First the subordinated debtholders would seek to protect their position, if endangered, by taking out a compensatory loan, rendering their discipline ineffective. Second, the economy would be deprived of short-term par value deposits, which have been a popular instrument for at least several centuries.

Circumscribe Bank Assets.   A fourth proposal recognizes a need for short-term par deposits, seeks to continue to provide them, and to protect their value by limiting their possible uses. Kareken (1985) and Litan (1987) have proposed that the proceeds of transaction accounts should be invested by the DI only in short-term Treasury securities which would have limited interest rate and credit risks. Guttentag (1987) has made a variant of this proposal—transaction deposits could be offered by banks which could hold only readily marketable and market-to-market assets.

Enhance Market Discipline.   Kane (1987b) has suggested another, fifth way to discourage runs—at the bank as we know it. Depositors who fled during the last month of a failed bank's operations should be subject to the same haircut loss imposed on those that remain. Depositors might have two reactions to the proposal—run early, or form a consensus to lobby politically to delay the declaration of failure. The first reaction would make the recommendation work. However, the second appears more consistent with recent history and would destroy the proposed solution.

Kaufman (1987) has proposed protecting depositors at the bank as we know it by reverting to an earlier system of double or increased jeopardy for stockholders. When a bank fails, its stockholders' liability would be less limited than it is now. Owners would be called upon to put up additional capital to make depositors whole.

Adoption of three of these five choices—but not the second or third—should provide an improved set of incentives to depository institutions.

Pricing Assistance.   It has been shown earlier and in the appendices that in the past LLR assistance has often been subsidized assistance. The Federal Reserve has taken steps of late to reduce the subsidy, which has not been systematically eliminated in all circumstances, however. The problem arises basically because LLR assistance is priced as a markup over the discount rate, which is a *below*-market rate, in accordance with Federal Reserve policy. As Schwartz (1987a) points out, this pricing system makes the Federal Reserve the lender of *first* resort, when an institution needs adjustment, seasonal, or other extended credit.

Three issues arise with respect to the current system for pricing assistance. The first is technical: does a requirement to post excess

collateral impose a cost on borrowers that compensates for any subsidized rate received? The second issue is the concern that it is inappropriate to penalize institutions that are already experiencing
difficulties. The third difficulty is determining what is an appropriate
penalty to impose.

Excess Collateral

Some analysts argue that the subsidy a depository institution receives
on its discount window loan is offset by the heavy collateral it posts.
For example, in testimony before the U.S. House Subcommittee on
Domestic Monetary Policy, E. Gerald Corrigan, president of the Federal Reserve Bank of New York, estimated the book value of the
assets the Bank of New York pledged as collateral for its $23.6 bil-
lion loan at $36 billion, or 153 percent of the loan value. He argued
that the $12.4 billion "excess collateral" more than offset any inter-
est subsidy arising from the fifty-four basis point differential between the discount and federal funds rates on November 21, 1985.

However, it is not clear that the collateral argument is relevant to
the subsidy question. An institution continues to receive interest on
securities pledged to the Fed as collateral. Moreover, the BONY
pledged its real and financial assets. The borrower suffers financial
loss only if it relinquishes flexibility in deploying the asset or incurs
administrative costs for assistance. Excess collateral may well protect
the Federal Reserve from loss, but it does not eliminate a subsidy
and it is unlikely to avoid other moral hazard problems.

Is a Penalty Appropriate?

While the Federal Reserve is interested in limiting the moral hazard
inherent in subsidizing troubled institutions, it sees three reasons
why it should not charge a penalty rate for LLR aid. First, it feels
that penalizing an already troubled institution would only compound
its problems. Second, unlike the nineteenth century Bank of England,
the Federal Reserve is a public body, not a private corporation.
Therefore, it does not need a profit motive to induce it to act in the
public interest as lender of last resort. Its interests are taken care of
by requiring a high ratio of sound collateral-to-loan value so that it

does not incur a loss on its operations. Third, there is clearly a public good aspect to lender-of-last-resort assistance. If the costs to society of contagion are high, it may not be appropriate for the lender of last resort to charge a high rate that would exacerbate a current crisis.

There are counterarguments that can be made on this issue, however. For example, subsidizing a bank currently experiencing a crisis encourages others to undertake risks that can give rise to future crises. There may therefore, be a potential trade-off between (1) charging a high discount rate and exacerbating a current crisis, and (2) charging a low rate and increasing the number and severity of future crises.[10]

As discussed in Chapter 3, the Federal Reserve has been moving toward charging market or penalty rate that avoids improper incentives and lender-of-last-resort abuse. These preliminary steps are appropriate. Nevertheless, the steps are being taken hesitantly and the hesitancy sends mixed signals to the financial markets. Moreover, the FHLBanks continue to charge *no* penalty for LLR aid. Therefore, the trade-off between containing an existing crisis and preventing future crises remains to be resolved.

Arguments have been presented in this study and elsewhere for taking the longer perspective. A firm commitment by the Federal Reserve to provide discount window loans at high or penalty rates would reduce market uncertainty and promote market discipline (Kaufman 1987; Meltzer 1986). If market participants are convinced that they, not the public, will bear the full costs of their actions, they will change their attitudes toward risk taking and there might be, other things being equal, fewer crises down the road.

The Appropriate Penalty

A penalty rate is usually defined as an above-market rate. But it is not clear which market rate is appropriate to use as the standard of comparison, nor how much above this market rate is appropriate as a penalty. Is the appropriate market rate the federal funds rate at which banks lend overnight to sound institutions? Is the three-month Treasury bill rate (the rate on default-free short-term credit) appropriate for assistance of similar duration? Or, more fairly, should the comparison be made with the rate that a troubled institution would have to pay for collateralized funds in the private market? Given the risks attending the loan, and the legal and administrative costs of valuing and perfecting a claim to collateral, this last rate might include a high-risk premium. Lack of clear definition by the Federal Reserve in its pricing statements of the market rate which is relevant to the bank in crisis, makes deciding on an appropriate penalty rate difficult. Moreover, a price needs to be determined for depository institutions' legally granted, assured access option to borrow at the discount window.

It can be agreed, however, that the Federal Reserve's present pricing decree may not be its final word on this subject. The published penalty imposes a constant markup within maturity bands over the regular discount rate for credit granted for up to 150 days. Such an arrangement is not a finely tuned pricing tool. A 100 basis point penalty when the discount rate is 5 percent is relatively more substantial than when that rate is 12 percent. For the longest term assistance (over 150 days) a flexible, market-related rate is to be charged. But what that rate is in implementation, unknown. Moreover, the FHL-Banks currently impose no penalty.

Further public discussion of the appropriate pricing of discount window assistance is warranted. A public statement by the Federal Reserve describing the policy it adopts in light of the discussion would be effective in reducing uncertainty. It would also be equitable in letting institutions know the rules under which they are operating.

ACCOUNTABILITY

The third current concern is the lack of Federal Reserve accountability for its LLR actions. Classic writers admonished the LLR to clearly announce its policies before a crisis and to reassure the markets during a crisis. They did not prominently discuss *ex post* accountability. Today, there are general concerns about the Federal Reserve's lack of openness with respect to its LLR policies before, during, and after a liquidity crisis.

The argument is frequently made in support of secrecy that the central bank needs to maintain confidentiality to minimize moral hazard problems. An alternative argument can be made and in fact, was made in Chapter 5. Suppose the Federal Reserve were to preannounce a stringent aid policy. That policy might include giving assistance only to solvent institutions, in special circumstances, in exchange for acceptable collateral, and with the imposition of a penalty rate. If these conditions were adhered to, it is hard to believe that undue risk taking would be encouraged. Anti-social policies are fostered by the hopes of obtaining lenient, subsidizing aid—hopes that are based on the observation that some insolvent institutions have received, and still do receive, inexpensive assistance.

Thus, an efficient and equitable policy would require the Federal Reserve to clearly state permanent policies and procedures for handling crises. Then it should adhere to them. It should keep records regarding the handling of LLR assistance. These records should become available to the public after a period of time, years, if necessary.[11]

Where the most exceptional circumstances call for a rare relaxation of the regular provisions, the Federal Reserve should, after the event, be accountable to Congress for revealing the circumstances that caused aid to be given and the conditions of the assistance that was granted. The authors believe that it would be preferable for the accountability hearings to be held in public, but they could be held in private, if the potential revelation would shake public confidence. The revealed conditions would include the collateral accepted, the rates charged, the amounts of emergency aid given, and the period over which extended credit was granted. The Federal Reserve should declare whether it planned to reinstate the previous permanent conditions of aid, or whether its old conditions would be modified henceforth as a result of its recent experience.

Evidently, frequent or trivial deviations from the permanent procedures would make the central bank lose credibility. This situation is being rapidly approached today. The Federal Reserve attempts to maintain a posture of stringency, but is unconvincing in the execution. It is well-known that the stated rules will be relaxed to prevent the demise of large institutions whenever it is deemed in the public interest to keep them in operation. It appears that the integrity of central bank policies has become so unconvincing that private institutions with funds at risk had to be brought into the rescue arrangement for First Pennsylvania and Continental Illinois. Moreover, assistance has also been given to smaller institutions when they fail in large enough numbers in any area to cause concern and stir up political pressures—as happened in Ohio and Maryland in 1985, and nationally, among federally insured S & Ls during the crises of 1981–2 and 1985–7.

CONCERNS FOR THE FUTURE

There are two different kinds of concern about the Federal Reserve's future ability to perform its LLR role effectively and equitably. First, certain developments in the financial sector have changed, and are still changing, the ability of the Federal Reserve to continue its policy of giving aid only to depository institutions. It may find itself, in the future, forced to extend aid farther than it desired to NDFIs and IPCs. Second, the question arises whether the Federal Reserve's LLR safety net *should* be cast more widely to encompass non-depository firms, particularly NDFIs.

EXTENDING ASSISTANCE TOO FAR

There are three areas where the Federal Reserve may extend assistance too far. The first, discussed above, concerns the possible over-willingness to lend to insolvent depository institutions. The second and third areas involve firms utilizing banks in their organization to provide support for non-banking entities in contravention of current Federal Reserve policy. Bank holding companies and "non-bank banks" provide the opportunity for this diversion of aid.[12]

Banking and Thrift Holding Companies

A practical question that arises with respect to bank and thrift holding companies is whether the Fed can adhere to its stated policy of confining support to the depository institutions in the organization. Consistency with present policy would demand that the Federal Reserve *not* channel assistance through a bank to the non-bank affiliates or subsidiaries of the holding company. But such separation may be impossible to maintain.

Bank and multiple thrift holding companies are limited in the activities they can pursue to those that are deemed appropriate for a depository institution.[13] Consequently, extending aid to them would not be a drastic departure from principle. Unitary thrift holding companies (holding companies that include only one thrift) have broad powers, however, so the potential for unintended aid is greater in their case.

Clearly, in the case of Continental Illinois, the FDIC guarantee encompassed the creditors of the holding company as well as the bank. The question did not arise substantively, however, because it was the bank itself that was in trouble, and its problems in turn threatened the holding company. However, there may be occasions where the demise of non-bank entities threatens the bank or the complete holding company. Should the Federal Reserve use discount window assistance through the bank to aid the non-bank affiliate? Furthermore, regardless of what is the appropriate public policy in this regard, it may prove impossible to insulate the bank from the rest of the holding company (Eisenbeis 1983).

Non-bank Banks

Thus there is a problem in implementing stated policy with respect to bank holding companies. The problem is *a fortiori* more serious in the case of non-bank banks,[14] because non-bank banks may be owned by companies engaged in a much broader set of commercial and industrial activities than bank or thrift holding companies.

Consequently, the issue of insulating the non-bank bank from the rest of the company is a more serious one. Since a non-bank bank that offers transaction accounts is required to maintain reserves, it has access to the discount window. However, in the case of the non-bank banks owned by non-depository institutions, non-bank bank assets comprise only a very small part of total holding company value. The Federal Reserve is, therefore, concerned that the non-bank bank may become a vehicle by which lender-of-last-resort assistance may be channelled to entities not otherwise having direct access to LLR assistance such as, for example, an NDFI or IPC.

This concern has resulted in vigorous pressure from the Fed and others on Congress to restrict the creation of non-bank banks, require their nonbank owners to divest those already in existence, and to continue to limit the activities of bank holding companies to traditional patterns in order to preserve the separation of banking from commerce and industry.[15] Finally, H.R. 27, the Competitive Equality Banking Act, was passed in August 1987. It redefined a bank as "an FDIC-insured institution whether or not it accepts demand deposits or makes commercial loans" in order to close the non-bank bank loophole. It did not require their divestiture by nonbank owners but limited asset growth to 7 percent per annum at grandfathered non-bank banks.

SHOULD ASSISTANCE BE EXTENDED FURTHER?

To date, the Federal Reserve has allowed a crisis that originated outside the banking system to spread to the commercial banks. Once the crisis reached the banks, it was contained there and not allowed to spill over from banks to others—the approach adopted during the Penn Central crisis in 1972. Banks were also the lender of next to last resort to the Placid Oil Company, and so indirectly to the Hunts, their brokers and dealers, and COMEX in the silver debacle of 1980. The Federal Reserve provided discount window assistance to some commercial banks that participated in loans to the Hunt family.[16] It is not known whether the discount window loans were for adjustment credit or LLR assistance. While the Fed's role in the silver crisis appears to have been passive—press reports at the time attributed a more active, driving force type, role for the Fed.[17]

It is questionable whether this indirect approach to aid is adequate today.[18] Over the last decade financial markets have changed markedly. Banks are losing market share in the loan markets to NDFIs and IPCs and in the deposit markets to thrifts. Financial firms are beginning to look more alike. In earlier times, firms offering financial services could be easily characterized by the types of products they offered and in many cases, the markets served were localized. Today, the distinctions between the various participants in the industry have largely disappeared, and the markets in which lending is done and from which funding is obtained have both become national and international in scope.

The means of making payments for the acquisition of goods and services used to be confined to commercial banks. Today, this is no longer true. Many depository and non-depository institutions offer accounts that may be used as a means of making payments. Furthermore, the product offerings of these institutions—once severely constrained by regulation and tradition—are no longer uniquely the province of a particular type of institution. In addition to these considerations, as discussed in Chapter 4, the financial services industry has evolved into one in which virtually all participants have business relationships with one another. A problem affecting one of the participants is therefore much more likely to affect the affairs of other participants.

The development of telecommunications and electronic data processing and transmission capabilities has in many cases been the catalyst for the growth in business interrelationships. Funds for intermediation can be attracted virtually at an instant from around the globe. Funds are transferred to ultimate borrowers just as quickly. These changes imply that the avenues through which a previously localized problem can be transmitted to others have greatly expanded, and also that such problems may spread within the financial system almost instantaneously.[19]

The Federal Reserve policy of using the commercial banking system to contain crises is understandable, given the lender of last resort's need for information on the financial condition of an affected institution. The commercial banks doing business with a problem firm have non-public information about its condition. This situation has been well-illustrated during the Penn Central and silver market crises. Moreover, commercial banks still play an important role in the payments system, so they are a natural conduit for aid.

Despite these valid reasons for favoring commercial banks as vehicles for crisis remission, current Federal Reserve strategy could prove inadequate in the future. There is little reason to doubt that if a crisis were to develop in the non-depository sector, the Federal Reserve would overcome its stated policy of confining discount window assistance to DIs and provide assistance directly to NDFIs if that were the only means of containing the crisis. The concern is whether the Federal Reserve would be able to recognize the need, gather necessary information, and act quickly enough to contain the situation. Given the speed with which such crises could develop, there is reason to question the feasibility of a quick and decisive response to any NDFI crisis that cannot be contained through use of the commercial banking system.

What is needed is that the Federal Reserve determine what information is necessary to facilitate its prompt assistance to DIs and what would be needed to open the discount window to NDFIs and

IPCs. Then the Fed should make arrangements to obtain these data *before* a crisis occurs.

At present, NDFIs and IPCs have, in principle, different and inferior access to, and conditions for, LLR assistance. In practice, direct access is non-existent. There are three reasons for this dichotomy in treatment. First, banks, and only banks, are held to be special. Because they are special, they are heavily examined, supervised, and regulated and required to hold reserves.[20] Because they are special, they also are given ready access to LLR facilities. Second, access under preferential conditions is maintained as partial compensation for the costs incurred in maintaining non-interest earning reserves. Third, reserve requirements, examination, supervision, and regulation produce substantial amounts of information to the Federal Reserve and other regulators about the financial condition of banks. Ready access to such information makes it easier for the Fed to provide ready, non-punitive access to LLR facilities to these institutions.

Are Banks Special?

The Federal Reserve argues that banks are special and therefore they are particularly likely to need LLR aid, and moreover, that aid can be channeled effectively through them. Gerald Corrigan (1982; 1987) has written that banks are special because they simultaneously (1) offer transaction accounts, (2) are the conduit for monetary policy, and (3) the backup sources of liquidity for the economy. Saunders (1987) claims that banks are special because (4) commercial loans, their principal asset, are unique. Chapter 2 also pointed out that (5) banks are more highly leveraged than typical commercial or industrial firms. They are also at the hub of the payments system.

Chapter 3 expressed the view that the nature of many bank assets (illiquid because of asymmetric information that banks possess about their customers) and their liabilities (often immediately callable at par) exposes them to runs. For these reasons, banks have access to the lender-of-last-resort deposit insurance, and are supervised and regulated under the safety net. That is, items one and four above are convincing arguments for their special treatment.

Two other characteristics—being the transmitter of monetary policy stimuli and liquidity backstops for NDFIs and IPCs—are less telling identifiers. It is true that institutions holding reserves (DIs) currently pass on the Federal Reserve's monetary policy implementation via open-market operations to the rest of the economy. But monetary policy does not have to be conducted this way. Patinkin (1965) and Fama (1980) have pointed out that the price-level goal of monetary policy could be achieved if the central bank controlled both the price and the quantity of *any* valued commodity. At present this commodity is high-powered money (currency plus DI reserves), but it could be some other commodity such as licenses to make a spaceship journey to the planets.

At present banks are the backup sources of liquidity to the economy. They took this role during the Penn Central and silver crises, for example. But this position derives at least partly from the Fed policy of funneling aid through them. Emergency liquidity need not always be provided only by the banking system. Thrifts and NDFIs could offer that service. Similarly, they could access Fedwire to effect large fund transfers.

The final peculiarity of banks and thrifts—their low capital-to-asset ratios—could be ended abruptly as a matter of public policy. In fact the current regulatory trend internationally is to require higher capital ratios in banking to reduce the industry's vulnerability.

Are Thrifts Special?

The claims to being special are no longer characteristics confined to commercial banks. Since the MCA, all S & Ls, savings banks, and credit unions have been able to offer transaction accounts if they wish. Since the Garn–St Germain Act, S & Ls have also been able to provide demand deposits to their commercial customers. Offering transaction accounts and holding reserves makes both banks and thrifts the executors of monetary policy. The 1982 Garn–St Germain Act gave S & Ls nationwide the power to make commercial loans.[21] Possessing three of the attributes of being special, thrifts could also become the backup sources of liquidity to the economy—if they wanted to play that role and if the authorities chose to allow them to do so.

Consequently, thrifts already possess the powers—particularly the two that are here considered vital—to make them special. However, at present they are exercising these powers only peripherally to their main lines of business. For example, at the end of 1986, only 4.0 percent of thrift assets were funded by transaction accounts. Commercial loans comprised only 2.0 percent of assets, and consumer loans only 4.4 percent. Consequently, at present thrifts might appropriately be classed as only "potentially special," but already very vulnerable because of their low capital ratios.

Are Some NDFIs Special?

With regard to the first characteristic, the Monetary Control Act gives the regulators wide power to define a transaction account:

> In order to prevent evasions of the reserve requirements imposed by the Subsection, after consultation with the Board of Directors of the FDIC, FHLBB, and the NCUA Board, the Board of Governors of the Federal Reserve System is authorized to determine, by regulation or by order, that an account or deposit may be used to provide funds directly or indirectly for the purpose of making payments or transfers to third persons or others. (Monetary Control Act 1980, Section 103B.)

Such accounts could be, and in fact already are, provided by non-depository institutions. Money market mutual funds (MMMFs) constitute one example of a non-deposit transaction account. While a mutual fund is not conceptually an instrument repayable at par, in practice money market mutual funds operate as such. Consequently, they are exposed to runs. They are not insured, do not obey formal reserve requirements, and do not have access to the LLR. Instead they are protected from sharp decreases in value by the liquidity and creditworthiness of their assets.[22]

The quotation above shows that MMMFs would be subjected to reserve requirements, which at present appear to be the operational determinant of access to the discount window for adjustment or extended credit. Nevertheless, if NDFIs were required to hold reserves under Section 103B, as shown in the next section, they currently appear not to have access to the discount window, which is confined to depository institutions. Consequently, a situation could arise where non-depository firms would be offering transactions accounts and required to hold reserves, without having access to the discount window.[23] There appears to be a potential legal anomaly and inequity in the present arrangements.

Other NDFIs currently provide commercial loanlike services to compete with banks. Nevertheless, commercial paper and private placements are not funded by deposits. Consequently, in the current environment, runs should not present a problem to NDFIs.

Thus, banks have been special in the past. Banks and thrifts continue to be special today. But developments in the financial markets are making them less special as time passes. For example, the securitization, first of mortgages and now of commercial and consumer loans, is making these loans more marketable and less subject to asymmetric information. The day may not be too far away when DIs cease to be special. On that day, loans, transactions accounts, and emergency liquidity will be provided on a regular, significant, and possibly simultaneous—rather than an exceptional basis—by nondepository firms.

Holding Reserves

At present, access to the discount window is one of the privileges compensating DIs for holding reserves: "Any depository institution in which transaction account or nonpersonal time deposits are held, shall be entitled to the same discount and borrowing privileges as member banks." (Monetary Control Act 1980, Section 103.7)

It is time to question this philosophy and to ask whether access to assistance should still be preferentially preserved to depository reserve-holding institutions.

This issue is worthy of comprehensive debate. One of three possible outcomes from the debate can be foreseen. First, emergency access to the discount window would be divorced from the obligation to hold reserves.[24] The potential cost inequity would be dealt with by paying interest on reserves. Access would be granted, perhaps at the discretion of the Federal Reserve, to any deserving DI, NDFI, or IPC. Second, the present system of preferential access for DIs could continue. Third, the obligation to hold reserves could continue to carry privileges of discount window access, but the obligation to hold reserves could be extended to NDFIs that hold accounts (particularly transaction accounts) and are judged particularly exposed to generating or transmitting financial crises. Interest might or might not be paid on reserves; the financial entities that would be affected is a matter that would need further study. However, money market mutual funds, credit card issuers, and others whose demise could lead to a loss of transaction activity might be prime candidates for an expansion of reserve requirements and discount window access.[25]

Choosing the institutions for the LLR expansion would require an agreement on the answer to the question raised above—what has made banks special in the past? Which other institutions are special today? It has been argued here that the coincidence of offering par-valued, immediately callable deposits and making illiquid commercial or consumer loans (especially while possessing low capital ratios) determines specialness. When non-depository institutions evolve further to take on this dual role, the safety net of deposit insurance, examination, supervision, regulation, and access to the LLR should be extended to them.

ACCESS TO INFORMATION

To provide LRR access to NDFIs, the Fed would need additional information about them. At present the Fed has weekly information about deposit flows at all DIs that need to maintain reserves. The institutions are required to file reports about transaction accounts and non-personal time deposits that carry reserve requirements. These data put the Fed's Reserve banks into the position of being able to monitor deposit withdrawals that threaten to deteriorate into runs. The Fed typically also has ready access to other information about DIs, particularly those that are federally chartered, examined, supervised, and regulated. These data encompass portfolio composition and the potential viability of the institution and some evaluation of the soundness of its assets.

Such data access remains a practical reason for the discrepancy in the LLR treatment between DIs and NDFIs. The suggestion that LLR access be granted in practice, in emergencies, to NDFIs raises questions about how the Fed's data needs would be met. Would the Federal Reserve need to regularly examine, supervise, and regulate NDFI institutions? The answer should be "no." The Federal Reserve currently aids institutions that it does not examine, supervise, or regulate. For example, state chartered, state regulated, federally or privately insured institutions are outside Federal Reserve examination, supervision, and regulation authority, yet they have access to the discount window. In exercising its LLR function to these institutions, the Federal Reserve has to obtain solvency and collateral information elsewhere. There is only one thing that LLR grantees currently have in common—they maintain reserves and therefore report deposit flows. But even these requirements do not force a DI to have direct contact with, or provide any additional information flow to, the Fed. Reserves can be maintained indirectly, being passed through by a correspondent bank to the Fed.

While the Fed may not have direct access to information about the condition of all DIs to which it lends, it feels more comfortable in granting aid where it does have quickly available information. Moreover, even where immediate and direct access to information is lacking, information is typically available indirectly from another agency participating in the federal financial safety net. The federal insurer or charterer should be able to provide data within a short period of time.

Nevertheless, while information is, in principle, available from other agencies, in practice it is sometimes not readily accessible. Many of the difficulties in aiding S & Ls in Ohio and Maryland arose because these S & Ls were *not* federally insured. The states that chartered, examined, supervised, and regulated these institutions did not have information that was adequate for Fed purposes. In Ohio, the Federal Reserve Bank of Cleveland delayed aid while information on collateral values and solvency was obtained. In Maryland, the GAO was unable to obtain information about the condition of privately insured S & Ls. State law kept the data confidential. Despite the lack of data, the Federal Reserve Bank of Richmond lent readily in the Maryland crisis. Loans were provided while the financial condition of the borrower was still undetermined. Several Maryland recipients were later found to be insolvent, and a year and a half after the crisis two of them were still receiving discount window assistance.

In July 1987, during the period of sustained loss of deposits, the GAO requested access to the Federal Home Loan Bank Board's monthly data series to more closely monitor the liquidity position of individual S & Ls. It was told that the Federal Reserve also had a request pending for the same data. (The extent of deposit withdrawals was severe enough to raise the question whether the Fed would need to be involved in providing liquidity assistance.) The Bank Board staff person volunteered that the old Bank Board under Chairman Gray would most probably have rejected the request. Moreover, the new Board, installed that month under Chairman Wall, rejected the GAO request. In other words, data are not necessarily readily released by one agency to another.[26] Personalities and agency pride may be an obstacle to data sharing and public release.

Typically, the Fed relies on the chartering agency for federally insured institutions to declare bankruptcy. In the absence of the declaration, the Fed assumes solvency and is prepared to continue lending on the provision of appropriate collateral. This was not the situation in Ohio and Maryland. The Fed and other regulators sent federal examiners to make their own determination of solvency and to assess the value of collateral.

If it were decided that NDFIs should have access to the discount window, the Federal Reserve would need to make pre-crisis arrangements with institutions granted access to provide regular, even weekly data on changes in liabilities, and with federal non-banking regulators to obtain data on institution condition. The Fed would need to determine what data would be indispensible for LLR assistance to be provided. This process might involve the federal regulators in obtaining new and different kinds of information from those demanded in the past. Moreover, institutions to whom eligibility was newly extended might also be required to regularly maintain reserves directly or indirectly at the Fed. Not all financial institutions are federally regulated, however.[27] It would probably be more difficult for the Fed to obtain needed data from NDFIs that are not federally supervised.

To resolve this issue, institutions not currently covered by Fed services (LLR and other) could be given a choice between (1) offering deposits and/or close deposit substitutes and bearing the accompanying regulatory costs, including the provision of specified information; and (2) not offering these instruments that are prone to runs and so avoiding the accompanying regulatory burdens. Choosing to remain or become a depository institution means accepting both the costs in terms of additional regulation, examination, supervision, provision of information, and maintenance of reserves in exchange for discount window access and other financial safety net services. Alternatively, institutions could choose to bypass the additional requirements in exchange for foregoing direct access to the Fed. In effect, an incipient financial firm is free to determine what line of business—depository or NDFI—that it is in. Such a freely made choice would be consistent with equity as foreseen in the economic theory of superfairness (Baumol 1986).

Choice also conveys one of the attractive features of Corrigan's 1987 proposal for financial reform. The appropriate public policy would be to prevent access by those not offering deposits and so not undertaking the accompanying burdens and to make access, together with its burdens, available to any institution that could generate a widespread, quickly transmitted financial crisis. Because banks and thrifts are currently the only entities that can concurrently execute both of the special characteristics of banks recognized here to be relevant to special treatment, they should remain required to undertake the burdens of their role and enjoy the benefits of liquidity assistance from the Fed or the industry lender.

NOTES

1. The sharing of responsibility is described in greater detail in Chapter 3.
2. More research needs to be done on the relationship between market values and book values. (See Kane 1987b). If they move in parallel over the business cycle, book values may remain as useful proxies for the conceptually more relevant market values.
3. Thrifts may be particularly able to continue in operation while insolvent because uninsured deposits typically provide a very small proportion of their funding.
4. The Bank of England was not able to resolve all of its problems speedily, however.
5. In 1986, one heavily insolvent S & L had 118 percent of its assets funded by FHLBank advances.
6. The GAO (1987d) showed that only 11.3 percent of the 222 S & Ls that were insolvent using GAAP at the end of 1982 had "fully recovered" to have capital above the regulatory minimum 3 percent and profitability four years later. Of the 916 S & Ls that had low capital (positive but below 3 percent) in 1982, 27.8 percent had fully recovered by 1986, but another 20.3 percent had deteriorated into insolvency. Moreover, many of those that deteriorated became seriously insolvent and highly unprofitable, thus imposing higher book value costs on FSLIC in 1986 than in 1982.
7. See Garcia (1987b).
8. Creditors gain little but additional security when firms do well because they do not share in the firm's profits.
9. Market discipline at depository institutions is discussed further in Benston et al. (1986, chap. 1).
10. Benston et al. (1986, 119–120) provide two alternate proposals for pricing LLR assistance. Both proposals involve linking the rate charged for aid to the market value of an institution's assets.

11. The Federal Reserve already provides minutes several weeks after Federal Open Market Committee (FOMC) meetings that periodically determine monetary policy—another sensitive area that used to be determined in complete secrecy.

12. See U.S. General Accounting Office (1986b) for more detailed information on the structure and development of non-bank banks.

13. In the case of bank holding companies the Federal Reserve determines which activities are "closely related to" and "a proper incident" of banking.

14. Until August 1987, a bank was an entity which offered both demand deposits and commercial loans (unless it was a thrift). Therefore, a non-bank bank offered either demand deposits or commercial loans, but not both.

15. Corrigan (1987) in his proposal to reconfigure the financial services industry, maintains this separation.

16. See U.S. Congress, House of Representatives (1981, 146–47).

17. Brimmer (1984), Melton (1985), and the press at the time gave Chairman Volcker a more active, behind-the-scenes role in containing the crisis. See the Appendix for further information.

18. With respect to crises originating among manufacturing firms and local governments, Congress has time available to decide if it wants to provide assistance.

19. A run may occur as soon as the news of an event that threatens solvencies is released and depositions and creditors react to it. News is transmitted by wire services and appears momentarily on computer monitors and securities brokers' screens. It may be observed by the general public on the nightly television news or in the newspapers. Reaction to the news may be immediate—by wire—for the professionals and the same day by telephone or trip to the bank for owner of smaller deposits.

20. Reserves were initially required to insure bank liquidity in the face of the normal exigencies of depositor withdrawals. Today, reserve requirements are more an instrument of monetary policy.

21. Mutual savings banks already possessed commercial loan powers.

22. MMMFs may be less exposed to the fear of runs than are depository institutions because their liabilities are not legally payable at par. On withdrawal, fund holders receive their share of the net realizable value of fund assets. Running from an MMMF is rational only if the net realizable value deteriorates as the fund diminishes. Some stock mutual funds experienced liquidity problems during and following the market crash of October 1987.

23. Holding reserves would make MMMFs a conduit for monetary policy under the Corrigan criteria for specialness.

24. Regular day-to-day use of the adjustment credit facility would remain confined to reserve-holding institutions.

25. Corrigan (1987) proposes a new class of financial holding company that would offer uninsured transaction accounts (but not deposits), access the large-dollar payments system, and the discount window (but only in abnormal circumstances) would hold reserves, engage in the full range of financial activities, and yet would remain separate from commerce and industry.

26. GAO has the power to subpoena data, but prefers not to do so.

27. Insurance companies are state regulated, for example. Brokerage houses are self-(that is, industry) regulated, but subject to oversight by the SEC or Commodity Futures Trading Commission (CFTC).

8 FROM HERE, WHERE?

The text so far has described the development of LLR responsibilities in the United States up to the present day. In so doing, it has provided details concerning current LLR operations and has evaluated the adequacy of these arrangements. This chapter offers a synthesis of LLR evolution to date and then questions the direction of future changes.

The course for future LLR development is currently at a watershed. With a slight tilt in one direction, the Federal Reserve and other agencies could significantly increase the scope of their LLR activities. Impetus in another direction, however, could result in a complete reassessment of the federal financial safety net that would substantially reduce the range of LLR and other safety net activities. This chapter offers some first steps toward establishing the criteria that could help determine which path is to be recommended. That does not mean, of course, that any recommended direction is the one that the nation would necessarily follow.

PERIODS OF LLR EVOLUTION

The historic development of the LLR in the United States can be divided into five periods, which are summarized in Table 8-1. During the full span of years between the nation's creation and the present

189

Table 8-1. Periods of U.S. Central Bank Evolution.

Date	Phase	Description
1976–1912	I. Pre-Federal Reserve	Mostly private provision of bankers' bank services.
1913–32	II. Early Federal Reserve	Bankers' bank services confined to member banks.
1933–59	III. Post-Depression Federal Reserve	Fed and other public bodies provide liquidity and capital assistance to DIs, NDFIs and IPCs impacted by the Great Depression.
1960–73	IV. Crisis-Free Era	Federal Reserve attempts to revert to its limited, pre-Depression role.
1974–present	V. Crisis Escalation	In principle, discount window availability is extended to all DIs in 1980. In practice, there is ambiguity and pretense that the Fed's role is limited. Banks have priority.

day, LLR services have shifted from being a private initiative to becoming a public responsibility. In public hands, the role escalated during the Great Depression, then receded during the quiescent years of the 1950s and 1960s, but grew again during the financial crises of the 1970s and 1980s.

Period 1–Private Provision

The first period of LLR activity spans the interval between the nation's creation and the founding of the Federal Reserve in 1913. This period is dominated by the private provision of some central bank services (currency exchange, settlement, and liquidity assistance) and was described more fully in Chapter 2. During much of this period there was no central bank of the United States. Bankers' bank services were sometimes supplied by, for example, the First and Second Banks of the United States or the clearinghouses. At other times, however, no services were available.

Period 2–The Early Federal Reserve

The second period lasts from the start of the Federal Reserve system in 1913 until the legislative reaction to the Great Depression in the mid 1930s initiated a complete reconfiguration of the financial system. The establishment of the Federal Reserve provided, for the first time, a national system of twelve bankers' banks. Any commercial bank, regardless of its location within the United States, could join the Federal Reserve system if it met the conditions for membership. Every member enjoyed the benefits of membership, including access to the lender of last resort. The central bank's role was limited, however, to serving its members, rather than serving the economy or banks in general.

Other financial firms, including nonmember banks and thrifts that did not (or, for non-banks, could not) undertake the responsibilities of membership (for example, subscribe to Federal Reserve Bank stock or maintain reserves), did not enjoy the benefits either. That is, they had to make other arrangements, often through correspondent banks, to obtain bankers' bank services such as check clearing, currency exchange, net settlement, and liquidity assistance. The early central bank's role, therefore, was not economywide, financial sectorwide, or even all-bank inclusive.

Period 3–The Reaction to the Great Depression

The disasters of the 1930s changed the public's perspective on the proper role for the government. Thereafter, the Federal Reserve, as part of the establishment, shared in the responsibility for maintaining the health and stability of the economy and particularly the financial sector. Henceforth, in this third, activist, period of U.S. central bank history (which lasted until the late 1950s), the Fed had wide responsibilities. During "unusual and exigent circumstances," the Federal Reserve and other elements in the government would provide liquidity and capital assistance to people and troubled firms, financial and non-financial. The Reconstruction Finance Corporation, the Home Owners' Loan Corporation, other specially created rescue organizations, and Section 13b of the Federal Reserve Act all allowed loans to be made on favorable terms to financial institutions, firms, farmers, and homeowners to allow them to survive the rigors of the Great Depression.

Period 4–Retreat

By the late 1950s, it was acknowledged that the "unusual and exigent circumstances" of the Great Depression were over and that they were not about to recur in the aftermath of the Second World War. The Federal Reserve system, during this fourth, relatively crisis-free period until the mid 1970s, tried to revert to its earlier limited role as a bankers' bank to its members. Nevertheless, the Fed's bureaucratic instincts for self-aggrandizement and the public's expectations of government intervention led the Federal Reserve to undertake broader, economywide responsibilities. For example, monetary policy came to be conducted to achieve target levels for higher economic growth, lower inflation, and unemployment.

Period 5–Crisis Recurrence

When financial difficulties began to recur in the mid and late 1960s and deteriorated into crises in the mid 1970s and the 1980s, the Fed shouldered the responsibility of coping with the problems. Denying, during the 1970s, that it owed assistance to others beyond member banks, it conducted itself as though it did have that responsibility. While allowing only member banks to access the discount window, until passage of the Monetary Control Act, the Fed dealt with its broader obligations by other means. It relaxed monetary policy whenever signs of stress appeared in the financial sector, obtained Board approval for advances to nonmember banks and thrifts during credit crunches, and/or made arrangements for nonmember banks and other financial firms, businesses, and individuals to receive liquidity assistance indirectly through their member and/or correspondent banks.

The stock market crash of October 1987 dramatically illustrates the Fed's current *modus operandi.* The day after the crash, the new Board chairman announced the Fed's willingness to provide liquidity. Monetary policy's stance shifted from a tightening to defend the dollar and thwart inflation to an easing to avoid recession. Both short and long-term interest rates then fell sharply in response to vigorous open-market operations.

This fifth period is, therefore, one of some ambiguity for the public concerning the Fed's role and some unnecessary inconvenience for everyone in its execution. In order to preserve the fiction that it was confining aid to member banks before MCA and to DIs thereafter, the Fed has needlessly hampered itself by reducing the number of options it has had with regard to the ways in which it could provide aid.

This artificially constrained situation persists to this day. No one really doubts that the Fed would regard it as its duty (and an opportunity to extend its power) to contain a crisis originating among NDFIs or even IPCs. But the pretense that it might not act prevents the Fed from taking the positive actions it needs to take in order to make its crisis actions effective. It should have better access to data than it does. It should make pre-crisis arrangements for aid. Borrowing documents should be on the shelf and at least annually updated to speed assistance when needed. Facing the unknown is not a good reason for slowness in response, but it did hamper Fed operations in Ohio and possibly also in Maryland.[1]

FUTURE DIRECTIONS

A sixth period of central bank activity lies in the future. The Fed could move either in the direction of substantial escalation of, or reduction in, LLR responsibilities. Chapter 4 suggested that there are likely to be many opportunities for the Federal Reserve and other central banks to practice their crisis-handling skills at home and abroad in the future. Despite the five years of rising national (if not all-regional) prosperity that has followed recovery from the 1980 through 1982 recession, the numbers of insolvent, failed, and problem banks and thrifts have increased annually during the decade, at least through 1987.[2] The crash of 1987 reinforces this impression.

Many writers have pointed out that many current laws and regulations are obsolete and that the incentive system for banks and thrifts is wrong. Both of these inadequacies cause, or at least contribute importantly to, the contemporary problems. On the one hand, the strict regulations that were put in place after the Great Depression sought to insure financial sector stability by compartmentalizing markets and limiting competition. Each type of financial service provider had a little corner of the financial markets where, protected from the potential entry of others, it could exercise a circumscribed degree of monopoly power to insure its individual profitability and financial sector stability.

But times have changed. Economic thinking is now more consumer-oriented. A belief has resurfaced that financial services should be provided at the lowest possible cost and maximum convenience for the consumer. Technological change, particularly in the collection, storage, analysis, and transmission of data, have made the old financial market segmentation counterproductive. Yet the laws and regulations that govern financial sector activities have not changed with the times. Consequently, participants in the financial markets have become skilled in dodging regulation and undermining laws. In these circumstances, the possibilities for crisis abound.

Crises are the more likely because the incentives offered to depository institutions are currently misconstrued. A safety net that does not discriminate among safe and risky firms and endeavors, encourages anti-social amounts of risk taking. The permission for insolvent and low-capital firms to continue in operation under a policy of capital forbearance can also impose undue burdens on healthy members of an industry and its competitors. It can ultimately project unreasonable and unnecessary costs onto society if the weak drive out the strong in an unDarwinian "survival of the weakest" and if the taxpayer ends up footing at least part of an escalating bill for industry cleanup.[3]

Many of the best academic and policy-oriented minds have been warning in recent years that this situation should not be allowed to continue. Financial sector laws and regulations should be brought up to date, and the present destructive incentive system should be changed.

While reforming the system soon might avoid a deterioration of the present situation into even more serious crises, the establishment appears to be in no hurry to take the necessary steps. In these circumstances, the Federal Reserve needs must prepare itself for crisis duty.

WHEN SHOULD LLR ACTION BE TAKEN?

While it currently seems likely that the Fed and the rest of the safety net's role will escalate, there is still time to provide an impetus in the other direction, if that is appropriate. Many economists and policy-makers are complaining that the safety net, including the Federal Reserve, is currently too ready to suppress signs of financial stress when they appear by providing assistance to troubled DIs. Others believe that the Fed should be more active in crisis intervention. To take this disagreement beyond the political predispositions of the two sets of opponents, there needs to be a way to judge when safety net and/or LLR action is socially beneficial. Professor Paul Horvitz offers one relevant criterion:

> Delay is attractive to many. The Administration may seek to delay recognition of the losses until after 1988. Congressmen may favor pushing the problems past the next election. Some thrift managers may want to defer recognition until after their retirement. And some seem to believe that the inevitable can be postponed indefinitely.

> Forbearance is justified when it reduces the present value of expected future losses. It requires a hard-nosed economic calculation of FSLIC costs, and not a soft-hearted grant of mercy. (Horvitz 1987, 4)

This exhortation makes the present discounted value of costs to the insurer the criterion for action. Acts of Congress already require that the FDIC and FSLIC utilize a method of failure resolution that incurs the least expense to their insurance fund.[4] But insurer costs are usually measured as immediate outlays, so that the implications of present actions for future expenditures are not properly taken into account.

Moreover, such a calculation does not encompass all of the costs and benefits experienced by society's other agents, as a result of the actions taken. It excludes, to give just two examples, (1) the implicit costs imposed on society of moral hazard, that is, the risks to the insurer and the taxpayer (or the benefits to the receiver) of guarantees provided; and (2) the charges imposed on competitors, users of financial services, and the taxpayer by giving preferential treatment to failing firms.

Evidently, a full social accounting of the costs and benefits of LLR and other safety net actions would be a substantial undertaking. It is not one that is currently conducted when decisions are made whether and how to provide assistance to troubled firms. Moreover, such a comprehensive analysis will not be attempted here. Rather, this chapter aims to initiate the process of thinking about what a full accounting would involve.

The first step in the social accounting is to ask which parties stand to gain or lose from LLR action in the safety net. The answer to this question depends, at least partially, on the outcome of the action and the stage of bank deterioration at which it is taken.

Rationales for LLR Action

LLR action may enable a bank experiencing runs or other liquidity stresses to weather the storm and survive as a fully viable institution. The assistance given to BONY fits into this mold. No doubt, there are other examples of LLR assistance given to other firms that have fully recovered. The identity of these firms is not known because the Federal Reserve does not disclose the names of institutions it has aided. Senior Fed staff did, however, assure the authors that LLR assistance had been given in the past to banks that later went on to lead useful, profitable and fully capitalized lives.

Liquidity assistance may also be given to buy time for the insurer to implement a cost-saving method of resolution for failing firms. Conceptually, three options for final resolution are available: (1) The troubled institution may be liquidated and cease to exist. (2) It may continue to operate after being merged with or sold to another (preferably healthy) institution. Liquidation or merger can occur either before or after the institution becomes insolvent; insolvency as measured by any or all of the accounting net worth concepts discussed in Chapter 1. (3) The troubled firm may continue to operate as either independent or partially or totally nationalized after being given federal capital assistance.

On the other hand, resolution may be postponed. Three additional options for safety net action are available in this case: (4) The firm can continue to operate while under-capitalized. That is, it may be granted forbearance. (5) If liquidity assistance is not to be provided, runs may be stopped, at least temporarily, by declaring a bank holiday. In this situation, a bank is closed for a period during which it conducts *none* of its business. A bank holiday was declared in 1933 at the nadir of the Depression and again during the S & L crisis in Ohio in 1985. (6) A suspension of convertibility may be instituted. During the nineteenth century, suspensions prevented depositors from converting a bank's notes into specie and so reducing its reserve base. In those days suspensions were preferred to bank holidays as a method of curtailing deposit losses because they allowed the bank to remain open to conduct *some* parts of its business. McCullough (1987) discusses how a suspension could be conducted in the modern environment.

THE COSTS AND BENEFITS OF LLR ACTION

These six types of safety net action impose different costs and benefits on the numerous parties affected. Table 8–2 characterizes the costs of runs to depositors, creditors, borrowers, owners, managers, and other employees of the problem firm and also for other depository firms, the insurer, and the taxpayer. Two kinds of losses are represented in the table. An explicit financial loss is characterized by a "1" and an implicit or delayed cost or an inconvenience by a "2."

Use of the table for a social accounting of LLR action would be somewhat complex, as the relative efficacy of action would depend on the outcome of the run and the type of resolution adopted in the event of insolvency. For example, a suspension of convertibility might be held preferable to the provision of LLR assistance or to a bank holiday, but not to a federal infusion of capital or to a liquidation. LLR aid has sometimes been found to be unavoidable if a failed firm is kept in operation under a policy of forbearance. Moreover, the choice of action must involve a judgment of whose interests are to be protected and whose will be disregarded when there is a conflict of interests. And such conflicts usually occur. Moreover at present, as Kane (1987a) points out, often it is the bureaucracy's self-interest that is pursued, rather than its constituents'.

Runs—Their Outcomes

Many people get nervous when runs occur. They may be forced to pay time and attention to assessing the strength of their institution and its insurer. They may need to move their funds and their other business elsewhere if the solvency reassessment is adverse.

There are, conceptually, three possible outcomes to a run: (1) the bank may withstand the run, survive, and recover unaided; (2) it may recover after LLR and capital assistance and possibly other subsidies; or (3) it may deteriorate and fail, even after aid. No examples

Table 8-2. Who Loses From Bank Runs?

	Recovery		Deterioration
	Assisted	*Unassisted*	*Worst Case Scenario*
Depositors			
Insured	a	a	2
Uninsured	2	2	1/2
Creditors			
Secured	a	a	2
Unsecured	2	2	1/2
Borrowers			
Sound			2
Unsound			1/2
New	2	2	2
Other DIs			
Correspondent	2	2	1/2
Respondent	2	2	1/2
Competitors	?	?	?
Loan Participants			
Sound loans			2
Unsound loans			1/2
Suppliers			
Owners	1/2	1/2	1/2
Managers	2	2	1/2
Other Employees	2	2	1/2
Regulators			
Insurer	?		1/2
Federal Reserve [b]	c		c
FHL Bank [b]	c		c
Taxpayers	1/2		1/2

Notes: "1" represents an explicit cost.
          "2" represents an implicit cost or an inconvenience.
a. 1 and/or 2 if the insurer is known to be insolvent.
b. Fully collaterized.
c. An opportunity cost is experienced if aid is underpriced.

of the first outcome are known to the authors, although they expect that some unaided recoveries have occurred, particularly in the days before the central bank was founded. Pennsylvania First and Continental Illinois are possible examples of the second outcome. (It may be, however, that these banks may yet succumb.) These first two contingencies are listed in Table 8–2. Financial Corporation of America is possibly an example of the third outcome. It has been aided by capital infusions from the FSLIC and has received liquidity assistance from the FHLBank of San Francisco, yet as of September 1987 its survival was again threatened by the rise in interest rates occurring at that time. Other insolvent S & Ls, currently operating under forbearance, including those in the management consignment program, are also at risk from a rise in interest rates.[5] Scenarios where the institution deteriorates are catalogued in Table 8–3.

Recovery

Where an institution recovers, depositors, creditors, borrowers, managers, employees, and involved DIs should incur no losses, if the insurer is secure. Any losses from the runs should fall on the owners. Competing institutions may suffer from spillover and from having to compete with risk-taking, subsidized opponents that pay high interest rates and offer easy terms on loans, but they may also benefit if the troubled bank's customers send additional business their way.

The regulators will bear any costs, explicit and implicit, for any capital assistance or forbearance. The Fed will experience opportunity costs from any underpriced aid. Regulator costs ultimately fall on the taxpayer. Taxpayers lose when additional budget or off-budget outlays occur. They also lose when tax receipts fall, in the event that business deteriorates and incomes decline. Treasury receipts will also fall if the Fed's surplus income, annually transferred to the department, is reduced as a result of opportunity costs incurred in the provision of below-market aid.

Deterioration

If the bank experiencing the run deteriorates and fails, uninsured depositors, unsecured creditors, unsound borrowers whose loans may

Table 8-3. Who Loses From Run Resolutions?

	Liquidation		Merger		Forbearance		Bank	
	Before Insolvency[a]	After Insolvency[a]	Before Insolvency[a]	After Insolvency[a]	Recovery	Deterioration	Holiday	Suspension
Depositors								
Insured	2	2		b		b	2	2
Uninsured	2	1/2		1/2	2	1/2	2	2
Creditors								
Secured	2	2		b		b	2	2
Unsecured	2	1/2		1/2	2	1/2	2	2
Borrowers								
Sound								
Unsound	1/2	1/2	1/2	1/2		1/2		
New	2	2						
Other DIs								
Correspondent	2	1/2	?	1/2		1/2	2	2
Respondent	2	1/2	?	1/2		1/2	2	2
Competitors	?	?	?	?	1/2	1/2	1/2	2
Loan Participants								
Sound loans								
Unsound loans	1/2	1/2	1/2	1/2		1/2		

Suppliers				
Owners	1/2	1/2	2	1/2?
Managers	1/2	1/2	?	?
Other employees	1/2	1/2	?	?
Regulators				
Insurer	1/2	1/2	2	1/2
Federal Reserve[c]	d	d	d	d
FHL Bank[c]	d	d	d	d
Taxpayer	1/2	1/2	2	1/2

Notes: "1" represents an explicit cost.
"2" represents an implicit cost or an inconvenience.

a. Market value insolvency.
b. 1 and/or 2 if insurer is insolvent.
c. Fully collateralized.
d. 2 if aid is underpriced.

be called, DIs involved in troubled loan participations, respondent and correspondent banks, owners, managers, other employees, the insurance fund, and the taxpayer may all incur explicit and implicit losses. Competitors may gain or lose as losses arising from spillover or from competing with risky, subsidized firms are less than or exceed the profits from new business. The fully collaterallized Fed should suffer no explicit costs, but may experience opportunity losses.

This list constitutes a serious catalog of losers, which serves to emphasize why the authorities usually move decisively to aid a bank experiencing a run. If solvent when the run starts, unaided, the bank can quickly fail. If already insolvent, its negative net worth tends to deteriorate further at a fast pace as liquidity drains away and assets have to be sold at fire sale prices.

Losers from Liquidation

Exactly who loses from a run that does not lead to speedy recovery depends on the type of remedial action taken. The regulators may decide to liquidate a bank that is experiencing, or is exposed to, a run. Liquidation may occur before or after market-value insolvency.[6] Today, regulators employ several variations on the liquidation theme.[7] Here, however, a liquidation is taken to mean closing the firm, placing it in receivership, paying off or transferring deposits. In the process, uninsured depositors and unsecured creditors are put at risk, sound loans are bought by new lenders, unsound ones are called or placed for workout, owners forfeit all of their stake, managers and employees lose their jobs, and the bank ceases to exist.

Under this liquidation scenario, no depositor or creditor need incur losses if the bank is market-value solvent when liquidated. They will, however, suffer inconvenience as they need to establish business relationships with new suppliers. Other respondent DIs will also suffer—implicitly, from the loss of a solvent business partner and also explicitly, if that partner is insolvent, when they will lose at least part of their deposits maintained at their failed correspondent bank. Competitors may gain or lose as before. Owners, managers, and employees all forfeit their stake in the closed firm. The insurer may have to expend funds if the troubled bank's assets prove insufficient to cover the claims of insured depositors and secured creditors. The fully collateralized Fed incurs only opportunity losses, regardless of the borrower's insolvency. The taxpayer also stands to suffer, particularly if the firm is insolvent.

Losers from Mergers

If the troubled bank is merged with, or sold to, another firm rather than being closed, fewer people are affected. If merged while solvent, no depositor or creditor need suffer a loss of funds. Inconvenience should be caused to fewer people as new business relationships are automatically created by the merger. Only those that are unhappy with their new bank need to relocate. Sound loans and participations are likely to continue; unsound ones may be called. Some other DIs may gain if the new owner changes correspondent or respondent relationships, and some will lose. Owners may well have their stake reduced and managers and employees may, but not necessarily will, lose their jobs. During a merger, not all of these negative outcomes are certain to occur. The Fed will incur opportunity losses on any underpriced assistance given, and the insurer may be forced to expend reserves to encourage the merger or sale of an insolvent bank. In this case, the taxpayer will lose too.

Losers from Forbearance

Who loses under a policy of capital forbearance to an insolvent or undercapitalized bank depends on whether the institution recovers or deteriorates and does or does not receive capital and liquidity assistance.

If the firm recovers, few people experience explicit losses. Competitors may suffer, however, from having to meet the higher deposit rates offered by the weak bank, from losing business to a subsidized competitor, and from paying higher deposit insurance premiums to fund industry cleanup. The Fed, the taxpayer, and the insurer incur opportunity costs.

If the bank deteriorates, however, who losses depends on the form of resolution (liquidation or merger) chosen. But uninsured depositors and unsecured creditors are likely to lose, as are competitors, correspondent and respondent banks, unsound borrowers, participants in substandard loans, the insurer, the Fed (implicitly), and the taxpayer. The owners, managers and employees benefit in the short-run.

Thus, a policy of capital forbearance is a dangerous one for the regulators to pursue. It exposes many people to additional and avoidable losses.

Losers From Bank Holidays

The declaration of a bank holiday causes inconvenience and opportunity losses, at a minimum, to almost all customers of the bank. The costs fall unfairly on the owners, customers, depositors, and creditors of healthy banks that are typically put on holiday along with the troubled institutions. Bank holidays are usually declared over all institutions of a particular type in a certain area—the nation, during the Depression and the privately insured S & Ls in the State of Ohio in 1985—rather than being confined to institutions that are experiencing runs.

The only people not instantly, adversely affected are those owners, managers, and employees who at least temporarily are able to retain their stake in the sick firm. The regulators also gain at the outset by avoiding having to make difficult resolution decisions or take other more decisive actions. In the long run, the regulators and policymakers are likely to lose political capital during the public outrage that usually develops when the bank holiday inflicts losses and inconvenience on the voting public.

For these reasons, Federal Reserve Chairman Volcker strongly advised the state's governor against declaring a bank holiday in Maryland in 1985.

Losers From Suspensions

A suspension is aimed to conserve DI liquidity while allowing some of its customers to be served. Like bank holidays, suspensions have tended to be declared areawide. They also, therefore, impose unfairly on the customers, owners, and managers of sound banks subjected to the suspension.

Under a suspension, deposit withdrawals are limited, but other business continues. Thus, depositors are the ones most adversely affected by the withdrawal limitations. However, a suspended bank's business in general may be affected, as depositors seek to reduce their net position at the bank. Then there are likely to be fewer funds available for borrowers also. Respondent banks may find that the services provided by their suspended correspondent banks are curtailed or unavailable. Correspondent banks will receive fewer calls for services from suspended respondent banks. The loss of business may be compensated if servicing shifts to new financial firms rather than being reduced overall. Existing borrowers, managers, owners, and employees may initially, at least, all retain their existing positions at the troubled bank as a result of the suspension. These parties may well favor, therefore, a suspension over other alternatives that impose losses on them with a greater degree of immediacy and certainty.

During a suspension, the regulators may avoid giving immediate assistance, but help is more likely to be deferred rather than avoided altogether. This outcome was apparent after the suspensions (imposed as limitations placed on the amounts of funds that depositors could withdraw) in Ohio and Maryland in 1985.[8] The taxpayer will lose if the overall quantity of financial services and the value of taxable profits thereon are reduced.

A SOCIAL ACCOUNTING

It is apparent that many people have interests at stake that the regulators should consider when deciding whether to give LLR assistance and when determining the mode of resolution for failing banks and thrifts. It is also clear that some modes of resolution favor some groups relative to others.

Insured depositors, for example, are protected under all scenarios until policy mistakes make their insurer insolvent. Then they, healthy firms in the industry, and the taxpayer are in jeopardy, as in the 1985-7 S & L crisis. Owners, managers, employees, uninsured depositors, and unsecured creditors favor capital infusions, forbearance, bank holidays and suspensions—policies that delay the day of reckoning for them. The insurance agency, the insured depositors, others in the industry, and the taxpayer should favor prompt action, particularly merger, before insolvency.[9]

The present decision process for conferring aid pays scant attention to long-term issues and taxpayer interests. Immediate outlays to the insurance fund, as set out in the law and executed by the financial regulators, is the criterion currently used, but it is an inadequate one for determining aid.

All players' interests are not currently taken into consideration. Moreover, the catalog in Tables 8-2 and 8-3 makes it obvious that it would be exceedingly difficult to accurately conduct the indicated social accounting. Interests clearly conflict. Policymakers would need to determine not only the numbers of people affected by any decision, but also the extent of their individual losses plus a weighting scheme to apply to these loss estimates, in order to make the interpersonal comparisons that arise whenever interests conflict.

Evidently, policy is not currently formally constructed in this way. Nor is it likely to change in that direction. The calculations are too complex, too subject to judgment, prejudice, and lobbying pressures. In these circumstances, economists that favor government intervention admit that political decisions have to be made in these circumstances. Then they strive to make the political process fair and representative of all interests. Alternatively, fearing that the political process is rendered inequitable by the pressure of, for example, industry lobbyists, some centralists try to avoid the obstacles to valid social accounting by delegating the responsibility for making hard choices to the quasi-independent regulators, particularly the Fed.[10]

Free market economists, on the other hand, recommend turning to the private markets to make the necessary hard choices about the provision of liquidity assistance and insurance. Under a market-determined system of aid, only those that are prepared to pay the full, expected, actuarial cost of the assistance become eligible to receive it.

PUBLIC OR PRIVATE PROVISION
OF LLR ASSISTANCE?

This text was written in Washington, DC after the authors talked to the Federal Reserve, other financial regulators, and congressional staff. This setting has given the authors a bias toward regarding the

Federal Reserve as the inevitable LLR. Sprague, a former senior FDIC official, typified this view when he described in his book (1986) the private assistance given to First Pennsylvania National Bank and Continental Illinois as an aberration difficult to explain. Nevertheless, historically, in both the United States and the United Kingdom, private LLR assistance has been provided and continues to play a part in LLR assistance packages today.

If there were no public LLR, alternative private arrangements would undoubtedly develop. It is in the interest of banks and thrifts exposed to contagion to stem a crisis. Bank holidays, limited suspensions of convertibility, troubled bank borrowing from other private banks that sometimes operated in concert, and clearinghouse loan certificates have all played a LLR role in the past. These facilities existed before the Federal Reserve was created. Moreover, current academic research shows that the private facilities were more successful in coping with crises before World War I than was the Federal Reserve during the Great Depression (Schwartz 1987b).

Central Bank Advantages

Despite the relative success of private LLR facilities, the central bank has three advantages as LLR. First, it has almost unlimited power to provide liquidity support, because it can create money. Private agents have limited or no ability to print money and fewer resources, therefore, to lend to troubled institutions. Second, where the central bank regulates or supervises banks accessing the LLR or works in close cooperation with other financial supervisors, it should have access to needed information not available to others. Third, a trusted central bank, as was the Federal Reserve under a respected Chairman, benefits from the backing of the legislature, which gives it greater power than private alternatives are ever likely to possess. Fourth, it currently controls the domestic payment system.

Despite these advantages, the Federal Reserve may overstate its case. Anna Schwartz, in commenting on a draft of this book, writes:

> The Fed has a political interest in portraying itself as Horatius at the Bridge defending the financial system from imminent collapse. . . . The Fed now takes the position that any nonfinancial or financial failure can start a panic and it must always be ready to inject funds. (Schwartz 1987a)

Ultimately, however, the fear that contagious runs involve externalities that need to be addressed by a public institution acting in society's interest has been the most compelling justification for the centralized provision of LLR services. The Federal Reserve's actions on October 20, 1987 during the stock market crisis, is a case in point. No other body had the power to provide generalized liquidity through open-market operations to prevent the crisis from becoming contagious and immediately initiating a recession, or worse. The provision of liquidity through monetary policy is and must remain, therefore, a public responsibility.

Externalities: Deposit Insurance and Runs

The case for the public provision of LLR services, therefore, hinges on the severity of any externalities associated with bank runs. Professor George Kaufman (1987) points out that one of the serious externalities of bank runs before deposit insurance was their impact on the money supply. Small depositors' demands for cash increased, using up a greater proportion of high-powered money (currency plus bank reserves) and leaving fewer reserves available to back the (leveraged) supply of deposits. A substitution of currency for deposits if not compensated by the Fed, reduced the money supply. At the same time, fear of bank runs also raised bank demands for excess reserves. Both of these developments served to reduce the deposit multiplier and the money supply.[11]

After deposit insurance, small depositors who trusted their insurer had no need to run. Large, uninsured depositors became the focus of runs. Currency is not, however, a practical alternative for large depositors, who run to another bank or "to quality" by buying, for example, a Treasury security or a precious metal. But such purchases merely transfer the deposit to some other owner and probably to some other bank. Similarly, today most small depositors run to another bank or thrift, not to cash. Thus, modern runs need not seriously reduce the total quantity of reserves or the money supply. Deposit insurance has limited the impact of depositor runs on the money supply. As a consequence it has substantially reduced the seriousness of one of the major externalities of bank failures.

Nevertheless, it remains the responsibility of the central bank to avoid the sharp monetary contractions that set the stage for financial crises. Moreover, the central bank must limit crisis contagion among financial firms and prevent the transmission of problems to the real, producing and consuming, sectors of the economy. It uses monetary policy procedures to achieve these ends. It compensates via open-market operations for any second order, increased demands for currency and/or reserves that may occur during periods of stress and could reduce the money supply. This is the service that the Fed provided during the crash of October 1987 and which it failed to provide during the 1930s.

Externalities: Bank Runs and the Supply of Credit

The Federal Reserve has two principal avenues from which to provide LLR assistance.[12] It can use open-market operations to offer liquidity to the market in general, or discount window loans to target assistance to specific institutions. The provision of generalized liquidity is a central bank function.

So, a serious decline in the money stock is, with a well-funded system of deposit insurance, no longer such a serious threat to the economy as it was before 1934. Moreover, this threat can be dealt with by the central bank's monetary policy operations. The question, raised effectively by Goodfriend and King (1987), then arises whether there are any reasons remaining for making discount window loans to individual institutions. Having access to the discount window is akin to retaining an emergency line of credit with a private financial institution.

The answer to this question depends on whether there are any other externalities associated with financial crises that are sufficient to justify central bank, rather than the private provision, of line-of-credit services. Bernanke (1983) provides a positive answer to this question by showing that deterioration in credit availability during the Great Depression contributed substantially to the seriousness of the Depression.

External diseconomies from a reduction in the stock of financial knowledge and a loss of credit supplies suggest that discount window loans should be made available to financial institutions that supply credit. But credit-shortage diseconomies make no case that discount window access should be confined to banks or, more generally, to depository institutions. Justification of the current preference given to DIs requires a demonstration that bank loans are special and more valuable to society than other loans.

James (1987a, b) and others have produced research which shows that bank loans are special. In a world of asymmetric information, the granting of a bank loan is viewed by the markets as a vote of confidence in the viability of the borrower. The borrower's bank has special, inside information about the financial condition of the borrower—information based on deposit and credit relationships that possibly have taken a long time to establish. Disruptions of these special relationships that occur when banks fail and are closed reduce the stock of financial sector knowledge and involve a loss to society. The role of banks as lenders of "next to last" resort during financial panics has a special social value.

Today, the peculiar nature of DI deposits and banks' special access to private information remain the justifiable reasons for protecting DIs. They are, therefore, often merged rather than closed, given capital assistance to allow under-capitalized banks to continue in business, and granted forbearance. The public repeatedly demonstrates the value it places on deposits as a financial instrument. Policymakers recognize that the loss of the special lending relationships *could* decrease the supply of credit and cause a recession.

Banks Are Becoming Less Special

It remains to be pointed out that the special qualities of banks have decreased and many believe likely to continue to decline in the remaining years of the twentieth century.[13] The electronic age is making all forms of knowledge, including financial information, more readily available. Banks and thrifts are increasingly being placed in the position of using their special borrower evaluation techniques to originate but not retain loans. The loans they have originated are then standardized, guaranteed, securitized, and sold into the secondary markets to be held by both depository institutions and other investors. Securitized portfolios are more liquid than "plain vanilla" loans. Holding tradeable portfolios enables banks to sell assets in a credit crunch and be less in need of discount window assistance when facing deposit withdrawals.

Mortgages, automobile receivables, credit card and farm loans were all securitized in the second half of 1987. In addition, secondary markets were developing for non-securitized international debt and even for regular commercial loans. Commercial paper, and more recently junk bonds, are also playing a part in reducing the formerly, economically crucial role of the commercial and industrial (C & I) loan. The day may be approaching when the C & I loan has become as rare as an old-fashioned consumer loan since the advent of credit cards.

When this day comes, banks (and thrifts) will have ceased to be special and should then be less exposed to runs. They will have correspondingly less need for backup sources of liquidity. The private provision of discount window services would then become more feasible.

Policymakers should now be anticipating this day. In preparing for it, they should now be asking whether the difficulties, discussed earlier in this chapter, in determining social priorities for the appropriate granting of individualized liquidity assistance and in operating the safety net could then be safely left to market determination.

Nevertheless, even if the private markets assume the responsibility for providing emergency line-of-credit services to individual institutions, the Federal Reserve will retain its vital, not-to-be-delegated role as lender of last resort to the financial sector in general and to the economy.

NOTES

1. A paper, presented at one of the Federal Reserve systemwide research meetings, proposed that all institutions having regular legal access to the discount window should go through an annual "fire drill" to practice crisis management skills. The paper was poorly received.
2. The FDIC predicted during the third quarter of 1987 that commercial bank failures will be fewer in 1988. The outlook is less good for S & Ls, however, as their often unhedged positions deteriorate with rising interest rates.
3. It is well known that subsidies reduce costs. Garcia and Polakoff (1987) show that weak firms' costs of production are also lowered by forbearance.
4. The Federal Deposit Insurance Act mandates minimizing costs to the fund.
5. See GAO (1986a; 1987a; 1987d) for a discussion of the costs of delaying resolution, the relative lack of success of forbearance policies practiced

during the favorable (to the S & L-industry) years 1983-6 and the lack of signs of recovery among S & Ls in the MCP.

6.   Market-value net worth is the appropriate measure to use to determine resolution costs.

7.   Liquidations can be conducted in different variations by the bank and thrift regulators. A liquidation can involve closing the bank and paying off its depositors. Liquidation can also mean closing the thrift and transfering the (insured) deposits to another institution. See Garcia and Polakoff (1987) for a description of FHLBB liquidation methods, which currently include placing failed S & Ls in receivership or conservatorship. Under a conservatorship, the values of assets are preserved by the conservator and new management for all claimants on the institution including the owners.

8.   The suspensions in Ohio and Maryland have been described in Garcia (1987a).

9.   "Insured" depositors ran in Ohio and Maryland and nationwide in the S & L crisis of 1985-7. See the data on deposit losses in Appendix C.

10. A senior member of the staff of Senator Proxmire's Senate Banking Committee expressed this view.

11. The deposit multiplier is the ratio of the stock of money to the level of reserves.

12. For other subsidiary LLR actions undertaken by the Fed in the market crash of October 1988, see Garcia (1988).

13. It could be that the changes making banks less special are cyclical rather than structural, and that they might therefore be reversed.

APPENDICES
Failure Case Studies

OVERVIEW

This appendix contains three case studies. The S & L crises nation-wide in the period 1985-7 raise domestic U.S. issues. Those surround-ing the silver scare of 1980 and the Franklin failure gave rise to both domestic and international precedents. The silver crisis case study examines the Fed's role in a non-depository institution crisis.

DOMESTIC PRECEDENTS

The domestic U.S. cases show increases in the size and duration of liquidity support. Assistance was given to undeclared but in fact, in-solvent institutions. The range of accepted collateral was extended to include foreign assets at Franklin's London subsidiary. In the national S & L crises of 1985-7, FSLIC-guaranteed advances to insolvent S & Ls that ran out of acceptable collateral.

Changes have been made by the Federal Reserve in pricing—away from the heavy subsidies that Franklin received to smaller subsidies for Continental Illinois. The Federal Home Loan Banks, however, continue to charge the same rate for advances given to S & Ls regard-less of their condition and so subsidize emergency assistance.

In the final resolution of both of Franklin's and Continental's problems, the FDIC assumed the Fed's LLR loan to the banks. That is, to preserve FDIC reserves, the Fed lent the FDIC the funds to make capital injections into their banks, until the liquidation proceeds from sales of their assets became available to the FDIC to allow it to repay the Fed's loan.

The silver crisis case study shows a continued reluctance by the Fed to provide direct LLR assistance beyond depository institutions, and continues the tradition of private sector rescues.

INTERNATIONAL PRECEDENTS

The resolution of the Franklin crisis is regarded as an example of the way in which an international crisis should be handled. The Federal Reserve quickly notified foreign central banks that were likely to be involved of Franklin's problems. It provided liquidity support to the London branch when it lost deposits. It cooperated closely with the Bank of England over the question of collateral for the foreign branches' support and quickly notified other concerned central banks. Moreover, it took over the running of Franklin's foreign exchange operations to minimize FDIC losses and to limit the disruption to the foreign exchange markets.

These actions—particularly the Fed's liquidity support to the foreign branch—are viewed by U.S. researchers as models to be followed by others. But in one respect the model is not easily replicable. Franklin's foreign branch accepted Eurodollar deposits, so that the U.S. central bank had the central bank's competitive advantage of being the ultimate creator of dollar deposits. Offshore banking (for U.S. banks, the accepting of dollar deposits abroad) still predominates over foreign banking (for U.S. banks, accepting non-dollar deposits).

For other countries, however, a bank's foreign branches may be accepting deposits in the foreign currency. If the branch is located in the United States, it would have access to the Fed even though it would be expected to turn to its home central bank for liquidity support in an emergency. In this case, the parent's central bank does not have the Fed's advantage. It cannot create the foreign currency with which to replace lost commercial bank deposits. It can only use the stocks of the foreign currency it has on hand, can purchase, or borrow. But if the troubled bank were small this restriction should not present a problem. If the bank were large, international cooperation would be needed. If the parent bank had no central bank—because it was domiciled in a country that lacked one such as Hong Kong, for example—a problem could arise.

The case studies that follow are presented in chronological order of failure.

FRANKLIN NATIONAL BANK

On October 8, 1974, Franklin National Bank of New York became the largest bank failure in U.S. history at that time. Prior to its failure, Franklin National Bank (also referred to as Franklin) was the twentieth largest U.S. bank, with assets of $4.8 billion and deposits of $3.7 billion. Franklin's failure came almost one year after the first billion dollar bank failure, U.S. National Bank of San Diego, and coincided with the failures of Bankhaus Herstatt and the Israel-British Bank. The handling of Franklin's failure set precedents in the United States and abroad. The Federal Reserve, as lender of last resort, and the FDIC, as receiver of the failed bank's assets, both made departures from previous practice in resolving the crisis.

As background material, the causes of Franklin's failure will be briefly discussed. Events between April 1974 (just prior to Franklin's first emergency discount window loan) and October 8, 1974, when Franklin was declared insolvent and was purchased and assumed by European and American Bank and Trust (EAB) will be described. This analysis will highlight the evolution of the domestic lender-of-last-resort concept from its classic origins to 1974. It will also examine enhancement in the degree of cooperation among foreign central bankers during Franklin's failure.

THE CAUSES OF FRANKLIN'S FAILURE

Until 1964, Franklin[1] was solely a retail bank with seventy-three branches on Long Island, NY. In 1964, Franklin moved into New York City with the intention of capturing part of the growing international banking market. Between 1964 and 1969, Franklin doubled in size to $3 billion in assets (the twenty-sixth largest U.S. bank) and became a single bank holding company. In 1971, Franklin joined the New York Clearinghouse Association.

In its attempt to take advantage of the growing Eurodollar market, Franklin opened branches in Nassau, the Bahamas and London. In 1972, Michele Sindona purchased 21.6 percent of Franklin New York Corporation's stock. Although Sindona's background was questionable and concerns about the purchase were raised in the United States and England, no action was taken to block the acquisition.[2] Franklin's high growth strategy continued. For example, Sinkey describes the situation as follows:

> By 12/21/73 Franklin's banking business had evolved to its tripartite structure of retail, wholesale and international elements. The retail segment with its 73 branches on Long Island was the only strong and viable part of the business. The wholesale and international segments were weak links characterized by undue risk taking and inadequate spread management (Sinkey 1976, 163).

Franklin's original growth strategy entailed developing a large U.S. customer base and becoming a lead bank in Eurodollar loan syndications. Unfortunately, this strategy proved unsuccessful. In order to develop a domestic market, Franklin accepted the riskier loans which the other New York money center banks had rejected. Franklin experienced periods of losses due to its poor loan acceptance and pricing policies. Internationally, Franklin had entered the market too late to become a lead bank in Eurodollar loan syndications. It indiscriminately and massively entered into loan participations. In addition, Franklin was unable to expand its core deposit base much beyond its traditional Long Island branches and began to increasingly rely on volatile and costly short-term purchased funds.

As a result of its problems in the loan portfolio and the growing costly dependence on short-term purchased funds, Franklin began to rely on the foreign exchange operations of the bank as the prime profit-generating center for the bank. The foreign exchange operations were isolated from the rest of the bank. Its managers were instructed by Sindona to bypass reporting to the chief executive officer and the bank president and to report directly to the Board of Directors. Instead of generating profits for the bank, the foreign exchange operations were unprofitable and the losses were hidden by falsified documents and unrecorded transactions. Unstated foreign exchange losses mounted to over $33 million between January 1973 and March 1974.

In November 1973, Franklin's competitors became concerned about the bank's activities. Representatives from Morgan Guaranty met with officers of the Federal Reserve Bank of New York to express their concern over the volume of Franklin's foreign exchange activity. Morgan and other money center banks stopped trading foreign exchange with Franklin by the beginning of 1974. Franklin's foreign exchange losses triggered the crisis of confidence and a subsequent depositor run which led eventually to its failure.

THE CRISIS DEVELOPS

Staff at the Office of the Comptroller of the Currency (OCC) became aware of Franklin's mounting foreign exchange troubles in March 1973 and ordered a $1 billion retrenchment program (more than one-quarter of Franklin's assets). In October 1973, despite its problems, Franklin sought permission from the Federal Reserve to purchase Talcott National, a New York-based finance company. In studying the application, the Federal Reserve Bank of New York became so concerned that it set up a task force to monitor Franklin's performance on a weekly basis. It denied the application on May 1, 1974 because the takeover would complicate Franklin's retrenchment efforts. As the OCC feared, the denial triggered a crisis of confidence.

On May 10, 1974, Franklin New York Corporation announced that, due to unexpectedly large foreign exchange losses, it would not pay a quarterly dividend. As a result of the announcement, the bank began to lose uninsured deposits.[3] To replace them, Franklin borrowed at the Federal Reserve Bank of New York's discount window. By October 7, 1974, Franklin's discount window borrowing had reached over $1.7 billion. "This debt represented 47.3 percent of

[Franklin's] assets of $3.646 million—the largest fraction of a member bank's total resources ever provided by the Federal Reserve" (Brimmer 1984, 8).[4] The absolute loan size was also unprecedented at that time, although larger loans have been made since.

EVIDENCE OF CONTAGION

The failure of Franklin National coincided with that of Herstatt in Germany; Israel–British in Israel and London, where the secondary bank crisis was in progress; and the problems of real estate investment trusts (REITS) and an unprecedented (since the Depression) number of problem banks in the United States. There were, therefore, serious doubts about the stability of the banking system. Consequently, the spread between rates payable on large CDs compared to Treasury bills increased from an average, then, of 45 basis points before the crisis to 470 basis points in July 1974. This increase in spreads causes Carron (1982) to characterize the episode as a serious crisis. Lending rates rose—the prime rate increased from 8.75 percent before the Franklin demise to 12 percent after it. But panic did not develop, because the public perceived that the Federal Reserve was accepting its LLR role.

The Federal Reserve, as lender of last resort, is always concerned about the potential for a crisis to spread to other institutions. During the Franklin crisis, U.S. multinational banks experienced difficulties in raising funds in the international markets. Moreover, U.S. regional banks' access to the domestic money markets was curtailed (Brimmer 1984). For example, at year end 1973, twenty-five large regional banks obtained 23 percent of their liabilities in the form of domestic purchased funds. However, as the Franklin crisis unfolded, several regional banks suspended efforts to distribute their CDs in the national money markets.

In the international area, Franklin's immediate closure, following closely on Herstatt's failure, could have caused disruptions in the foreign exchange, loan syndication, and interbank markets.

RESOLVING THE CRISIS

The Federal Reserve, FDIC, OCC, the New York State Banking Commission, and the Department of Justice all played important roles in resolving the crisis. Reconciling the interests of different agencies took time.[5] It was obvious to the federal regulators as early as March 1973 that Franklin would not be able to work its way out of its problems and would have to be closed. The law required the FDIC to chose the least costly way of resolving a bank insolvency. The FDIC determined that a deposit payoff would not be the least costly solution because of Franklin's size and poor asset quality (which would translate into substantial loans for the FDIC).[6]

The FDIC, under Section 13(c) of the FDIC Act, had the authority to directly infuse capital into Franklin if the FDIC ruled that Franklin was "essential" to providing adequate banking services in its community. Essentiality, in 1974, was interpreted to mean that without the bank's presence in a community, the availability of banking services would be seriously impaired. Given the highly competitive nature of banking in New York, it could not be convincingly argued that Franklin was "essential" to its community so that it should be given a capital infusion to allow it to remain in operation. Therefore, the FDIC and OCC decided that the FDIC would attempt to find a purchaser for Franklin. The number of realistic purchase-and-assumption candidates was limited by Franklin's size and existing banking and anti-trust laws.

SETTING UP THE BIDDING PACKAGE

In disposing of a failed bank, the FDIC usually presents potential purchasers of the failed institution with a "clean bank." Hirshhorn describes this procedure as follows:

> Rather that auctioning the failed bank in its exact condition at the time of its closing (which would, by definition, have a negative value), the FDIC first restructures the bank's balance sheet. This usually involves removing assets from the bank's portfolio that are nonperforming, questionable or otherwise difficult to evaluate. At the auction a uniform package is offered to bidders. This package consists of deposits and other unsubordinated liabilities and a like amount of assets, less the amount of the premium bid. (Hirshhorn 1985, 3)

Once a bidding package is constructed, interested banks submit sealed bids for the institution. Normally, the bank submitting the highest bid purchases the institution.

As the crisis developed in mid 1974, the FDIC worked to make the bank a viable merger candidate. The FDIC shrank Franklin's size and assumed its discount window loan in order to attract bidders for the bank.

The assumption of a lender-of-last-resort loan was not unusual in the disposition of a failed bank. The method of repayment, however, was unprecedented. Normally, the FDIC immediately repays the discount window liability to the Federal Reserve out of its trust fund. The Franklin loan, however, if repaid immediately, would have exhausted one-third of the FDIC's trust. Instead, the FDIC signed a three-year note in order to repay the loan (Spero 1980).

Recognizing the capital drain that the purchase of Franklin would cause the successful institution, the FDIC also arranged to provide the assuming institution with a medium-term capital note of $10 million, with the opportunity to draw a further $5 million if required. The Federal Reserve agreed to allow the purchasing bank to borrow funds at the discount window if necessary immediately after the Franklin purchase (Willie 1974).

THE RESOLUTION

When the OCC declared Franklin insolvent on October 8, 1974, it was taken over by a foreign consortia, EAB. The EAB paid a premium of $125 million for the clean bank. It assumed $1.37 billion in deposits and $0.24 billion in other liabilities and acquired $1.49 billion of Franklin's assets. The FDIC assumed $314 million of Franklin's liabilities and acquired $2.17 million of Franklin's assets rejected by the EAB, in addition to assuming the $1.7 billion discount window liability.

The unprecedented takeover of a failed U.S. bank by a foreign concern was necessitated by a confluence of restrictions. The acquiring bank would need to be large to take Franklin over and run it successfully. Given the prohibition of interstate banking in force at that time, only New York City's largest banks would be both viable and eligible candidates. But these were ruled out by existing antitrust laws and fears of establishing a large conglomerate banking power in New York. A large foreign consortium was the only feasible option.

LLR PRECEDENTS

In order to provide the time needed to solve the crisis, lender-of-last-resort assistance to Franklin set many precedents. It clearly demonstrates that the Federal Reserve's modern interpretation of its domestic and international roles as lender-of-last-resort differs from the classic prescription. Franklin's assistance was large, both absolutely and relatively, of long duration, and was given to a *de facto*, but undeclared, insolvent bank.

Occurrence of a run suggests that depositors suspect that the institution is economically insolvent. In times of crisis, economic net worth is likely to be lower than book-value net worth. Regulatory practice has been not to close a bank until it is undisputably bankrupt. Yet classic principles maintain that the LLR should not lend to an insolvent institution. But the regulatory practice of delaying closure may require it.

The lender of last resort can traditionally sidestep the solvency issue by agreeing to lend as long as the problem bank has adequate collateral. In Franklin's case the Federal Reserve expanded the range of acceptable assets to include foreign assets. For the first time, the Federal Reserve provided discount window loans to cover withdrawals from Franklin's London branch. Previously, the Federal Reserve had used discount window assistance to compensate only for losses of domestic deposits. It should be noted that the Franklin London branch accepted primarily Eurodollar deposits. That is, it was engaged in "offshore banking." Therefore, the Fed had the traditional central banker's comparative advantage of being able to create the currency in which the run is occurring.

The Federal Reserve set another precedent by providing management and operational assistance to the bank by taking over the running of its problem foreign exchange portfolio.

Under the classic model of lender-of-last-resort operations, Franklin would have been declared insolvent and permitted to fail. Insured depositors would then have been paid off by the FDIC. Crisis contagion would have been forestalled by the Federal Reserve lending directly to solvent banks experiencing difficulties as a result of Franklin's demise, and by an easing of open-market operations to provide liquidity to the markets in general. In 1974, however, Franklin's failure was postponed to prevent closing the bank and paying off depositors and to allow a purchaser to be found.

Furthermore, under classic lender-of-last-resort operations, Franklin would have been penalized by charging a high rate for its lender-of-last-resort assistance. Instead, it received a subsidy.

THE SIZE AND DURATION OF FRANKLIN'S ASSISTANCE

Franklin's deposit outflows are shown in Table A-1. They were heaviest in the early months of the May to October crisis as uninsured depositors ran from the bank. Discount window assistance grew correspondingly and encompassed a period of five months. According to Brimmer (1984, 12), "by May 17, the loan was up to $960 million. It stood at $1.17 billion on May 31; by the end of July it was up to $1.39 billion. A peak of $1.7 billion was ultimately reached."

Table A-1. Interest Rate and Dollar Subsidy, Franklin National Bank, May-October 1984.

Month	Discount Deposit Outflow	Minimum Window Rate	Interest Replacement Rate	Rate Subsidy	Dollar Subsidy
May	$1,214MM	8.50%	11.18%	2.68%	$2.06MM
June	356	8.50	11.54	3.04	3.09
July	121	8.50	12.95	4.45	5.25
August	79	8.50	12.62	4.12	5.14
September	96	8.75[a]	11.74	2.99	3.61
October	28	10.00	12.59	2.59	0.86
Total	$1,894				$20.01
Average		8.75	11.53	2.78	

Sources: Derived from information provided by Spero (1980) and Board of Governors of the Federal Reserve (1978).

a. On September 26, 1974, Franklin's discount window loan rate was increased to 10 percent. The discount rate of 8.75 percent represents a weighted average.

COVERING INTERNATIONAL DEPOSIT
OUTFLOWS

In addition to the size and duration of the discount window loan, the international scope of the loan's coverage was unprecedented. Franklin was losing international as well as domestic deposits. Brimmer (1976) estimates that Franklin lost over 60 percent of its Eurodollar deposits. Spero (1980) notes that foreign deposits represented a large block (33 percent) of total deposit outflows. As much as one-quarter of the discount loan was applied to the coverage of foreign deposit outflows and to shore up the London branch which faced a severe mismatching of the maturities of its asset and liability portfolios.[7] Brimmer describes the deterioration at the London branch and the extent of Federal Reserve assistance channeled to it:

> On May 3, the branch had a net claim of $7 million on its New York parent. By July 31, it owed Franklin $352 million. This amount (equal to 25 percent of the Federal Reserve loan then outstanding) was used to offset part of the attrition in the branch's Eurodollar deposits. [Brimmer 1976, 12]

The ratio of the market value of the collateral (as determined by the Federal Reserve) to the discount window loan outstanding is usually well above 1. In the case of Franklin, the Federal Reserve Bank of New York held $2 billion worth of collateral on a $1.7 billion loan. In June 1974, the Federal Reserve set a precedent by accepting the assets of Franklin's London branch as collateral for the discount window loan (Brimmer 1976). The London assets were largely comprised of loan participations that originated with other international banks. They were considered to be of a higher quality than Franklin's domestic loans because the originating banks supposedly used more prudent loan acceptance and pricing practices than Franklin. Therefore, these assets were particularly attractive to the Federal Reserve as collateral.

FRANKLIN'S INTEREST RATE SUBSIDY

As discussed in Chapter 3, the Federal Reserve in the past has frequently provided discount window support at subsidized rates.

Table A-2. Minimum Replacement Cost of Funds for Franklin National Bank.

Month	Instrument[a]	Outflow[b]	Weight	Rate[c]	Weighted Rate
		($ M)	(%)	(%)	(%)
May	Foreign Deposits	317	26.11	11.17	2.92
	Domestic CDs	246	20.26	11.20	2.27
	Federal Funds	595	49.01	11.31	5.54
	Repurchase Agreements	56	4.61	9.74	0.45
	Total	$1,214			11.18

Source: Data derived by the authors from information provided by Spero (1980).
  a. The estimate assumes similar instrument replacement. That is Franklin would have replaced an outflow of CDs by borrowing in the CD market, at the current market rate.
  b. All deposit outflows are assumed covered by discount window loans.
  c. The rate applied to foreign deposits is the three month Eurodollar rate.

Franklin, for example, was able to borrow from the Federal Reserve Bank of New York at the basic discount rate from May 10, 1974 until September 25, 1974. It was only during the last two weeks of discount window borrowing that the Federal Reserve assessed Franklin a premium over the discount rate of 125 basis points, raising the loan rate to 10 percent. However, after its loan rate was raised, Franklin continued to receive an interest rate subsidy from the Federal Reserve. If Franklin had not received Federal Reserve assistance it would have had to borrow in the markets. Private lenders would have charged higher rates (even on a collateralized loan) than did the Federal Reserve. For example, even the federal funds rate, which provides a lower bound estimate of the market rate to relatively risk-free borrowers, averaged 10.6 percent over the same time period.

The interest rate subsidy was estimated by subtracting the discount window loan rate from a derived minimum replacement cost of funds for Franklin. The minimum replacement rate, estimated in Table A-2, is a weighted, average cost of capital for the instruments being replaced. This rate is a lower bound of possible replacement cost of funds since it does not include any risk premium that Franklin, as a problem bank, would have had to pay for funds raised in the markets.[8]

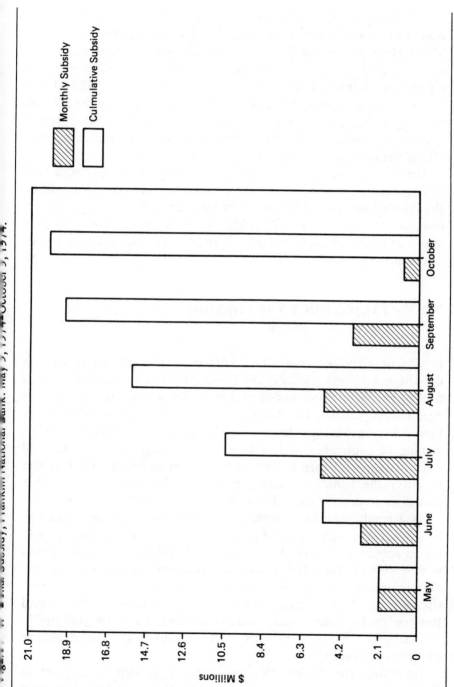

Source: Derived from information supplied by Spero (1980) and Board of Governors (1978).

The average minimum replacement cost of funds was 11.53 percent over the five-month period of Franklin's discount window borrowing. The average rate Franklin was paying on its discount window loan was 8.75 percent over the same period. Therefore, Franklin received, on average, an interest rate subsidy of 278 basis points or $20.01 million in interest savings. Table A-2 and Figure A-1 show the accrued monthly subsidy that Franklin received. It followed the same growth pattern as Franklin's discount window drawings, accumulating rapidly in the first two months and tapering off thereafter.

The monthly subsidy received fell in the last two months of borrowing for two reasons. First, the Federal Reserve raised the rate on Franklin's loan from 8.5 percent in May through August to 10 percent in October. Second, Franklin decreased the amount of new drawings at the discount window, possibly in response to the higher discount rate.

TAKING OVER THE FOREIGN EXCHANGE BOOK

In order to further assist the FDIC in establishing an acceptable deposit assumption package, the Federal Reserve assumed Franklin's foreign exchange book on September 26, 1974. Even though the foreign exchange book had been "cleaned up," potential bidders for Franklin were reluctant to acquire that part of the bank. By the beginning of September, it had become increasingly difficult to find other foreign exchange traders to enter into contracts with Franklin to cover the bank's remaining exposure. There was also fear that parties to contracts favorable to Franklin might not honor them.

As a result, Franklin's foreign exchange operations continued to be subject to a high degree of risk, and potential bidders were unwilling to acquire the failing bank unless its foreign exchange operations were excluded. The FDIC could not take over Franklin's foreign exchange operations because it lacked the necessary funds and expertise and would have encountered conflicts of interest.[9] The Federal Reserve, on the other hand, considered it imperative for stability in the foreign exchange markets that all of Franklin's foreign exchange contracts be honored.

Therefore, the Federal Reserve decided to step in and act as Franklin's agent when Franklin was unable to purchase sufficient foreign currencies to fulfill its contracts. In fact, the Federal Reserve successfully managed the execution of Franklin's existing foreign exchange contracts without incurring losses.[10] As, Spero (1980) notes, this was the first time that the Federal Reserve had managed part of a failing bank's operations.

If Franklin's foreign exchange contracts had been renegotiated, Franklin's foreign exchange losses could have been substantially higher and there would have been severe disturbances in the foreign exchanges markets. The Federal Reserve received the cooperation of foreign central banks in persuading their commercial banks to honor their outstanding contracts with Franklin.

INTERNATIONAL COOPERATION

The Federal Reserve foresaw the need to obtain the Bank of England's cooperation in utilizing the assets of Franklin's London branch as collateral early in the crisis (Spero 1980). Consequently, it notified the Bank of England of Franklin's problems on May 13, 1974 (just three days after Franklin began to borrow from the Federal reserve). Governor Richardson offered the Bank of England's complete cooperation.

Secrecy was held to be vital in order to avoid further shocks in the international financial markets. To allow the Federal Reserve to acquire the London assets for collateral without the public becoming aware of, and concerned about, the implications of the central banks' actions, the Bank of England set up a series of short-term renewable trusts in which the Federal Reserve received unperfected title to the assets of the branch.[11] The Federal Reserve began accepting the London assets as collateral on June 14, 1974. Before the crisis ended, over one-quarter of Franklin's collateral at the Federal Reserve came from the London branch (Spero 1980).

DISPOSITION OF THE LONDON BRANCH

The status of the London branch was also important in the final resolution of the Franklin crisis. Since the London branch had the highest quality assets; the ability to assume the London branch was critical to potential bidders. Since the Federal Reserve had not perfected its claim to the assets being used as collateral, the Bank of England could have blocked the transfer of the assets, ordered a separate liquidation of the branch, or seized the branch's assets for distribution to the British creditors. Instead, it reached an agreement with the Federal Reserve on September 20, 1974. As a consequence, after receiving advance notice of Franklin's failure, the Bank of England arranged an immediate transfer of the title to Franklin's London branch to the purchaser provided that all of Franklin's British tax liabilities were met. The Bank of England and the British banking community, for example, could limit their potential losses by cooperating with the Federal Reserve in facilitating Franklin's acquisition. By aiding in the disposition of the London branch, the Bank of England avoided liquidating the branch itself. Instead, the branch was merged with a viable bank, EAB, at very little monetary cost to the Bank of England or the British creditors.

HANDLING OF THE FRANKLIN CRISIS:
A MODEL OF DOMESTIC AND
INTERNATIONAL COOPERATION

The analysis of the failure of Franklin helps to demonstrate the changes that have taken place in the role of the lender of last resort in the case of a large, U.S.-based, international bank. Precedents in lender-of-last-resort actions were established concerning (1) the size of the discount window loan, (2) the duration of the assistance, (3) the management of Franklin's foreign exchange book by the Federal Reserve, (4) the coverage of foreign deposit outflows, and (5) the use of foreign assets as collateral.

Moreover, there was a shift in the lender-of-last-resort emphasis from providing short-term liquidity assistance to providing liquidity assistance in order to keep the bank open until a formal resolution could be arranged by the other regulatory agencies. Despite the changes in operations, the objective of the Federal Reserve, as lender of last resort, remained to protect the financial system. Henceforth, however, this objective would extend beyond the domestic financial markets to encompass the international financial system as well.

The case of Franklin also demonstrated the ability of foreign central bankers to work together quickly and decisively to forestall a potential international crisis, when this was in their collective self-interest. However, it appears that differences remain in interpretation of the degree of comprehensiveness of lender-of-last-resort action. Those differences concern aiding unsound institutions. Some countries will preserve unsound banks. Others will not. "Some countries were reluctant to agree to anything like blanket support of all banks, good and not so good." (Reid 1982, 117)

NOTES

1. Material in this section is drawn from Spero (1980), Sinkey (1976), Brimmer (1984), and Wille (1974).
2. Sindona was suspected to have been involved in fraudulent dealings over his European holdings.
3. Brimmer (1984) notes that Eurodollar deposits declined by 57.5 percent, domestic CDs by 76 percent, federal funds by 57 percent, and repurchase agreements by 54 percent from May to July 1974. If Franklin could raise purchased funds at all, it was only at a large premium (Sinkey 1976).
4. This statement remained true as of July 1987. Assistance to Franklin covered a greater proportion of assets than that to Continental Illinois (see below). Continental's aid was larger, however, in dollar value.
5. The Department of Justice was concerned that the ultimate resolution of the Franklin crisis would not violate existing anti-trust and banking laws. The New York State Banking Commission's approval was required in the event of a state-chartered institution's purchase of Franklin.
6. Wille (1974) estimated that if the bank were closed and the insured depositors (deposits up to $20,000 were given federal deposit insurance coverage at that time) were reimbursed, the total cost to the FDIC would have approximated $750 million.
7. Franklin had funded fixed-rate medium-term loans with short-term CDs. As interest rates were rising at this time, Franklin could not sell its assets to reduce its funding needs without realizing losses that would have made it book-value insolvent as well as market-value insolvent.
8. Sinkey (1976) asserts it is reasonable to assume that Franklin would have been required to pay a 100–250 basis point premium over market rates during these five months of discount window borrowing.
9. A complete description of the Fed's handling of the exchange book is given in Wille (1974). For example, Wille pointed out the potential conflicts which would arise if the FDIC took over the foreign exchange operations: "if these unexecuted contracts ended up in FDIC's hands as possible receiver, FDIC might have a fiduciary duty to (Franklin's) creditors and owners not to honor those which were unfavorable to the Bank, and

to demand performance of those which favored the bank." (Wille 1974, 27)

10.   Kane (1987a) points out that the Fed incurred costs in assuring Franklin's exposure. While it did not occur any losses, it incurred opportunity costs of staff time and lost interest on part of its portfolio. (The Federal Reserve operating surplus is remitted to the Treasury.)

11.   Title to the assets could not be perfected without notifying the recipients of the loans. Therefore, the Federal Reserve's title to the London assets was never perfected, in order for secrecy to be maintained.

THE 1980 SILVER CRISIS[1]

During the last week of March 1980, it appeared that default by Nelson and William Hunt on their silver obligations might engender a serious disruption of the U.S. financial system. Futures contracts were the primary vehicle through which the Hunts amassed both their huge physical holdings of and control over silver; for this reason, several of the futures industry's largest broker/dealers were placed in immediate jeopardy when the Hunts proved unable to honor their commitments in a timely fashion. The failure of even one of these broker/dealers threatened a financial chain reaction that could have compromised the viability of commodity clearinghouses and their members, other broker/dealers and their customers, banks, and public companies and their stockholders.

Although financial catastrophe was averted, the silver crisis underscored the potential fragility and interdependence of the financial system. Final resolution of this episode was made possible, in large measure, by a lender-of-last-resort function assumed by a number of private commercial banks led by Morgan Guaranty and First Dallas (attempting to avoid silver-related lending losses and acting with the tacit acceptance of Federal Reserve Board Chairman Paul Volcker, despite pre-existing Fed policy discouraging credit extension for speculative undertakings).

Before examining the final bailout and rationale underlying Fed tolerance of this action, the sections that follow will provide an overview of conditions leading to this *denouement*. To this end, a discussion is first provided outlining basic fundamentals underlying components of silver supply and demand.

ECONOMIC FUNDAMENTALS UNDERLYING SILVER SUPPLY/DEMAND

Silver Supply

Globally, silver bullion is available from the following three sources:

1. Newly mined supplies;
2. Recycled product; and
3. Existing stocks held by individuals, firms, and governments.

By country, the major silver miners are Mexico, Canada, the Soviet Union, Peru, the United States, and Australia. As a point of information, a significant portion of the world's silver production derives as a byproduct from base-metal (copper, lead, and zinc) mining operations; the quantity of newly mined silver produced, therefore, is dependent to a significant degree upon supplied amounts of these non-precious base metals. Production data are shown in Table B–1.

Silver extractions from existing industrial scrap, silverware, jewelry, and coins represent a second source of the metal. The silver contained in these existing items represents a major part of the metal mined throughout history; hence, the supply of silver bullion potentially available through this avenue exceeds by a substantial margin the world's annual mined production. Finally, institutional, individual, industrial, and governmental holdings (stocks) comprise a third silver source.

India plays a potentially significant role in global silver supply, inasmuch as that country is believed to possess the world's largest "above ground" silver stocks. Estimates place these holdings between three and five billion ounces. In February 1979, however, the Indian government embargoed silver exports.

The vastness of (post–February 1979) restricted Indian silver resources is placed in perspective when consideration is given to the size of similar such stocks believed to be in existence throughout the rest of the world. For 1979, world government, silver bullion stocks were estimated at 321.8 million ounces. Silver stocks approved for delivery by commodity exchanges and held by U.S. industrial concerns totaled 145.2 and 23.7 million ounces respectively. As of 1979, 746.5 million ounces of silver in coin form were estimated to be available worldwide.

As indicated by the estimates set forth in Table B-1, mining production of silver did not demonstrate significant sensitivity to the volatile economic climate characterizing the decade between 1969–79. On the other hand, it does appear that supplies of silver from existing secondary sources (previously identified as industrial scrap, silverware, jewelry, and coins) were responsive to states of flux in the economic climate. As an example, there was a marked correlation between silver prices, which rose sharply beginning in 1973 followed by a steep decline in mid 1974, and the supply of silver provided by recycling and stock drawdown during this period. It should be noted that while the recycled silver supply is price-sensitive in the "short run," such supplies are nonetheless constrained in the "very short run" by refining and physical collection capacities.

Silver Demand

Silver is used in the manufacture of consumption and capital goods. Examples of the former include photographic film, silverware, and jewelry. Electronic, electrical, and catalytic products are representative of a number of capital goods requiring silver as a production input.

Estimates of 1979 world industrial/commercial demand for silver are placed in the area of 432.8 million ounces. For that particular year, demand exceeded production by approximately 81 million ounces. In fact, throughout the period 1969–79, demand surpassed mined and recycled production of silver by amounts ranging from 81 to 182 million ounces annually. Such shortfalls were met by drawdowns of available world silver stocks.

As demonstrated by Table B-1, industrial/commercial demand for silver remained fairly stable throughout 1969–79—a period characterized by oil price shocks, rising inflation, and unprecedented volatility in nominal U.S. interest rates.

While industrial and commercial uses of silver are readily estimated and manifest relatively stable levels throughout the decade under examination, the same characteristics did not hold with respect to

Table B-1. Estimated World Silver Production, Consumption, and Stock Liquidation: 1969–79 (*in million troy ounces*).

Date	Primary Silver Production	Production From Salvage and Other Miscellaneous Sources	Total Silver Production
1979	271.0	80.5	351.5
1978	265.0	86.5	351.5
1977	267.4	80.2	347.6
1976	247.0	76.1	323.1
1975	241.5	73.2	314.7
1974	237.4	65.7	303.1
1973	245.8	64.8	310.6
1972	239.7	56.3	296.0
1971	238.4	41.7	280.1
1970	251.9	35.2	287.1
1969	241.3	14.6	255.9

Date	Silver Consumption	Drawdown of World Silver Stocks	Indian Exports
1979	432.8	81.3	33.5
1978	433.5	82.0	45.5
1977	436.7	89.1	40.6
1976	451.8	128.7	70.0
1975	415.6	100.9	66.0
1974	436.9	133.8	42.0
1973	492.5	181.9	26.0
1972	424.3	128.3	6.0
1971	378.6	98.5	16.0
1970	365.8	88.7	16.0
1969	390.6	134.7	25.0

investor demand. As is the case with a number of other capital assets (real estate and gold, for example), silver is perceived to be a store of value during inflationary periods. This belief becomes pronounced when real rates of return on financial instruments fall to negative levels. Unlike industrial/commercial demand, however, there is no accurate indicator of investor (capital-asset) demand for silver.

Table B-1. continued

Date	Drawdown of World Stocks Held Outside India
1979	47.8
1978	36.5
1977	48.5
1976	58.7
1975	34.9
1974	91.8
1973	155.9
1972	122.3
1971	82.5
1970	72.7
1969	109.7

Source: Commodity Futures Trading Commission (1981, 75).

Previous discussion documents a state (from 1969–79) of relative price insensitivity (inelasticity) as concerns both newly mined silver production and industrial/commercial silver utilization. On the other hand, it is clear the short-run supply function of recycled and existing silver stocks was relatively elastic with respect to price. Given both the modern day state of capital mobility and avenues (such as futures markets) for its expression, it is also asserted that there was the potential for (very short-run) price-elastic investor demand with respect to silver. These conditions provide a foundation for exploring the fundamental behavior underlying silver price movements during the "crisis" period of interest.

A further understanding of the dynamics underlying investor demand for silver, however, requires consideration of the state of the U.S. economy over the time horizon matching the period during which silver demonstrated extreme price volatility. The following section summarizes the U.S. economic scenario at that time.

GENERAL ECONOMIC CONDITIONS

Over the four quarters encompassed by the period 1979–80, the U.S. economy experienced OPEC-induced (Organization of Petroleum

Exporting Countries) supply shocks, accelerating inflation, rapidly rising rates of interest, and continued deterioration in the relative value of its currency. During this time, real GNP (Gross National Product) exhibited sustained growth.

At mid January of the first quarter of 1980, the United States entered into a "stagflationary" cycle, with future prospects dimmed by the OPEC cartel's announcement of yet another hike in crude oil prices.

Following is a chronicle of trends distinguishing the January 1979– March 1980 period.

January–June 1979

Strong, real economic growth is manifest and accompanied by rising prices. Capacity utilization and the industrial/production index are at high levels. Business borrowing is brisk, with consumer installment credit fueling retail sales advances. Augmented by oil price increases, inflation advances towards record heights. Business productivity and profitability demonstrate marginal erosion.

July–September 1979

Real GNP growth continues, though mitigating factors continue to be present. Capacity utilization, new orders for materials and consumer goods, and housing starts begin to decline. The Consumer Price Index (CPI) rises to 14 percent in third quarter 1979, up from the 12.7 percent level exhibited over the first half of the year. Consistent with advancing energy costs, expectations are for still higher levels of inflation. The dollar approaches record lows. Third quarter money growth targets are exceeded by the Fed for the first time during the year. Real rates of interest are negative.

October 1979–Mid January 1980

With unemployment up slightly, the economy continues to expand. The CPI is 18.6 percent during January 1980. On October 6, 1979, the Fed announces a shift in operating target emphasis—from Fed funds rate to bank reserve management. Interest rates climb.

World financial uncertainty is heightened by political unrest. In early November, American diplomatic personnel are taken hostage in Iran. Two weeks later, extremists sieze Saudi Arabia's Grand Mosque. In December, the Soviet Union invades Afghanistan.

Mid January 1980–March 1980

The U.S. economy enters into recession, while inflation continues to accelerate. OPEC announces a 33 percent increase in its crude oil prices. Motivated by the spiraling inflationary cycle, the Fed re-emphasizes its existing credit controls and restrictions on extensions of credit for speculative undertakings. The dollar begins to rise in value as real interest rates turn positive.

In summary, January–December 1979 represented a period during which existing conditions (among them being states of accelerating inflation and negative financial rates of real return) were not at conflict with speculative investor demand for capital assets. Whether the Hunt group's activities were deliberately directed toward price manipulation of the silver market is a matter upon which this study will not dwell. Suffice it to say there were a number of economic bases for their speculative behavior. The extent to which this speculation was exercised, resulting in price influence and market endangerment, is the issue towards which attention is now turned.

INVESTOR DEMAND FOR SILVER

Hunt and ContiCommodity Group Holdings

Nelson Bunker and William Herbert Hunt believed (and acted upon this belief) as early as 1973 that silver represented an "excellent investment" (U.S. Securities and Exchange Commission 1982, 32). Given the commodity shocks occurring at that time and the accompanying interest rate volatility, it is reasonable to deduce why the Hunts looked to capital assets as a speculative store of wealth.

In fact, two groups held large, long (net purchase) silver positions in both the cash and futures markets during the crisis period under review. The group with the largest overall positions in these markets was composed of members of the Hunt family and International Metals Investment Company (IMIC)—an institution controlled by various Hunt family members and a number of Arab investors. The second group consisted primarily of several foreign traders/entities (Naji Robert Nahas, Banque Populaire Suisse, Norton Waltuch, Gilian Financial, and ContiCapital Management, Inc.) conducting most of their trading activity through ContiCommodity Services, Inc. Information available does not indicate whether this second group acted in concert with the Hunts.

The Hunt group became fairly active in silver during the mid 1970s. At the end of 1975, as shown in Table B–2, the Hunts held net-long positions of 15,876 silver futures contracts. Immediately prior to this time, the Hunts also owned 44.4 million ounces of physical silver stored in vaults registered with the CBOT (Chicago Board of Trade). These futures and physical holdings indicate the group had combined actual/potential control over more than 123 million ounces of silver. This last figure is placed in perspective when considered in relation to worldwide silver consumption for 1979—a total of 432.8 million ounces. Following 1975, the Hunt group's holdings of silver futures contracts declined sharply to a low point of 3,141 contracts (net-long) in June of 1976 and then increased to 5,393 contracts (net-long) by the end of 1978. Most of the trading activity in these accounts during this period consisted of either the closeout of futures positions or rollover of expiring futures positions (nearing maturity) to more distant delivery dates.

By September 30, 1979, the Hunts had increased their net-long futures position to 24,722 contracts (approximately 120 million ounces). From October 1979 to January 1980, they also began taking delivery, at futures contract maturity, of large quantities of physical silver. Consequently, there was a decrease in their net futures positions (but not in their overall silver exposure). Contributing to the futures reduction were three large EFP (Exchange for Physical) transactions conducted in mid January 1980 with Englehard Minerals & Chemicals Corporation and Sharps Pixley, Inc.

During February 1980, members of the Hunt group made further reductions in their futures positions, primarily by accepting delivery on CBOT (futures) contracts. Also, several positions in nearby delivery months on the COMEX (Commodity Exchange, Inc.) were rolled forward into contract months with mid 1980 maturities. During the first three weeks of March, the futures position of the Hunt group declined only slightly.

Table B-2. Estimated Silver Contract Ownership by Hunt-Related Accounts (*5,000 troy ounces per contract*).

Date	Net Futures Positions			Stocks Owned on		
	COMEX	CBT	Totals	COMEX	CBT	Other[a]
9/30/75	6,917	4,560	11,077	N/A	N/A	N/A
12/31/75	6,865	9,011	15,876	N/A	8,883	N/A
3/31/76	6,092	5,324	11,416	N/A	N/A	N/A
6/30/76	4,061	-920	3,141	N/A	N/A	N/A
9/30/76	3,890	578	4,468	N/A	N/A	N/A
12/31/76	3,910	571	4,481	N/A	N/A	N/A
3/31/77	3,288	259	3,547	N/A	N/A	N/A
6/30/77	4,540	816	5,356	N/A	N/A	N/A
9/30/77	5,277	1,518	6,795	N/A	N/A	N/A
12/31/77	5,826	2,016	7,344	N/A	N/A	N/A
3/31/78	6,459	2,224	8,683	N/A	N/A	N/A
6/30/78	4,200	2,451	6,651	N/A	N/A	N/A
9/30/78	2,481	3,047	5,528	N/A	N/A	N/A
12/31/78	4,076	1,317	5,393	N/A	N/A	N/A
3/31/79	6,655	1,699	8,354	1,986	7,369	N/A
5/31/79	8,712	4,765	13,477	1,986	7,369	N/A
6/30/79	9,442	3,846	13,288	1,986	8,069	N/A
7/31/79	10,407	4,336	14,743	1,986	8,069	N/A
8/31/79	14,941	8,700	23,641	1,986	8,069	N/A
9/30/79	15,392	9,330	24,722	3,170	8,069	N/A
10/31/79	11,395	7,444	18,839	3,170	9,444	5,583
11/30/79	12,379	5,693	18,072	3,170	9,444	5,583
12/31/79	13,806	5,921	19,727	3,170	10,644	5,583
1/31/80	7,432	1,344	8,776	3,888	10,644	12,447
2/29/80	6,993	789	7,782	3,888	12,761	12,447
4/02/80	1,056	388	1,444	4,938	12,761	12,447

Source: Commodity Futures Trading Commission (1981, 103).

a. Since silver stocks owned in locations other than exchange vaults is not known with certainty, the data presented should be interpreted as minimum estimates of stocks held by the Hunt group in other locations.

Table B-3. Estimated Silver Contract Ownership by Conti-Related Accounts (*5,000 troy ounces per contract*).

| Date | Net Futures Positions | | Stocks Owned on | | |
	COMEX	CBT	COMEX	CBT	Other[a]
8/31/79	8,560	0	6	0	N/A
9/30/79	9,023	0	1,471	0	N/A
10/31/79	9,315	0	2,263	0	N/A
11/30/79	7,741	0	2,308	0	400
12/31/79	5,132	0	5,771	0	400
1/31/80	4,002	0	6,365	0	750
2/28/80	4,010	0	6,365	0	750
4/02/80	2,667	0	7,565	0	750

Source: Commodity Futures Trading Commission (1981, 106).

a. Since foreign traders are not required routinely to report futures positions to the CFTC and because accurate estimates of physical silver owned in foreign depositories are not available to the CFTC, the data presented in this table represent minimum estimates of these futures and cash market positions in silver during the indicated period.

As indicated in Table B-3 Conti Group investors established relatively large positions (in relation to world silver consumption during the year) on the COMEX at or about August 1979.

The futures positions of the Conti Group increased only marginally from August to October 1979. Thereafter, the combined positions of this group declined steadily, reaching 2,667 contracts at the beginning of April 1980. Silver stocks owned by the Conti Group increased rapidly in the period covered by Table B-3, reaching a peak of 7,565 contracts (37.8 million ounces) in the first week of April 1980. These cash-silver positions were achieved largely through deliveries on maturing futures contracts.

It is conservatively estimated that the combined actual and potential silver holdings of the Hunt and Conti Groups represented roughly 20 percent of world demand during late 1979. Clearly, such a market concentration embodied a force inherently capable of exerting significant influence upon the price of silver.

FUNDAMENTAL AND TECHNICAL INFLUENCES UPON SILVER PRICES
(January 1979–March 1980)

The Rise in Price

During the decade encompassing 1969–79, silver's supply and demand characteristics provided a fundamental basis for its later, pronounced rise in price. Throughout this time horizon, industrial/commercial silver demand exceeded production of newly mined supply. The February 1979 Indian embargo could have exacerbated this existing imbalance.

Additionally (as this study's earlier description of the January 1979–March 1980 period made clear), the U.S. economic climate exhibited continued and accelerating rates of inflation, a weakening currency, rampant investment uncertainty, and frequent, negative returns on financial assets. These conditions induced commodity price increases and generated an (investor) search for assets that would function as satisfactory stores of wealth.

In conjunction with the dynamics set forth above, massive futures purchase positions assumed by the Hunt and Conti Groups, relative to readily available stocks, rendered silver susceptible to significant price increases in the event the (futures) delivery option was vigorously exercised. In retrospect, the aforementioned groups utilized this delivery option (and its EFP derivative) to an unprecedented degree. During the critical first quarter of 1980, expectations of additional massive deliveries may have further fueled the escalation in silver prices.

The Decline in Price

Among the more significant factors underlying the abrupt turn in the price of silver during first quarter 1980 were:

Reduced Demand Factors

1. Input substitution (away from silver) and reduction of industrial/commercial demand, relative to supply, as consequences of the

recession and the emergence of a long-run, elastic response function. Specifically, there was a 24 percent decline in silver use during 1980 relative to the preceding year—down to 119.7 million ounces from the 157.2 million ounce level recorded for 1979;

2. The imposition by both the COMEX and CBT of retroactive margin increases and reduced position limits, as well as a liquidation-only trading regime (for long-position holders). These measures were intended to rectify perceived position concentrations in the silver futures market;

3. Rapidly escalating short-term rates of interest, rendering more costly traders' efforts to acquire and carry silver bullion or finance silver futures margin requirements (as illustration, during the period February 15–March 28, 1980, the prime rate rose to 19½ percent from 15¼ percent);

4. A relative increase in the value of the dollar, resulting in the re-emergence of that currency as an alternative (to precious metals) store of wealth;

5. Capital-investment diversion towards U.S. government and other interest-bearing securities carrying record (high) yields; and

6. A perceived easing of international political tensions;

Increased Supply Factors

1. Full capacity operation of refineries transforming coins, scrap, and other silver forms into bullion;

2. An increase of 1.6 million ounces, between January 2 and March 1980, of COMEX silver stocks;

3. The mid March (1980) futures selling/delivery activity of a number of large traders; and

4. The end of March forced selloff of Hunt positions. During the last week of that month, Hunt interests were failing to meet margin calls. Approximately 10.24 million ounces of physical silver and 4,000 long futures contracts were liquidated by the Hunt's intermediating broker/dealers. The combination of the increased silver supplies (delineated above) with significant reductions in Hunt Group silver holdings/control produced a sudden, substantial increase in the relative availability of silver bullion, thus exerting additional downward pressure on the price of silver.

As regards the COMEX and CBT exchanges' suspension of active trading in silver futures during March 1980 (the liquidation-only trading regime), it is not unreasonable to suspect that large purchase positions (as were held by the Hunt and Conti Groups), suddenly constrained in the manner they were, may well have been vulnerable to and resulted in the market's anticipation of a terminated price spiral.

It would be convenient if a single factor could be pinpointed as the causal event leading to the near catastrophe in silver. If this were possible, the focus of required action would be accordingly direct. To date, however, no such solitary rationale has been unambiguously identified. Rather, it appears that an accumulation of circumstances provided a conducive setting for events that subsequently occurred.

In any event, the (March 1980) sudden break in silver prices found many major brokerage intermediaries overexposed with respect to large-customer position concentrations. By permitting such exposures, the brokerage houses themselves contributed to forces that ultimately provoked the silver crisis. As the financial institutions that were the first to be jeopardized by the unfolding silver scenario, the predicament of these broker/dealers is now accorded explicit treatment.

THE CRISIS

The six broker/dealers carrying Hunt silver positions at the end of March 1980 were Bache, Halsey, Stuart, Shields, Inc. (Bache); Merrill, Lynch, Pierce, Fenner & Smith, Inc. (Merrill Lynch); Dean Witter Reynolds, Inc. (Dean Witter); A. G. Edwards & Sons, Inc. (Edwards); E. F. Hutton & Company, Inc. (E. F. Hutton); and Paine, Webber, Jackson, & Curtis, Inc. (Paine Webber). At year end 1979, these firms intermediated for the Hunt Group a total of 17,444 long silver futures and forward contracts. As of December 31, 1979, the Hunts also held with these firms and their affiliates 14.9 million ounces of silver bullion—posted as collateral for silver loans. Two of the firms, Bache and Merrill Lynch, accounted for 80 percent of the futures contracts and 87 percent of the physical silver held at year end by the six brokers. Not surprisingly, these two firms were placed in the most immediate jeopardy when the market finally turned against the Hunts.

Had the Hunt defaults compromised the net-capital positions of Bache and Merrill Lynch below permissible regulatory levels, these firms would not have been allowed to conduct additional transactions—in effect, rendering the COMEX clearinghouse vulnerable to a massive default. A momentary digression is in order. The settlement feature (clearing system) of a futures exchange is "closed," in the sense that daily profits resulting from contract liquidation or revaluation against the exchange's closing settlement price (the market), are remitted by contract losers to gainers through the intermediary function interposed by the clearinghouse.

Had Bache or Merrill Lynch (both clearing members) been unable to fulfill their obligations as a consequence of the Hunt defaults, clearinghouse rules would have called for the attempted transfer of these entities' contract positions to other clearing members. This procedure, however, would not have made good liabilities owed to the system—itself composed of numerous members. In this particular case, these other members most probably would not have received substantial monies due them, despite the application of (limited) emergency funds maintained by the clearinghouse. Hence, it is possible they would have been unable, in turn, to independently cover yet-to-be received funds that were owed to their customers. (As a point of information, the clearinghouse would, at this point, impose finite assessments upon solvent members as a means by which to attempt restoration of systemwide integrity.) Had total remittance been attempted, individual broker insolvencies might have erupted. To the extent remittance could not be effected, customers' financial integrity could have been compromised. Inasmuch as the commercial banking sector was heavily involved in funding the day-to-day activities of commodities broker/dealers (who, in turn, were substantially funding the Hunts), the latters' insolvency could have jeopardized the status of the banking system. A "snowball" effect may well have occurred. Efforts to forestall impending insolvency through legal recourse would not have addressed short-run problems of illiquidity.

To continue, the silver represented by the Hunt's broker-intermediated futures positions, irrespective of physical silver holdings, reflected a market value of $3.35 billion at December 31, 1979. Equity in Hunt accounts, however, including securities holdings, physical silver, and unrealized silver and other commodity futures gains was only $1.1 billion. In short, the futures positions were vulnerable to a market downturn.

Within the brokering establishments carrying the largest Hunt positions, the decision to assume the risks associated with such substantial holdings was made at the executive committee level or by the firms' highest ranking officer. Certain of these decisionmakers possessed extensive information of a general nature concerning the Hunt's reputation for great wealth and silver market experience. They were, however, without current or specific knowledge as to the extent of the Hunt's silver trading activities with other firms, the concentration of such positions, or the liquidity available to support these holdings in the event of a market downturn. This information was never demanded from the Hunts.

The Behavior of Silver Prices During the Crisis

From a intraday spot high of approximately $50 on January 17, 1980, the bull market in silver subsequently exhibited a steep decline. By the end of January, spot prices had fallen to approximately $34 per ounce. During February and early March, spot prices ranged between $31 and $38.50, but on March 10, the decline resumed, with spot prices falling from $29.75 to $10.80 by March 27. The rapidly declining prices generated margin calls on the Hunt's net-long futures positions as well as calls for additional bullion deposits (in order that required collateralization ratios be maintained on their broker-extended loans). During this period, the Hunts were also engaged in the purchase of substantial amounts of silver, underlying maturing futures contracts, as well as separately transacting for delivery of silver from a number of commodity dealers.

Institutional Exposure

With the declining market generating sizeable cash requirements (variation margin) on their futures exposures, the Hunts borrowed directly from banks, three of the six aforementioned brokers (the banking system representing the real source of this funding), commodity merchant firms, individuals, and Placid Oil Company (a petroleum concern owned by Hunt family trusts). Table B-4 indicates the Hunt credit buildup. (In Table B-4 the proportion of broker/Placid Oil financing exemplifies the interdependence of the

Table B-4. Hunt Silver-Related Loan Balances (*in $ millions*).

	August 1, 1979	January 17, 1980	March 27, 1980
Broker Lenders			
Bache, Halsey, Stuart, Metals Company	38.0	43.7	235.5
Merrill, Lynch, Pierce, Fenner & Smith	—	54.0	169.0
ACLI International, Inc.	29.8	80.5	134.2
E. F. Hutton & Co., Inc.	—	100.5	100.0
Mocatta Metals, Corp.	50.4	25.5	25.5
Subtotal	118.2	304.2	664.2
Banks			
Swiss Bank Corp.	70.0	150.0	200.0
First National (Chicago)	30.0	10.0	100.0
Citibank	—	25.0	90.0
First National (Dallas)	—	—	79.2
Bank Leu	—	—	50.0
Credit Lyonnais	10.1	15.0	30.0
J. Henry Schroder Bank	5.0	18.0	29.0
Saudi Finance Corp.	—	—	26.0
Bank Arab, International	—	—	10.0
Subtotal	115.1	218.0	614.2
Other Lenders			
Placid Oil Co.	—	—	100.0
Naji Nahas	—	—	29.5
Subtotal	—	—	139.5
Total	233.3	522.2	1,417.9

Source: Brimmer (1984, 51).

financial system, inasmuch as such funding represented, to a significant degree, "indirect" lending from the banking community.)

The Broker/Dealer Dilemma Revisited

On Thursday, March 13, 1980, International Metals Investment Company (IMIC) informed Merrill Lynch that it would be unable to meet a $45 million margin call on its silver position because of what it asserted were administrative problems. IMIC was a Hunt-controlled entity transacting its silver futures speculation through Merrill Lynch. The following Monday, March 17, the Hunts apprised Bache they did not have the cash necessary to meet $44 million in variation margin calls.

IMIC and the Hunts proceeded to offer silver bullion to Merrill Lynch and Bache (as well as other forms of physical silver) in lieu of cash as margin calls mounted during the ensuing two weeks. In essence, this arrangement rendered additional funding a *fait accompli*, since clearinghouse requirements for cash necessitated Bache and Merrill Lynch's independent fulfillment, through their bank credit lines, of this immediate obligation. In other words, cash the Hunts did not make available to Bache and Merrill Lynch had to be obtained immediately by these brokers in order to fulfill exchange requirements. This strategy was embraced as a necessary evil in the hopes a market turnaround would end the cashflow dilemma and thereby eliminate the brokers' realization of critical losses.

The Hunts continued to pay cash to the other four brokers until March 25 and 26, when they ceased all cash payments/bullion deposits and informed their brokers that they were illiquid. It was at this point that liquidation of the Hunt accounts became inevitable. The Hunts also defaulted on obligations to banks and commodity dealers. The most notable of these was a $432 million installment due (March 26) towards the purchase of 28.5 million ounces of silver from the Englehard Minerals & Chemicals Corporation.

On March 27, when silver prices reached their crisis low of $10.80, unsecured debit balances in Hunt accounts, representing potential losses to the intermediating firms, had increased substantially—notwithstanding the Hunt's cash or collateral deposits during the intervening period. These potential losses were not identified and addressed initially, since prevailing industry practice dictated futures valuation at the daily (futures) settlement price(s)—even under circumstances of "limit" market movements. (In other than the current or nearby delivery month [the spot month], exchange price fluctuations are constrained by pre-designated ranges, or limits.) Such a regime was used not only to ascertain the extent of required margin calls, but also to determine whether a customer's unsecured debit balance necessitated a chargeoff against regulatory capital. In the "limit-down" market prevailing in silver at the time, use of these practices assigned an unrealistically elevated value to the Hunt's accounts.

Under then-existing circumstances, the spot price more closely reflected the true value of the Hunt's silver futures contracts. Legitimately "market-to-market" as they were at futures prices, Hunt accounts at each firm *appeared* (until very late March) to be in equity. Actual deficits occurred in a number of cases, however, when Hunt contracts were liquidated on March 27 and 28 at or near the spot price.

The uncertainties associated with the crisis continued into the week of March 31. At Bache, bullion that collateralized its bank loans (loans to Bache that the broker obtained in order to fund its Hunt-related lending) was insufficient to cover outstanding balances. Publicly, Bache incorrectly announced on March 28 that it had liquidated Hunt positions without a loss. (Bache, as well as several other brokers, were soon to have trading in their shares suspended by the New York Stock Exchange when it became apparent that serious losses, in fact, were involved.) When Bache informed its bankers on Sunday, March 30 and Monday, March 31, of a $17 million collateral deficiency on its loans, the fully collateralized lenders (Citizens and Southern, Barclays, Bankers Trust, and First National of Oklahoma) insisted on immediate repayment and were bought out of the credit by those that were less-than-fully collateralized (First National of Chicago, Irving Trust, Harris, Northern Trust, Marine Midland, and U.S. Trust). This was not accomplished until the early morning hours of April 1. Failure to reach such an agreement would have placed Bache in default (technically, it had now reached this stage) and subjected the exposed lenders to serious losses.

Under the newly structured credit arrangement, Bache proceeded, thereafter, to liquidate remaining bullion in the Hunt accounts. Following this action, the broker received remaining cash shortfalls from Placid Oil (after the final bank bailout) as settlement for the Hunt's remaining obligations.

At Merrill Lynch, the IMIC account was $64 million in equity on March 28, valuing remaining futures contracts at futures settlement prices. At spot prices, however, remaining loans and debit balances exceeded by $83 million all of the collateral in the IMIC account. The Hunt family and related entities, meanwhile, held on deposit approximately $295 million in other accounts with the firm. Merrill Lynch management believed that Hunt family members were willing to support the IMIC account from the time of its inception, but it was not until March 27 that Merrill Lynch sought a written guaranty of this from the Hunts.

Five days later, after initial resistance on the part of the Hunt's attorneys, Nelson and William Hunt executed a personal guaranty that enabled the firm to utilize assets in Hunt family accounts and thus avoid charging against net capital the unsecured, IMIC debit balance. Relying upon this guaranty, Merrill Lynch held open IMIC positions until Hunt interests paid off their deficit. Merrill Lynch's strategy, obviously, was undertaken in order to avoid realization of substantial losses. The final Hunt repayment, as well as terminal restitution to a number of other brokers, was accomplished, ultimately, by receipt of a $1.1 billion loan structured by a consortium of banks and extended to Placid Oil (which, in turn, "downstreamed" these funds to the Hunts).

Separately, the Hunts had, outstanding, a $702 million forward (silver) purchase obligation with Englehard Minerals & Chemicals Corporation. Settlement on the initial installment of the Englehard transaction was due March 26. With no apparent prospect for payment, the commodity dealer felt its only recourse would be the initiation of a lawsuit. This action would have triggered a condition of bankruptcy for the Hunts, resulting in forced liquidation of massive amounts of silver and silver obligations. Hence, Hunt creditors and their customers would most probably have been placed in financial jeopardy. The alternative, as Englehard perceived it, was negotiation of bank credit (with the Hunts as either direct or indirect recipients) in such a manner so as to facilitate the dealer's repayment. Ultimately, the Hunts were able to satisfy their obligation with Englehard (at the Boca Raton bankers' conference—March 29, 1980) by directly conveying to that firm interests in a number of petroleum licenses, as well as permitting it to assume ownership of silver deposited as collateral.

THE ROLE OF THE FEDERAL RESERVE

A Federal Reserve report indicates "that the four domestic banks which were the largest lenders to the Hunts all used the discount window during February/March 1980" (U.S. Congress, House of Representatives 1981, 58); a two-month period when the volume of bank credit extension to the Hunts totalled approximately $800 million. While the Fed has downplayed the possibility that discount window borrowings were indirectly utilized to fund the Hunts, it does not totally rule out this possibility. Such a circumstance, if it occurred, would contravene long-standing Fed policy prohibiting speculative lending funded by discount window drawdowns. If, indeed, this activity took place, it did so without the knowledge of the Fed Chairman, Paul Volcker: "During this period, we had no knowledge, apart from rumors reported in the press, of the size or value of the Hunt positions in the silver market, or of any bank lending against silver" (U.S. Congress, House of Representatives 1981, 146).

The Fed (October 23, 1979) had imposed and reiterated (March 14, 1980) its policy restricting credit extension for the purpose of funding speculative undertakings. Yet, Fed Chairman Volcker did not overrule the consortium banks' $1.1 billion debt restructuring extended on behalf of the Hunts.[2] This loan, officially dated April 28, 1980, came at a time when normal consumer credit was virtually unavailable.

Volcker became aware of the acute nature of Bache's predicament, a direct consequence of the Hunt defaults, only as recently as March 26, 1980, when a Bache representative urged him to consider closing the COMEX. Quoting Volcker directly from Congressional testimony:

> The first indication I had of any potentially serious financial consequences arising from the sharp fall of the silver price was in an urgent call at midday on Wednesday, March 26, from a leading brokerage house, indicating that Hunt interests were failing to meet substantial margin calls and that certain loans the brokerage house had with banks, secured by Hunt silver, were either undermargined or in imminent danger of becoming undermargined. (U.S. Congress, House of Representatives 1981, 15)

Volcker was present, as were Englehard representatives and the Hunt brothers, three days later during a March 29, 1980 bankers' conference held in Boca Raton, Florida. Although the conference had been scheduled independently of the crisis, it was used by Englehard and silver-lending banks at risk to address the urgent matters now at hand. Again, at that time, the head of the Federal Reserve did not reject a contemplated, speculative credit package that direcly contradicted existing government policy. (As mentioned previously, it was at the Boca Raton conference that Englehard directly negotiated a settlement strategy with the Hunts. This action was taken after the at-risk banks rejected the Englehard/Hunt refinancing proposal put forth. Nevertheless, Englehard's settlement, while mitigating the urgency underlying implementation of a financing package, did not eliminate the bank's independent requirement for such an arrangement. Thus, the banks continued to work towards this goal.)

As Volcker later testified (before the House Commerce, Consumer, and Monetary Affairs Subcommittee), it was not clear whether he possessed the authority to veto such a financing package. In response to a Subcommittee member's inquiry positing Volcker's authority to render mandatory (within one-half hour) existing voluntary credit constraints, the Fed chairman offered the following reply: "I can't. It would require action by the President." (U.S. Congress, House of Representatives 1981, 147)

It is evident that banks with Hunt exposures were acting in their self-interest by restructuring their outstanding indebtedness. Had they not done so, their direct loans to the Hunts could not have been repaid when due. Additionally, their "indirect" loans (to brokers) may have been jeopardized as well.

Given the market dislocations and losses, apart from those associated with the Hunts, that may very well have resulted without the bailout, evidence points towards Fed acceptance (non-rejection might be a more apt characterization) of the banks' proposal in light of the lack of viable alternatives. Again, from Volcker's Subcommittee testimony:

> The credit referred to in recent press articles first came to my attention in a general way at the initiative of one of the lead banks involved on Easter weekend. By that time, lending banks had more fully appraised their overall exposure to Hunt interests and had reached at least tentative conclusions regarding the value of available Hunt assets and those of key Hunt-related companies. A small group of banks developed a concept over the next few days about a method of restructuring the Hunt silver indebtedness in a manner that would greatly strengthen the security position of creditors with outstanding silver loans or contracts. . . . The new bank loans would be to and secured by the assets and earning power of perhaps the strongest of the Hunt-related companies, the Placid Oil Co.

> Control over the silver and silver contracts, with appropriate safeguards, would pass into the hands of that same company. Silver-related loans to the Hunts would be paid off. The immediate purpose would be to protect more securely the interests of existing Hunt silver creditors, bank and nonbank. . . .

The credit in question was negotiated between a syndicate of banks, including the then existing creditors, and the Hunt interests. It was entirely a transaction between these private parties operating in their own natural interests. (U.S. Congress, House of Representatives 1981, 149–50)

The press at that time attributed a more active role to the Federal Reserve. Chairman Volcker was there portrayed as orchestrating a Hunt-family bailout in smoke-filled hotel rooms in the middle of the night during the bankers' conference at Boca Raton. But a statement in the Senate a few weeks later by another member of the Board of Governors disputes this notion.

The amount of credit is, of course, very large and the circumstances under which it arose are clearly extraordinary. . . . The credit is, and always has been, a strictly private transaction in which business, credit and other judgments have been made by the parties themselves with no guidance, suasion or other efforts by the Federal Reserve to influence the nature and the terms of the credit other than those related to the limitations on speculation. (Partee 1980, 60)

Further underscoring the privately initiated aspects of the bailout, the following is excerpted from a statement by E. Gerald Corrigan (now of the New York Fed):

While we did, of course, have an interest in the outcome of these negotiations, no official of the Federal Reserve initiated or participated in the negotiations. The Federal Reserve's primary concern was that the terms and conditions of the loan agreement were consistent with the Special Voluntary Credit Restraint Program then in effect. In particular, the Federal Reserve had a concern that the proceeds of the loan not be used directly or indirectly to support any renewed speculative activity by the Hunts and that the silver be liquidated in an orderly manner. More generally, the Federal Reserve, in consultation with other government agencies involved, felt it appropriate that the situation be resolved in an orderly fashion.

The various agreements constituting the credit were executed as of April 28, 1980. Consistent with the position taken by the Federal Reserve, those agreements did provide rigorous covenants prohibiting renewed speculation by the Hunts. In addition, it was understood that the lead banks would provide periodic reports about the credit to bank examination personnel. In light of these stipulations and arrangements, the Federal Reserve interposed no objections to the loan. Again, it was only because of the coincidence of the Special Credit Restraint Program then in effect that the Fed was able to seek the commitments against further speculation contained in the loan agreements. (U.S. Congress, House of Representatives 1981, 150)

At congressional hearings, several representatives voiced their perception as to the inequity of the Hunt credit. After all, many smaller business enterprises at the time were constrained (by the Fed's role in promulgating credit restrictions) from receiving loans that would have been employed towards the production of real output. The Hunt loans resulted from their speculative activities—a seemingly undeserved "reward" for non-productive enterprises. In the minds of a number of congressmen, the Hunt loan added insult to injury, in view of the industries negatively affected by the rise in silver prices—such price increases occurring, at least to some degree, as a result of the Hunt's speculative role.

Whether or not the cause of equity was served during the silver crisis, it is likely that Fed's tolerance of the bank bailout was necessitated solely by the magnitude of the situation. As has been the case in other recent crises of similar proportions, government actions in this instance were geared toward forestalling widespread financial disruptions. Given the interdependence of the present financial framework, issues of social equity may assume new dimensions when the viability of an entire system is perceived to be at risk.

Reinforcing this conclusion are comments by Andrew Brimmer, a public governor at the COMEX during the time of the crisis (and also a former member of the Board of Governors of the Federal Reserve):

> The potential crisis was checked by a timely decision by the Federal Reserve Board to permit commercial banks to lend to commodity speculators—although the grant of such loans was clearly inconsistent with the credit controls the Federal Reserve Board then had in place. . . . The Federal Reserve has defended its decision to permit this breach in its credit restraint program by citing the threat to the overall financial system if the transaction had been blocked. In its judgment, a repudiation by the Hunts of their silver-related indebtedness would have dragged down a number of broker-dealers, and market prices not only of silver but also of publicly-traded securities as well may have collapsed. The Federal Reserve concluded that such a risk to the financial system had to be prevented from materializing. (Brimmer 1984, 41)

In retrospect, it appears that the Fed's peripheral role in resolving the silver crisis emanated from that body's subjective/objective assessment that the cause of social welfare would best be served by acceding to private sector initiatives. Until it is feasible to assess in a more formal manner the all-inclusive costs and benefits among crisis alternatives, the resolution of parallel future events will again be based primarily upon the subjective judgment of officials concerned. This being the case, at least one lesson from the silver crisis seems straightforward. That is, the nature of such subjective decision processes ensures that actions taken to address similar future occurrences shall again become the focal point of a great deal of criticism and debate.

NOTES

1. This Appendix was written by Michael Pollakoff.
2. Federal Reserve disapproval of bank financing of speculative activities goes back to its origins early in the century and was reiterated after the stock market crash of 1929.

THE S & L CRISIS OF 1985-87

It has been pointed out that well-insured depository institutions can continue to function even when they are insolvent. They can do so because a large part of their costs of doing business—their interest expense—does not have to be paid out as cash when it is incurred. Rather, it can be credited to depositor accounts until the owner withdraws the funds.

DISINTERMEDIATION

Nevertheless, deposit withdrawals have presented a problem at federally insured S & Ls at times in the past. Figure C-1 shows two periods of deposit losses—in 1981-2 and 1985-7. In the first of these periods, before interest rate deregulation, the liquidity problem was called "disintermediation." The second incidence of deposit losses cannot be attributed to disintermediation, however. Under disintermediation, depositors moved their funds from accounts whose interest rates were constrained by interest rate ceilings, which were imposed on S & Ls for the first time in 1966. When the rate constraint became binding; depositors relocated their funds elsewhere; increasingly, to unregulated money market mutual funds (MMMFs) during the late 1970s and early 1980s (Cargill and Garcia 1985).

During periods of disintermediation, net new-deposit inflows were negative. Figure C-1 illustrates the disintermediation phenomenon,

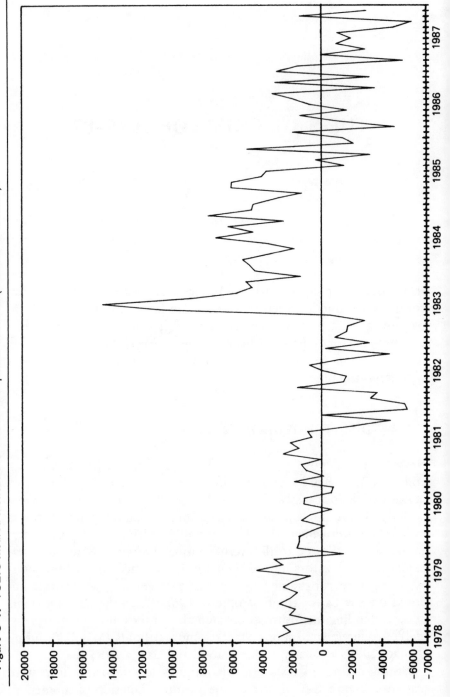

Figure C-1. FSLIC-Insured Institutions: Net New Deposits Received (*Millions of Dollars*).

which last occurred between January 1981 and October 1982. This period was acknowledged to be one of crisis for the S & L industry. The two main causes of the strain were (1) exposure to interest rate risk accompanied by unexpectedly high market rates, and (2) disintermediation. The industry lost money because the average rate paid on its deposits (some of which had already been deregulated) exceeded that received on its assets (typically, fixed-rate mortgages). The losses made some S & Ls book-value insolvent, while much of the industry had no economic net worth. In addition, S & Ls faced a serious liquidity shortage.

ENDING DISINTERMEDIATION

The Garn–St Germain Depository Institutions Act of 1982 addressed these two industry problems. It created the money market deposit and SuperNOW accounts which offered market-determined interest rates to compete with the MMMFs and it gave the industry additional asset powers to reduce exposure to interest rate risk (Cargill and Garcia 1985).[1] Congress also passed a "non-binding resolution" asserting that the full faith and credit of the U.S. backed the insurance funds.

As the figure shows, the act was highly successful in ending disintermediation. A surge of money poured into the new accounts in the early months of 1983. Despite seasonal fluctuations, net new deposit flows were positive each month until January 1985. During 1985, however, deposit flows were frequently negative. Beginning in August 1986 they became systematically negative (with May 1987 providing the one exception). Deposit losses were again a problem.

BUILDING UP TO THE MID 1980s CRISIS

The liquidity strains of 1985–7 were not attributable to disintermediation. By 1986 all interest rate caps had been removed from bank and thrift accounts, except for the zero-rate restriction on demand deposits that was largely irrelevant to thrifts, which offered other interest-paying checking accounts.

The causes of the mid 80s thrift crisis were perceived to be twofold. First, credit risk exposure was causing increasing numbers of

Table C-1. Incidence of Insolvencies by State, December 1986.

State Ranked by Percentage of GAAP-Assets Insolvent Institutions	All in State		GAAP-Insolvent			
	Total Number Thrifts	Total Assets ($ billions)	Number of GAAP-Insolvent	Percentage State Thrifts	Assets of GAAP-Insolvent Thrifts	Percentage State Assets
Wyoming	11	$1.3	2	18.2	$0.6	49.4
Idaho	9	1.5	3	33.3	0.6	40.3
Oregon	20	9.7	10	50.0	3.9	40.3
Arkansas	39	8.3	12	30.8	3.1	37.7
Oklahoma	53	10.1	16	30.2	3.3	32.3
Texas	281	97.3	81	28.8	28.6	29.4
Louisiana	102	15.6	28	27.5	4.3	27.8
Minnesota	37	16.1	8	21.6	4.3	26.6
Mississippi	45	4.8	7	15.6	1.0	21.3
Maryland	95	18.9	12	12.6	3.8	20.2
Alabama	37	8.5	5	13.5	1.6	18.4
Illinois	267	65.3	56	21.0	11.4	17.4
Nebraska	23	9.1	8	34.8	1.3	14.7
South Carolina	49	10.4	3	6.1	1.5	14.3
Indiana	115	12.7	14	12.2	1.8	13.8
New Mexico	25	5.9	3	12.0	0.8	13.4
Utah	14	5.9	3	21.4	0.7	12.5
Iowa	52	9.1	7	13.5	1.0	10.6
New Jersey	139	50.2	21	15.1	5.3	10.6
North Carolina	139	19.3	5	3.6	1.8	9.4
Ohio	232	51.8	18	7.8	4.6	8.9
Tennessee	64	10.6	10	15.6	0.9	8.9
Florida	149	83.0	20	13.4	7.4	8.9
West Virginia	18	2.1	2	11.1	0.2	8.4

State					
Missouri	85	21.9	12	14.1	1.7	7.7
Pennsylvania	169	38.1	4	2.4	2.9	7.5
Montana	11	1.2	1	9.1	0.1	7.4
Virginia	66	22.9	7	10.6	1.5	6.7
North Dakota	6	3.9	2	33.3	0.2	6.2
Kansas	58	16.9	7	12.1	1.0	6.0
Georgia	67	16.2	9	13.4	0.9	5.9
Kentucky	67	7.2	4	6.0	0.4	5.4
New York	86	48.3	6	7.0	2.4	5.0
California	216	310.4	32	14.8	14.8	4.8
Arizona	14	21.6	1	7.1	1.0	4.8
Michigan	51	34.8	6	11.8	1.6	4.7
Washington	43	17.1	5	11.6	0.6	3.6
Colorado	38	15.9	6	15.8	0.6	3.5
Massachusetts	33	7.0	1	3.0	0.2	2.2
Connecticut	31	11.3	1	3.2	0.2	1.4
Wisconsin	79	15.8	1	1.3	0.1	0.8
Alaska	4	0.6	0	0.0	0.0	0.0
Delaware	4	0.4	0	0.0	0.0	0.0
District	6	4.3	0	0.0	0.0	0.0
Guam	2	0.1	0	0.0	0.0	0.0
Hawaii	6	3.7	0	0.0	0.0	0.0
Maine	15	1.2	0	0.0	0.0	0.0
Nevada	7	4.1	0	0.0	0.0	0.0
New Hampshire	12	1.8	0	0.0	0.0	0.0
Puerto Rico	10	5.6	0	0.0	0.0	0.0
Rhode Island	3	3.6	0	0.0	0.0	0.0
Vermont	4	0.4	0	0.0	0.0	0.0
Total	3,220	$1,165.3	460	14.3	$124.2	10.7

Note: GAAP net worth includes Income Capital Certificates.
Source: Data derived by the authors from FHLBB Reports of Income and Condition.

thrifts to become insolvent whether their net worth was measured by RAP, GAAP or market values. (See Table 1-4 in Chapter 1.) Some S & Ls had made mistakes in handling their new asset powers and others had fraudulently abused the powers. The resulting insolvencies were widely spread across the country. Table C-1 shows the total numbers of S & Ls in each state, the numbers and percentages and GAAP-insolvent S & Ls ranked by the percentages of state assets.

Second, the deteriorating financial condition of the FSLIC (see Table C-2 prevented it from dealing with many of the escalating insolvencies, so that a backlog of "zombie" institutions had accumulated and were waiting to be addressed.[2] As it became increasingly apparent during 1986 and early 1987 that the federal insurer was approaching insolvency, deposit withdrawals accelerated, as is illustrated in Figure C-1.

The situation among federally insured S & Ls had unpleasant similarities to the scenarios in Ohio and Maryland. The industry's problems had accumulated over a number of years. The regulators had not vigorously dealt with them—rather, they showed signs of being unduly influenced by the industry and its lobbyists in trying to cover up the problems. FSLIC was declared insolvent by the GAO early in March 1987. Quiet runs began occurring in Texas, where many of the industry's problems had been pinpointed by the press. In the meantime, Congress, trying to avoid new budget commitments in the twilight era of the Gramm-Rudman-Hollings law, was slow in, and divided over, addressing the industry's inadequacies and deciding how much money to provide to the bankrupt FSLIC.

The House and Senate produced very different rescue bills and the conference committee formed to reconcile the differences met during July 1987 for an unusually long time. During the conference, the president repeatedly threatened to veto the bill, including the version produced by the conference committee, which then took the unusual step of reconvening to change the bill just enough to gain presidential acquiescence. These events were, no doubt, disturbing to depositors. Deposit outflows cumulated to $21.9 billion, or 2.5 percent of initial deposit levels between September 1986 and June 1987.[3]

The president signed the Competitive Equality Banking Act of 1987 on Monday August 10, 1987.[4] The act included provisions for recapitalizing the FSLIC by borrowing funds in the capital markets—borrowings that would be repaid in thirty years from the proceeds of zero-coupon bonds purchased from the capital reserves of the Fed-

Table C-2. FSLIC Insurance Fund Reserves *(in billions of dollars)* 1980-86.

December	Primary Reserves[a]	Secondary Reserves[b]	Total Reserves
1980	5.67	0.79	6.46
1981	5.70	0.60	6.30
1982	5.69	0.61	6.30
1983	5.76	0.66	6.42
1984	4.89	0.72	5.61
1985	3.78	0.77	4.55
1986	(6.33)	0.00	(6.33)

Sources: U.S. General Accounting Office (1982; 1983; 1984c; 1985; 1986c; 1987d).

a. Primary reserves are immediately usable by the FSLIC because they derive from the regular and special assessment premiums paid by thrifts to the FSLIC and from any interest earned on insurance fund investments.

b. In the early 1960s, falling FSLIC reserves led to legislation requiring thrifts to prepay insurance premiums into a secondary reserve account. Although the requirement was eliminated in the 1970s, some prepaid premiums and accumulated interest remained. The secondary reserve was not readily available for FSLIC use, as it remained an asset on S & L books until the FSLIC was declared insolvent in 1987 and the GAO determined that "The Corporation has exercised its authority under—the National Housing Act—to use its secondary reserve to help absorb operating losses." (GAO 1987d, 6)

eral Home Loan Banks. H.R. 27 also repeated the pledge of U.S. full faith and credit to back the insurance funds, but not the recap bonds.

On the same day Governor Bill Clements of Texas, said in a speech that depositors would receive cash for only part of their deposits. For the remainder they would get an IOU from the government: "The federal government is finally going to belly-up to this problem, and when they do, they're going to pay off those depositors like 30 cents on the dollar and give them a piece of paper, like a bond." (*Amarillo Daily News*, 11 August 1987, 1)

The next day, the front page of the *Washington Post*'s Business Section headlined runs in Amarillo, Tx. The new chairman of the Federal Home Loan Bank Board, M. Danny Wall, in office barely six weeks, immediately called a news conference to refute the governor's claims and reassure depositors. Such statements, he said:

are uninformed. To say that depositors may end up with only 30 cents on the FSLIC-insured dollar is a complete fiction . . . that has absolutely no basis in fact. I assure all FSLIC-insured depositors in Texas and across the country that there is no reason to be concerned about the safety of federally insured money. (FHLBB Press Release, 11 August 1987)

Headlines on the runs eventually left the newspapers, but regulators, policymakers and depositors remained concerned about the situation.

PROVIDING LIQUIDITY ASSISTANCE

Questions arise as to how the deposit outflows in both periods were being replaced and whether they could be contained. While S & Ls have equal access to the Federal Reserve, as do member banks for LLR assistance under the 1980 act, Federal Reserve regulations require that thrifts use their special industry lenders before approaching the Fed. The liquidity resources of the FHLBanks are finite and much less extensive than those of the central bank.

Moreover, the criteria that determine which S & Ls among many the FHLBanks will assist are unclear in this industry. For example, the Federal Home Loan Bank of San Francisco handled the large 1984 run at Financial Corporation of America (FCA),[5] after the Board of Governors refused assistance. But under the agreement to share liquidity responsibilities reached by FHLBB Chairman Richard Pratt, and Federal Reserve Chairman Paul Volcker in 1981, the Fed gave LLR assistance to twenty-one S & Ls in early 1982. It is not known if the Fed lent to S & Ls during the liquidity crisis of 1985-7.

Past precedent is not well-known in this arcane area, so what information is available will be presented and analyzed in order to throw some light on the question of how any continuing or even escalating runs would be handled.

THE FEDERAL HOME LOAN BANK SYSTEM

In discussing its creation, the FHLB system writes:

More than 1,700 thrifts failed in the Great Depression and their depositors lost $200 million, about one-third of the value of their deposits. Unable to meet burgeoning demands for withdrawals, many otherwise healthy thrifts simply froze their depositors' accounts in place. Customers feared they would lose their entire savings, and many, desperate for cash, resorted to selling their passbooks at a loss on the black markets. . . .

On July 16, 1932 . . . Congress approved the Federal Home Loan Bank Act, which President Hoover signed into law six days later. The Federal Home Loan Bank Act's primary purpose was to rescue the failing savings and home-financing industry by channeling cash to thrift institutions. (Federal Home Loan Bank System 1987, 8)

The funds to be provided could be long-term to promote industry growth or short-term to replace lost deposits. The FHL Banks are, however, privately incorporated with responsibilities to their industry members. Their legal authorization states:

The primary credit mission of the Federal Home Loan Banks is to provide a reliable source of credit for member institutions. . . . Advances generally shall be made to credit worthy members upon application for any sound business purpose in which members are authorized to engage. Such purposes include, but are not limited to: making residential mortgage, consumer, and commercial loans, covering savings withdrawals, accommodating seasonal cash needs, restructuring liabilities, and maintaining adequate liquidity. (U.S. CFR 1987, 531.1)

Growth in Advances

The FHLBanks meet their credit mission by borrowing in concert with agency status in the capital markets. The individual banks use their share of the proceeds to make advances of differing maturities to their members. Overall usage of advances has grown since their initiation, both in dollar value and as a percentage of S & L assets, as the data in Table C-3 show. At the end of 1940, there were $171 million in advances outstanding, which constituted 5.8 percent of S & L assets. These figures had risen to $100.1 billion and 8.6 percent of assets at the end of 1986. The table also shows that until 1980, S & Ls had more regulatory capital than advances. By 1980 the ratio of advances to assets had risen above the ratio of RAP capital to assets, which was only 4.6 percent at that time.[6]

Use of Advances

When S & Ls were subjected to Regulation Q, some deposits were withdrawn when market rates exceeded the caps. Research has shown that FHLBank advances were used to fund industry growth

Table C-3. Federal Home Loan Bank System, Member Institutions, Regulatory Net Worth, and FHLBank Advances: 1940–86.

December	Number of Member Institutions	Total Value of Member Assets ($ billions)	FHLBank Advances ($ billions)	Members' RAP-Net Worth ($ billions)	Percentage of Assets	
					Advances	RAP-Net Worth
1940	2,277	2.93	0.17	0.19	5.84	6.56
1945	2,475	6.12	0.19	0.41	3.02	6.73
1950	2,860	13.69	0.75	0.99	5.50	7.19
1955	3,544	34.20	1.38	2.30	4.04	6.73
1960	4,098	67.43	1.97	4.73	2.91	7.02
1965	4,508	124.58	5.97	8.50	4.79	6.83
1970	4,365	170.65	10.47	11.91	6.14	6.98
1975	4,078	330.26	17.51	19.18	5.30	5.81
1980	4,055	620.63	47.01	32.58	7.57	5.25
1	3,785	658.53	25.73	27.94	3.91	4.24
2	3,349	699.52	33.78	25.72	4.83	3.68
3	3,183	819.17	41.26	32.98	5.04	4.03
4	3,136	978.51	65.40	37.92	6.68	3.88
1985	3,246	1,069.40	84.40	46.82	7.89	4.38
6	3,220	1,164.11	100.07	52.93	8.60	4.55

Source: Federal Home Loan Bank Board (1986, 9).

Figure C–2.   Actual Versus Predicted FHLB Advances.

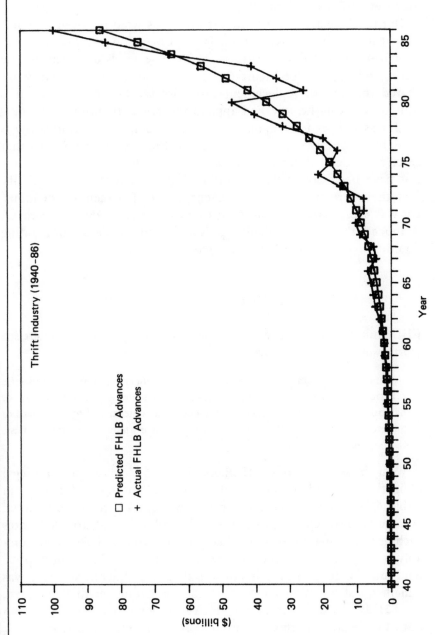

Thrift Industry (1940–86)

□ Predicted FHLB Advances
+ Actual FHLB Advances

($ billions)

Year

and replace lost deposits (Silber 1973; Jaffee and Quandt 1980; Morrisey 1971; and Kent 1983).

During the early 1980s, interest rate caps were removed in a process of interest rate deregulation. The last occasion on which disintermediation occurred was early in 1982. The levels of advances rose during this year. (See Figure C-2.) On this occasion the FHLBanks shared the deposit replacement task with the Federal Reserve. It is not known whether the Fed applied the same conditions for aiding thrifts as it does for helping banks. For example, no information is available about the capital condition of the twenty-one S & Ls that received Federal Reserve assistance early in 1982. They may or may not have been book-value insolvent, but there is a high probability that they were market-value insolvent, as 90–95 percent of the industry was economically insolvent at that time (Kane 1986a). Moreover, it appears that the FHLBanks apply different standards for granting liquidity assistance than does the Federal Reserve.

The FHLBanks' Role

FHLBank regulations declare that advances may be made to "creditworthy members." Moreover:

> Advances may be limited or denied if a member engages in unsafe or unsound practices, has inadequate regulatory capital, is sustaining operating losses, or has other financial or managerial deficiencies, as determined by the board of directors of its Federal Home Loan Bank, that bear upon its creditworthiness. (U.S. CFR 1987, 531.1 [d])

With these regulations, FHLBanks in 1986-7 were under no legal obligation to lend to their weak members. But some did. Data in Table C-4 show that advances rose more quickly than the national average to insolvent S & Ls nationwide and in several troubled states such as California, Louisiana, Oklahoma, Oregon, and Texas. Presumably, their FHLBanks were following the traditional LLR precept to lend immediately on the basis of sound collateral, while solvency was still in question. With good collateral, valued higher than the loan, the FHLBanks were not at risk. However, some troubled S & Ls ran out of collateral and this presented a problem to the regulators.

FHLBank Collateral Requirements

FHLBanks are required by legislation to obtain security for advances made. The law allows the FHLBB to determine what collateral is acceptable. The Board's regulations specify that, "A Bank shall require each borrowing member to pledge collateral sufficient, in the judgement of the Bank, to secure advances obtained. . . ." (U.S. CFR 1987, 525.7[a]) Eligible collateral consists of any property which is an authorized investment for the member institutions and which is (1) a non-delinquent residential mortgage; (2) a U.S. federal government or agency security; (3) a deposit in a FHLBank; or (4) other property acceptable to the FHLBank where its value is readily ascertainable and the bank is able to perfect its security interest in it.

Running Out of Collateral: FSLIC Guarantees

Some thrifts ran out of eligible collateral in the mid 1980s and turned to the FSLIC for assistance. The FSLIC began to guarantee some of the advances provided by the FHLBanks.

The data series on guaranteed advances begins in December 1985 and is shown in Table C-5. At that time, seven of the twelve district banks were provided with guarantees for advances made to their members. The San Francisco FHLBank was then the heaviest recipient, holding $1.3 billion of the total $2.1 billion of advance guarantees. The total value of guarantees peaked at $3.7 billion January 1987, when ten of the twelve FHLBanks were receiving guarantees. At that point, the Dallas bank was the heaviest user, with $1.7 billion of the total. San Francisco was close behind with $1.4 billion in guarantees.

The value of guarantees decreased in March 1987. The auditors of the Dallas bank threatened to give the bank a qualified opinion, because the value of FSLIC guarantees was questionable given FSLIC's impending insolvency. The FSLIC, therefore, made good on $947.4 million to honor its pledge to the Dallas FHLBank, and the total value of guarantees declined correspondingly.

FSLIC's policies and procedures for guaranteed advances specify that guarantees be provided for advances only if the insured association is a supervisory case that is (1) book-value insolvent, (2) cash-insolvent, or (3) is losing money so that it will soon become book-

Table C-4. Deposits and FHLBank Advances, All FSLIC Insured Institutions, QIV 1986.

Designation	Net Worth Category	Total Deposits	% Change Deposits	Large CDs	% Change CDs
Total	Less than or = to 0%	87.70	-7.10	7.68	-13.34
Industry	Between 0 and 3%	72.68	0.13	9.44	-4.81
	Greater than 3%	75.81	2.57	10.56	6.38
	Total Industry	76.40	0.77	10.01	1.35
Alabama	Less than or = to 0%	93.93	-1.15	6.25	2.32
	Between 0 and 3%	88.55	-1.46	6.67	-17.27
	Greater than 3%	74.75	0.85	10.92	--1.48
	Total State	79.22	0.23	9.77	-1.92
California	Less than or = to 0%	93.38	-3.46	11.84	-17.54
	Between 0 and 3%	55.12	-0.35	12.02	-0.56
	Greater than 3%	73.63	3.65	17.74	6.89
	Total State	70.27	2.42	16.13	4.45
Florida	Less than or = to 0%	85.16	-22.06	12.71	-32.17
	Between 0 and 3%	84.19	0.56	10.82	3.46
	Greater than 3%	74.70	1.65	8.59	3.30
	Total State	77.26	-1.48	9.34	-2.80
Louisiana	Less than or = to 0%	87.86	-5.36	6.46	-24.92
	Between 0 and 3%	91.96	-0.62	5.60	-8.26
	Greater than 3%	76.21	5.22	5.78	-3.41
	Total State	82.90	0.48	5.93	-12.00
Oklahoma	Less than or = to 0%	92.26	-0.54	5.87	-4.03
	Between 0 and 3%	83.66	-1.44	9.53	-2.52
	Greater than 3%	81.04	4.33	5.30	-10.81
	Total State	85.23	1.32	6.41	-6.26
Oregon	Less than or = to 0%	72.67	-0.67	3.85	3.88
	Between 0 and 3%	88.38	-0.24	7.47	-0.78
	Greater than 3%	69.24	0.63	6.93	19.58
	Total State	71.17	0.06	5.71	14.02
Texas	Less than or = to 0%	92.14	-2.13	7.94	-9.21
	Between 0 and 3%	84.59	1.17	11.47	-25.80
	Greater than 3%	74.68	3.36	10.22	-3.59
	Total State	82.49	0.90	9.89	-13.02

Source: Data derived by the authors from FHLBB Reports of Income and Condition.

Table C-4. continued

Brokered Deposits	% Change Brokered Deposits	Advances	% Change Advances	Number of CDs	% Change Number of CDs
3.96	-10.38	11.42	5.98	42,971	-13.51
3.48	3.21	9.61	8.84	105,819	-6.39
3.86	5.64	7.80	9.89	347,491	6.32
3.78	3.10	8.59	9.06	496,281	1.37
0.00	0.00	2.98	177.52	528	-15.92
0.00	0.00	4.02	-9.65	263	-8.68
1.27	-7.64	5.96	36.77	2,413	6.86
0.95	-7.64	5.28	40.43	3,204	0.95
9.84	-0.87	13.46	1.64	6,816	-12.26
7.44	2.59	10.68	5.82	33,615	11.40
8.00	3.70	9.63	9.09	137,261	6.43
7.95	3.17	10.06	7.77	177,682	6.46
6.06	-35.42	7.11	14.56	2.798	-33.70
0.19	-16.47	6.96	3.15	6,360	-8.74
1.70	23.74	7.52	5.82	27,342	4.05
1.74	-0.63	7.39	6.06	36,500	-2.58
3.35	0.21	13.90	3.54	1,099	-37.02
0.87	-12.20	3.10	1.84	1,228	-13.95
7.37	78.45	6.75	-9.31	3,219	-10.68
4.83	49.84	7.94	-2.51	5,546	-18.15
1.22	-11.99	9.75	26.13	560	-14.50
0.23	-21.88	10.23	-2.72	702	-6.40
0.19	-16.85	9.00	37.64	1,430	2.51
0.53	-13.84	9.51	22.06	2,692	-3.86
2.43	0.84	26.88	34.96	666	-12.25
0.00	0.00	6.74	-13.89	175	0.00
0.25	-0.41	18.46	-3.64	1,819	8.92
1.12	0.68	21.52	12.42	2,660	2.15
6.73	-7.35	12.21	32.19	11,893	-12.94
8.28	10.47	8.78	12.59	14,005	-41.12
6.51	3.55	5.75	26.07	24,956	8.02
7.05	2.21	8.47	24.34	50,854	-16.01

Table C-5. FHLBank Advances, FSLIC Guarantees, and Collateral
Deficiencies: 1985–87 (*$ billion*).

		Advances	Guaranteed Advances	Collateral Deficiencies
1985	J	70.51	N/A	N/A
	F	71.47	N/A	N/A
	M	71.67	N/A	N/A
	A	72.79	N/A	N/A
	M	74.16	N/A	N/A
	J	75.90	N/A	N/A
	J	77.76	N/A	N/A
	A	80.13	N/A	N/A
	S	81.49	N/A	N/A
	O	82.57	N/A	N/A
	N	82.72	N/A	N/A
	D	84.40	2.10	N/A
1986	J	82.63	2.10	N/A
	F	82.50	2.13	N/A
	M	82.52	2.14	N/A
	A	86.29	2.15	N/A
	M	86.35	2.35	N/A
	J	88.85	2.45	N/A
	J	90.90	2.61	N/A
	A	91.70	2.63	N/A
	S	91.73	2.83	N/A
	O	92.64	3.28	N/A
	N	93.46	2.29	N/A
	D	100.03	3.59	N/A
1987	J	95.46	3.73	1.54
	F	95.08	3.46	1.20
	M	96.74	3.58	0.45
	A	98.72	2.59	0.40
	M	100.50	2.38	0.20
	J	102.78	2.37	0.21
	J	102.93	2.93	0.70

Source: GAO (1988) and data provided to the authors by the Federal Home Loan Bank
Board.

value insolvent, (4) has insufficient collateral to obtain an advance without a guarantee and (5) has agreed to be merged when FSLIC can find a suitable merger partner. Such advances are granted only for limited purposes—to meet net depositor withdrawals, fund outstanding loan commitments, repay borrowings that cannot be rolled over, renew advances, allow collateral to be retrieved during foreclosure proceedings or when mortgages become fully paid up, or for other specifically approved purposes.

The FSLIC obtains whatever (ineligible) collateral it can to secure the guarantees. There have been occasions, however, when the FSLIC has not been able even to obtain sufficient ineligible collateral. In these circumstances advances are sometimes made despite a shortage of collateral. Six FHLBanks made advances on the basis of FSLIC guarantees despite the fact that the insurance agency had been unable to obtain even sufficient ineligible collateral to secure its exposure. In January 1987, of the $3.73 billion of guaranteed advances, $1.54 billion were deficient in collateral.

FSLIC Insolvency

The GAO declared the FSLIC insolvent in March 1987. Thereafter, the agency was unable to provide new guarantees. Nevertheless, the deposit withdrawals at insolvent S & Ls continued to be a problem. The FHLBanks themselves were then forced to stretch beyond their previous notions of acceptable collateral to secure a loan. In this situation, FHLBB regulations decree that, "If eligible collateral for outstanding advances becomes deficient and the bank cannot correspondingly reduce the amount of the advances, it may obtain *any* collateral to strengthen its position." (U.S. CFR 525.9, 1987 *emphasis added.*)

ISSUES RELATED TO THE FHLBANKS' ACTIONS

Three major issues (two new and one recurring) have arisen in recent years with respect to the FHLBanks' provision of LLR assistance to troubled S & Ls. First, the FHLBanks have been more ready than the Federal Reserve to aid insolvent firms. Second, the FHLBanks have been lending to S & Ls that lack adequate collateral. Third, the FHLBanks are providing subsidized aid at below-market rates.

Table C-6. Dollar Values of Deposits and FHLBank Advances, All FSLIC-Insured Institutions, 1986.

Designation		Deposits (billions $)	Large CDs (billions $)	Brokered Deposits (billions $)	Advances (billions $)
Total Industry	Less than or = to 0%	108.98	9.53	4.92	14.17
	Between 0 and 3%	186.12	24.16	8.92	24.62
	Greater than 3%	595.17	82.93	30.27	61.26
	Total Industry	890.27	116.62	44.10	100.05
Alabama	Less than or = to 0%	1.48	0.10	0.00	0.05
	Between 0 and 3%	0.52	0.04	0.00	0.02
	Greater than 3%	4.78	0.70	0.08	0.38
	Total State	6.77	0.83	0.08	0.45
California	Less than or = to 0%	13.81	1.75	1.45	1.99
	Between 0 and 3%	39.81	8.68	5.37	7.72
	Greater than 3%	164.52	39.64	17.86	21.51
	Total State	218.14	50.07	24.69	31.22
Florida	Less than or = to 0%	6.27	0.94	0.37	0.62
	Between 0 and 3%	11.99	1.54	0.03	0.99
	Greater than 3%	45.87	5.28	1.05	4.61
	Total State	64.12	7.75	1.45	6.13
Louisiana	Less than or = to 0%	3.80	0.28	0.14	0.60
	Between 0 and 3%	3.14	0.19	0.03	0.11
	Greater than 3%	5.96	0.45	0.58	0.53
	Total State	12.90	0.92	0.75	1.23

THE S & L CRISIS OF 1985–87   275

Oklahoma	Less than or = to 0%	3.01	0.19	0.04	0.32
	Between 0 and 3%	1.84	0.21	0.01	0.23
	Greater than 3%	3.76	0.25	0.01	0.42
	Total State	8.61	0.65	0.06	0.96
Oregon	Less than or = to 0%	2.83	0.15	0.09	1.05
	Between 0 and 3%	0.24	0.02	0.00	0.02
	Greater than 3%	3.80	0.38	0.01	1.01
	Total State	6.87	0.55	0.11	2.08
Texas	Less than or = to 0%	26.37	2.27	1.93	3.49
	Between 0 and 3%	22.26	3.02	2.18	2.31
	Greater than 3%	31.68	4.34	2.76	2.44
	Total State	80.30	9.63	6.87	8.24

Source: Data derived by the authors from FHLBB Reports of Income and Condition.

Aid to Insolvent S & Ls

At the end of 1986, 14.2 percent of the $100.1 billion advances outstanding were held by insolvent thrifts. (See Table C–6.) On average, the 460 GAAP-insolvent S & Ls relied heavily on FHLBank advances at a time when they were suffering declines in total deposits, and especially in large CDs and brokered funds. (See Table C–4.) Advances rose sharply, particularly in those states such as Alabama, Florida, Oklahoma, Oregon, and Texas, which contained many problem S & Ls that were losing deposits. Consequently, advances funded a larger proportion of assets (14.2 percent) at insolvent S & Ls than nationwide, where the proportion was 8.6 percent. The reliance by insolvent S & Ls on advances was particularly heavy in California (13.5 percent), Louisiana (13.9 percent), Oregon (26.9 percent), and Texas (12.2 percent). In short, it appears that advances were being given in disproportionately large amounts to insolvent S & Ls and, in many circumstances, to replace lost deposits.

At the time these advances were made, these S & Ls had no guarantee that their problems would be resolved. Indeed, the FSLIC then had insufficient funds to take care of their problems. The Federal Reserve's latest pronouncement (Federal Reserve Bank of Cleveland 1986) in this regard said that aid would be given to insolvent firms only when some other governmental agency had guaranteed a resolution. In contrast, some FHLBanks have been lending to insolvent S & Ls (sometimes as lender of last resort and sometimes in the more normal course of business) without an effective guarantee of resolution. Where the FSLIC had provided guarantees for undercollateralized advances, these guarantees had been potentially worthless, given the FSLIC's approaching insolvency.

Collateral and FSLIC Guarantees

The classic, and the Federal Reserve, approach to LLR aid is to lend immediately to those that have good collateral to offer, while answers to questions about solvency are sought. The Fed has stretched beyond its usual list of acceptable collateral to attach bank buildings and foreign assets, but its policy is *not* to lend when there is inadequate or no collateral.

FHLBank regulations require collateral for advances. These regulations define what is "eligible" collateral. Nevertheless, some troubled S & Ls ran out of eligible collateral and used the FSLIC to guarantee their advances. Guarantees were sometimes secured by adequate but ineligible collateral, but sometimes by insufficient collateral.

Pricing Advances

The third departure from received LLR practice is the FHLBanks' provision of aid at below-market rates.

The twelve FHLBanks combine together to borrow in the capital markets. The facts that they have agency status and are well-capitalized allows them to borrow at a low risk premium. Each FHLBank individually sets the rate it charges for the advances it makes to its members. Rates are fixed at the time of issue but vary with maturity and date of commitment. They do *not* vary according to the economic condition of the borrowing thrift. Advances may not be priced below the rate that a large, well-capitalized thrift could obtain on its own account, particularly if its FHLBank is charging a high markup over cost of funds. But it would seem most likely that they are priced below market for insolvent thrifts, at least in some districts.

SUMMARY

Thus, the FHLBanks provided and still are providing aid to troubled S & Ls at below-market rates. This issue is not a new one, but has been a recurring problem for the Federal Reserve. Nevertheless, provision of Federal Reserve subsidies in the past have been relatively isolated events and the institutions in trouble have had their problems resolved. In the current S & L crisis, large numbers of insolvent institutions are being aided when no resolution for their problems was in sight. Moreover, aid has been inadequately collateralized in a number of cases.

These practices violate three of the classic and modern precepts for LLR aid. First, no penalty is being imposed. Second, aid is being given to insolvent firms that lack a foreseeable resolution. Indeed, the FHLBanks are subsidizing insolvent institutions, which is unfair to their healthy competitors (both banks and thrifts) and to society. Third, the FSLIC and possibly the FHLBanks are exposed by under-collateralized advances. The taxpayer may ultimately have to cover any losses from the risky activities of institutions allowed to continue in business with FHLBank assistance.

Questions Remaining

Dangerous precedents have been set by FHLBank practices regarding the use of advances and it was not clear, as of September 1987, that the FSLIC, even after recap, can move fast enough to close, reorganize, or merge failed S & Ls that are experiencing deposit withdrawals. Several questions remain to be addressed about how the liquidity needs of 460 thrifts that were insolvent at the end of 1986 can be met during the remainder of 1987 and beyond.

Will the FHLBanks carry the burden despite their legal obligation to lend only to "creditworthy" members and their perceived obligation to make positive profits for their member institutions?[7] If the FHLBanks do not lend to stem any runs, or if one or more of the regional FHLBanks exhausts its capacity to lend, will resources be transferred from still solvent and liquid FHLBanks to the troubled bank?[8] Will the FSLIC lend to thrifts experiencing runs? Would the FSLIC's resources then be sufficient to meet depositor withdrawals?

Will the Federal Reserve again be drawn into the arena? If so, should it lend directly to the troubled S & Ls despite their lack of collateral? Should the Fed lend to the FHLBanks which have collateral but no legal obligation to aid their insolvent members? Should the Fed lend to the FSLIC, which may still, even after recap, have insufficient collateral to pledge for Fed lending? Should the Fed buy the bonds issued under recap if they do not sell well in the market? Such purchases might present problems as there are constraints on the types of assets that the Fed can hold in its portfolio. It is obligated to hold Treasury securities to back the stock of currency in circulation. Recap bonds are not Treasury securities and the 1987 act explicitly states that they do not carry the full faith and credit of the United States.

Neither the FHLBanks nor the FSLIC are depository institutions under the MCA, so the Fed would need to use its extended authority to lend, with Board approval, under Section 13.3 of the Federal Reserve Act (or with rigid collateral under Section 13.13). The S & L crisis of 1986–7 has raised many questions, which still remain unanswered.

NOTES

1. The DIDMCA of 1980 had earlier relaxed some restraints on S & L portfolios.
2. The term "zombie" was first used by Professor Edward Kane. Garcia and Polakoff (1987) characterize a "zombie" as an unprofitable and seriously insolvent S & L.
3. Deposit levels were relatively stable over this period, however, because interest credited to depositors' accounts roughly balanced deposit withdrawals.
4. H.R. 27 is inappropriately named. It has been characterized as neither pro-competitive nor equitable.
5. The *Wall Street Journal*, 18 August 1987 said that FCA had repaid $1 billion of its $3.1 billion advance from the FHLBank of San Francisco.
6. RAP-net worth exaggerates the accounting measure of capital because it includes deferred losses, appraised equity capital, income capital, and net worth certificates.
7. A senior official of one of the FHLBanks, in conversation, has stated that his bank's mission is to make money for its members and *not* to provide LLR assistance to member thrifts in difficulties.
8. The FHLBB instructed the Federal Home Loan Mortgage Corporation (Freddie Mac) to lend via repurchase agreements to Financial Corporation of America from 1984 onwards to help meet the thrift's liquidity needs.

REFERENCES

Aliber, Robert Z. 1985. "External Shocks and Financial Stability." *The Search for Financial Stability: The Past Fifty Years.* San Francisco: Federal Reserve Bank of San Francisco, June.

———. 1987a. "Bagehot, The Lender of Last Resort, and the International Financial System." University of Chicago. Unpublished paper.

———. 1987b. Comments on a draft of this book, June 1987.

Anderson, William J. 1987. Statement before the Subcommittee on Commerce, Consumer Protection, and Competitiveness, House Committee on Energy and Commerce, October 14.

Avery, R., G. Elliehausen, A. Kendell, and P. Spindt. 1986. "The Use of Cash and Transactions Accounts by American Families." *Federal Reserve Bulletin* (February).

Bagehot, Walter. 1873. *Lombard Street: A Description of the Money Market.* New York: Scribner, Armstrong. Reprint. Homewood, Ill.: Dow Jones-C Irwin, 1962.

———. 1921. *Lombard Street: A Description of the Money Market.* Edited by Harley Withers. New York: E.P. Dutton and Company.

Barth, James, R. Daniel Brumbaugh, and Daniel Saueraft. 1986. "Failure Cost of Government Regulated Financial Firms: The Case of Thrift Institutions." Research Working Paper #123. Office of Policy and Economic Research, Federal Home Loan Bank Board. Washington, D.C. October.

Barth, James R., and Robert E. Keleher. 1984a. "Financial Crises and the Role of the Lender of Last Resort." Federal Reserve Bank of Atlanta, *Economic Review* (January): 58–67.

———. 1984b. "Is There a Role for an International Lender of Last Resort?" *Journal of Bank Research* (November/December).

281

Baumol, William, J. 1986. *Superfairness*. Cambridge: MIT Press.

Beckhart, Benjamin Haggott. 1972. *The Federal Reserve System*. New York: American Institute of Banking.

Bennett, Barbara. 1986. "Off-Balance Sheet Risk in Banking: The Case of Stand-by Letters of Credit." Federal Reserve Bank of San Francisco, *Economic Review*. (Winter): 19-29.

Benston, George J., Robert A. Eisenbeis, Paul M. Horvitz, Edward J. Kane, and George C. Kaufman. 1986. *Perspectives on Safe and Sound Banking: Past Present and Future*. Study commissioned by the American Bankers Association. Cambridge, Mass.: The MIT Press.

Benston, George J., and George G. Kaufman. 1987. "Risk and Solvency Regulation of Depository Institutions: Past Policies and Current Options." Paper presented at the American Enterprise Institute Conference on the Financial Markets, November.

Bernanke, Ben S. 1983. "Nonmonetary Effects of the Financial Crisis in the Propagation of the Great Depression." *American Economic Review* 73, no. 3 (June).

Board of Governors of the Federal Reserve. 1966. *annual Report.*

_____. 1970. *Annual Report.*

_____. 1971. *Reappraisal of the Discount Window Mechanism.*

_____. 1978. *1973-1977 Annual Statistical Digest.*

_____. 1980. *The Federal Reserve Discount Window.*

_____. 1982. *Annual Report.*

_____. 1985. *Federal Reserve Bulletin.* January.

_____. 1986a. *Federal Reserve Bulletin.* February.

_____. 1986b. *Flow of Accounts, Financial Assets and Liabilities Outstanding Year-End 1962-85.*

Booth, James R., Richard L. Smith, and Richard W. Stoltz. 1984. "Use of Interest Rate Futures by Financial Institutions." *Journal of Bank Research* 15 (Spring): 15-20.

Brimmer, Andrew F. 1976. "International Finance and the Management of Bank Failure: Herstatt vs. Franklin National." Presentation before a joint session of the American Economic Association and the American Finance Association, September 16.

_____. 1984. "The Federal Reserve as Lender of Last Resort: The Containment of Systemic Risks." Paper presented at the American Economic Association Meeting, December 29.

Cargill, Thomas F., and Gillian G. Garcia. 1985. *Financial Reform in the 1980s.* Stanford, Calif.: Hoover Institution Press.

Carron, Andrew S. 1982. "Financial Crises: Recent Experience in U.S. and International Markets." *Brookings Papers on Economic Activity* 2: 395-418.

Commodity Futures Trading Commission. 1981. *Report to the Congress in Response to Section 21 of the Commodity Exchange Act.* Pub. L. No. 96-276, 96th Cong., 2d sess., Section 7, 94 Stst. 542, June 29.

Cone, Kenneth. 1982. "Regulation of Depository Financial Institutions." Ph.D. Diss., Stanford University (November).

Conover, C.T. 1984. Statement before the House Committee on Banking, Finance and Urban Affairs, September 19.

Corrigan, Gerald E. 1982. "Are Banks Special?" *Annual Report.* Minneapolis: Federal Reserve Bank of Minneapolis.

_____. 1983. *Banks Are Special.* New York: Federal Reserve Bank of New York.

_____. 1985. Statement before the Subcommittee on Domestic Monetary Policy of the House Committee on Banking, Finance and Urban Affairs, December 12 (reprinted in *Federal Reserve Bulletin*, February 1986).

_____. 1987. *Financial Market Structure: A Longer View.* New York: Federal Reserve Bank of New York, January.

Dale, Richard. 1982a. *Bank Supervision Around the World.* New York: The Group of Thirty.

Dale, Richard. 1982b. "Safeguarding the International Banking System." *The Banker* (August).

Diamond, D.W., and P.H. Dybvig. 1983. "Bank Runs, Deposit Insurance and Liquidity." *Journal of Political Economy* 91: 401-19.

Eisenbeis, Robert A. 1983. "How Should Bank Holding Companies Be Regulated?" Federal Reserve Bank of Atlanta, *Quarterly Review* (January): 42-47.

Ely, Bert. 1985. "Yes, Private Sector Depositor Protection Is a Viable Alternative to Federal Deposit Insurance." Federal Reserve Bank of Chicago, *Proceedings of a Conference on Bank Structure and Competition*: 338-53.

England, Catherine. 1985. "A Proposal for Introducing Private Deposit Insurance." Federal Reserve Bank of Chicago, *Proceedings of a Conference on Bank Structure and Competition*: 316-37.

Fama, Eugene E. 1980. "Banking Regulation in the Theory of Finance." *Journal of Monetary Economics* 6 (January): 39-58.

Federal Deposit Insurance Corporation. 1986. *Reports of Income and Condition.* Schedule RC-1—Commitments and Contingencies. New York. December.

Federal Home Loan Bank Board. 1982. *Savings and Home Financing Source Book.* Washington, D.C.

_____. 1986. *Savings and Home Financing Source Book.* Washington, D.C.

Federal Home Loan Bank System. 1987. *A Guide to the Federal Home Loan Bank System.* Washington, D.C.: FHLBS.

Federal Reserve Act. 1913. 12 U.S.C. Chapter 6, 38 Stat. 251. Washington, D.C., December 23, 1913 and subsequent amendments.

Federal Reserve Bank of Cleveland. 1986. *Annual Report for 1985.* Cleveland: Federal Reserve Bank.

Federal Reserve Bank of Chicago. 1985. "Operating Circular No. 10." Chicago: Federal Reserve Bank. Revised March 8.

Federal Reserve Bank of New York. 1983. *Annual Report.*

_____. 1983. "Monetary Policy and Open Market Operations in 1982." *Quarterly Review* 18, no. 1 (Spring): 37–54.

_____. 1985. *Annual Report.*

_____. 1985. *Fedpoints 37: Security Loans to Dealers.* New York: FRB.

_____. 1986. *Recent Trends in Commercial Bank Profitability: A Staff Study.* New York: FRB.

Federal Reserve Board. 1914. *Annual Report.* Washington, D.C.: FRB.

Friedman, Milton, and Anna J. Schwartz. 1963. *A Monetary History of the United States: 1876–1960.* Princeton: Princeton University Press.

Garcia, Gillian G. 1987a. "The 1985 S & L Crises in Ohio and Maryland." Unpublished paper, August.

_____. 1987b. "FSLIC Is 'Broke' in More Ways Than One. In Catherine England and Thomas Huertas, eds., *The Financial Services Revolution: Policy Directions for the Future.* Norwell, Mass.: Kluwer Academic Publishers, 235–49.

_____. 1988. "Lessons from the Crash of '87: Systemic Issues." Federal Reserve Bank of Chicago, *Proceedings of a Conference on Bank Structure and Competition* (forthcoming).

Garcia, Gillian G., and Elizabeth Plautz. 1987. "The Failure of Continental Illinois National Bank." Unpublished paper, July.

Garcia, Gillian, and Michael Polakoff. 1987. "Does Capital Forbearance Pay and If So, For Whom?" Federal Reserve Bank of Chicago, *Proceedings of a Conference on Bank Structure and Competition:* 285–305.

Goldfeld, Stephen M., Dwight M. Jaffee, and Richard E. Quandt. 1980. "A Model of FHLBB Advances: Rationing or Market Clearing?" *Review of Economics and Statistics* 62, no. 3 (August): 339–47.

Goodfriend, Marvin, and Robert G. King. 1987. "Financial Deregulation, Monetary Policy, and Central Banking." Paper presented at the American Enterprise Institute Conference on the Financial Markets, November.

Guttentag, Jack. 1987. "Financial Innovations and the Merging of Commercial and Investment Banking Activities." Federal Reserve Bank of Chicago, *Proceedings of a Conference on Bank Structure and Competition:* 41–48.

Guttentag, Jack, and Richard Herring. 1983. *The Lender of Last Resort Function in an International Context.* Essays in International Finance, No. 151. Princeton, N.J.: Princeton University. May.

Hackley, Howard H. 1973. *Lending Functions of the Federal Reserve Banks: A History.* Washington, D.C.: Federal Reserve Board.

Havrilesky, Thomas M., and John T. Boorman. 1976. *Current Issues in Monetary Theory and Policy.* Arlington Heights, Ill.: AMH Publishing Corporation.

Hirschhorn, Eric. 1985. "Bidding Levels in Purchase and Assumption Auctions." Federal Reserve Bank of Chicago, *Proceedings of a Conference on Bank Structure and Competiton:* 369–388.

Horne, Karen. 1985. Statement before the Subcommittee on Commerce, Consumer, and Monetary Affairs of the House Committee on Government Operations, April 3.

Horvitz, Paul M. 1987. "Determining the Exceptions to the Rule in Capital Forbearance." *American Banker* (June 12): 4.

Humphrey, David B. 1985. "Payment Finality and Risk of Settlement Failure: Implications for Financial Markets." Draft, May 13.

Humphrey, Thomas M. 1975. "The Classical Concept of the Lender of Last Resort." Federal Reserve Bank of Richmond, *Economic Review* (January/February): 1–15.

Jaffe Stephen, and Richard Quandt. 1980. "A Model of FHLBB Advances: Rationing or Market Clearing?" *Review of Economic and Statistics* 62, no. 3 (August): 347–57.

James, Christopher. 1987a. "Are Bank Loans Special?" Federal Reserve Bank of San Francisco, *Weekly Letter*, July 24.

_____. 1987b. "Some Evidence on the Uniqueness of Bank Loans." *Journal of Financial Economics* 19, no. 2 (December): 217–36.

Jones, Jesse H. with Edward Angly. 1951. *Fifty Billion Dollars: My Thirteen Years with the RFC (1932–1945).* New York: The Macmillan Company.

Kane, Edward J. 1986a. "Appearance and Reality in Deposit Insurance: The Case for Reform." *Journal of Banking and Finance* 10, no. 2 (June): 169–225.

_____. 1986b. *The Gathering Crisis in Deposit Insurance.* Cambridge, Mass.: MIT Press.

_____. 1987a. Comments on a draft of this book (June).

_____. 1987b. "Who Should Learn What from the Failure and Delayed Bailout of the ODGF," Federal Reserve Bank of Chicago, *Conference on Bank Structure and Competition*: 306–26.

Kareken, John H. 1985. "Ensuring Financial Stability." *The Search for Financial Stability: The Past Fifty Years.* Federal Reserve Bank of San Francisco, June.

Kaufman, George G. 1987. "The Truth About Bank Runs." In Catherine England and Thomas Huertas, eds., *The Financial Services Revolution: Policy Directions for the Future.* Norwell, Mass.: Kluwer Academic Publishers, 9–40.

Kaufman, George C., Larry R. Mote, and Harvey Rosenblum. 1983. "The Future of Commercial Banks in the Financial Services Industry" in *Financial Services: The Changing Institutions and Government Policy.* Edited by George J. Benston. Englewood Cliffs: The American Assembly, Columbia University. Prentice-Hall Inc.

Kennedy, Susan Estabrook. 1973. *The Banking Crisis of 1933.* Lexington: University of Kentucky Press.

Kent, Richard J. 1983. "The Demand for Federal Home Loan Bank Advances by Savings and Loan Associations." *Housing Finance Review* 2, no. 3 (July): 191–208.

Kindleburger, Charles P. 1985. "Bank Failure: The 1930s and the 1980s." In *The Search for Financial Stability: The Past Fifty Years.* San Francisco: Federal Reserve Bank of San Francisco, June.

Koehn, Michael, and Anthony M. Santomero. 1980. "Regulation of Bank Capital and Portfolio Risk." *Journal of Finance* (December).

Koppenhaver, Gary D. 1987. "Standby Letters of Credit." Federal Reserve Bank of Chicago, *Economic Perspectives.* (July/August): 28–38.

Lanier, Henry W. 1922. "A Century of Banking in New York: 1822–1922." New York: George H. Doran.

Litan, Robert E. 1987. *What Should Banks Do?* Washington, D.C.: The Brookings Institution.

Longstreth, Bevis. 1983. "In Search of a Safety Net for the Financial Services Industry." *The Bankers Magazine* 166 (July/August).

Maisel, sherman J. 1973. *Managing the Dollar.* New York: W.W. Norton and Company.

McCall, Alan S., and Victor L. Saulsbury. 1986. "The Changing Role of Banks and Other Private Financial Institutions." Federal Deposit Insurance Corporation, *Regulatory Review* (April): 1–7.

McCulloch, Huston, J. 1987. "The Ohio Crisis in Retrospect: Implications for the Current Federal Deposit Insurance Crisis." Federal Reserve Bank of Chicago, *Conference on Bank Structure and Competition*: 230–51.

Melton, William. 1985. *Inside the Fed: Making Monetary Policy.* Homewood: Dow Jones-Irwin.

Meltzer, Allan H. 1986. "Financial Failures and Financial Policies." In George, G. Kaufman and Roger C. Kormendi, eds., *Deregulating Financial Services: Public Policy in Flux.* Cambridge: Ballinger Publishing Co.

Merrick, John, and Stephen Figlewski. 1984. *An Introduction to Financial Futures.* Occasional Papers in Business and Finance #6. New York: Salomon Brothers Center for the Study of Financial Institutions, Graduate School of Business, New York University.

Minsky, Hyman P. 1977. "A Theory of Systemic Fragility." In Edward I. Altman and Arnold W. Sametz, eds., *Financial Crises: Institutions and Markets in a Fragile Environment.* New York: John Wiley.

Miron, Jeffrey A. 1986. "Financial Panics, the Seasonality of the Nominal Interest Rate, and the Founding of the Fed." *American Economic Review* 76 (March): 125–40.

Morrissey, Thomas F. 1971. "The Demand for Mortgage Loans and the Concomitant Demand for Home Loan Bank Advances by Savings and Loan Associations." *Journal of Finance* (June): 687–98;

Nash, Nathaniel. 1986. "Mending the Financial Safety Net." *New York Times,* October 7.

Okun, Arthur M. 1975. *Equality and Efficiency: The Big Tradeoff.* Washington, D.C.: The Brookings Institution.

Partee, J. Charles. 1980. "Interim Report on Financial Aspects of the Silver Market Situation in Early 1980." Senate Committee on Banking, Housing and Urban Affairs, May 21.

Patinkin, Don. 1965. *Money, Interest and Prices: An Integration of Monetary and Value Theory,* 2d ed. New York: Harper and Row.

Regulation A. 1980. 12 CFR Subchapter A. Part 201—Extensions of Credit by Federal Reserve Banks. Washington, D.C.: U.S. Government Printing Office.

Reid, Margaret. 1982. *The Secondary Banking Crisis 1973-75.* London, England: MacMillan.

Robertson, Ross M. 1968. *The Comptroller and Bank Supervision: A Historical Appraisal.* Washington, D.C.: Office of the Comptroller of the Currency.

Saunders, Anthony. 1987. "Bank Holding Companies: Structure, Performance, and Reform." Paper presented at the American Enterprise Institute Conference on the Financial Markets (November).

Schwartz, Anna J. 1987a. Comments on a draft of this book (June).

_____ . 1987b. "The Lender of Last Resort and the Federal Safety Net." *Journal of Financial Services Research* 1, no. 1 (October): 1-17.

_____ . 1987c. "Financial Stability and the Federal Safety Net." Paper presented at the American Enterprise Institute Conference on the Financial Markets, (November).

Shafer, Jeffery R. 1982. "The Theory of a Lender of Last Resort In International Banking Markets." *Recent Developments in the Economic Analysis of the Euro-Markets.* (September): 127-45.

Silber, William L. 1973. "A Model of Federal Home Loan Bank System and Federal National Mortgage Association Behavior." *Review of Economics and Statistics,* 53, no. 3 (August): 308-20.

Sinai, Alan. 1976. "Credit Crunches—An Analysis of the Postwar Experience." In Otto Eckstein ed., *Parameters and Policies in the U.S. Economy,* Data Resources Series, Vol. 2. Amsterdam: North Holland, 244-74.

Singer, Mark. 1985. *Funny Money.* New York: Alfred A. Knopf.

Sinkey, Joseph F., Jr. 1976. "The Collapse of Franklin National Bank of New York." *Journal of Bank Research* (Summer): 113-22.

_____ . 1986. *Commercial Bank Financial Management in the Financial Services Industry,* 2d ed. New York: Macmillan Publishing Company.

Spero, Joan Edward. 1980. *The Failure of Franklin National Bank.* New York: Columbia University Press.

Sprague, Irvin H. 1986. *Bailout: An Insider's Account of Bank Failures and Rescues.* New York: Basic Books Inc.

Thompson, James B., and Walker F. Todd. 1987. "Interbank Exposure in the Fourth District." Unpublished paper, Federal Reserve Bank of Cleveland.

Thornton, Henry. 1939. *An Inquiry into the Nature and Effects of the Paper Credit of Great Britain (1802).* New York: Rienhart and Co., Inc.

Timberlake, Richard, H. Jr. 1984. "The Central Banking Role of Clearinghouse Associations." *Journal of Money, Credit and Banking* 16, no. 1 (February): 1–15.

Todd, Walker F. 1986. "Outline of an Argument on Solvency." Unpublished paper, October 22.

U.S. Congress. House of Representatives. 1981. Committee on Government Operations. *Silver Prices and the Adequacy of Federal Actions in the Marketplace 1979–80.* Washington, D.C.: Government Printing Office.

_____. 1984. *Inquiry into Continental Illinois Corp. and Continental Illinois National Bank.* Hearing Before the Subcommittee on Financial Institutions Supervision, Regulation and Insurance, Committee on Banking, Finance and Urban Affairs, Serial No. 98–111, September 18, 19 and October 4.

_____. 1985. Committee on Banking, Finance and Urban Affairs. "The Federal Reserve Bank of New York Discount Window Advance of $22.6 Billion Extended to the Bank of New York." Serial No. 99–65, December 12.

U.S. General Accounting Office. 1982. *Examination of Financial Statements of the Federal Home Loan Bank Board and Related Agencies.* GAO/AFMD-82–58, March.

_____. 1983. *Examination of Financial Statements of the Federal Home Loan Bank Board and Related Agencies.* GAO/AFMD-83–65, April.

_____. 1984a. *Federal Financial Institutions Examination Council Has Made Limited Progress Toward Accomplishing Its Mission.* GAO/GGD-84–4, February 3.

_____. 1984b. *Guidelines for Rescuing Large Failing Firms and Municipalities.* GAO/GGD-84–34, March 29.

_____. 1984c. *Examination of Financial Statements of the Federal Home Loan Bank Board and Related Agencies.* GAO/AFMD-84–47, May.

_____. 1984d. "Comparison of the Elements of the Continental Illinois Rescue with GAO's Large Loan Guarantee Guidelines Report: More Lessons Learned?" Memo, December.

_____. 1985. *Examination of Financial Statements of the Federal Home Loan Bank Board and Related Agencies.* GAO/AFMD-85–60, July.

_____. 1986a. *Thrift Industry Problems: Potential Demands on the FSLIC Insurance Fund.* GAO/GGD 86–48BR, February.

_____. 1986b. *Financial Services: Information on Nonbank Banks.* GAO/GGD 86–46FS, March 21.

_____. 1986c. *Financial Audit: Federal Savings and Loan Insurance Corporation's 1985 and 1984 Financial Statements.* GAO/AFMD-86–65, July.

_____. 1986d. *U.S. Treasury Securities: The Markets, Structure, Risks and Regulation.* GAO/GGD-86–80BR, August 20.

_____. 1986e. *Deposit Insurance: Analysis of Reform Proposals.* GAO/GGD 86–32, September.

_____. 1987a. *Thrift Industry: The Treasury/Federal Home Loan Bank Board Plan for FSLIC Recapitalization.* GAO/GGD-87–46BR, March.

_____ . 1987b. *Financial Audit: Federal Savings and Loan Insurance Corporation's 1986 and 1985 Financial Statements*. GAO/AFMD-87-41, May.

_____ . 1987c. *Financial Services: Developments in the Financial Guarantee Industry*. GAO/GGD-87-74, May 25.

_____ . 1987d. *Thrift Industry: Forbearance for Troubled Institutions 1982–1986*. GAO/GGD-87-78BR, May.

_____ . 1987e. *Thrift Industry: The Management Consignment Program*. GAO/GGD-87–115BR, September.

_____ . 1988. *Thrift Industry: FHLBank Advances Program*. GAO/GGD-88-46BR, March.

U.S. Securities and Exchange Commission. 1982. *The Silver Crisis of 1980*. Staff Study, October.

Volcker, Paul A. 1984. Statement before the Senate Committee on Banking, Housing and Urban Affairs, Washington, D.C., July 25.

_____ . 1985. Statement before the Subcommittee on Domestic Monetary Policy, House Committee on Banking, Finance and Urban Affairs, December 12 (reprinted in *Federal Reserve Bulletin*, February 1986).

Wille, Frank. 1974. *The FDIC and Franklin National Bank: A Report to Congress and all FDIC Insured Banks*. Boca Raton, Fla.: Savings Bank Association Convention. November 23.

Wolfson, Martin H. 1986. *Financial Crises: Understanding the Post War U.S. Experience*. Armonk and London: M.E. Sharpe, Inc.

Zweig, Phillip L. 1985. *Belly Up: The Collapse of the Penn Square Bank*. New York: Crown Publishers, Inc.

INDEX

Access to assistance
  evaluation criteria for equity and,
    114–115
  Federal Reserve and, 148
  portfolio composition and, 115
  region or organization structure and,
    115, 149
  reserve requirements and, 182–183
  runs and, 209–210
  size and type of business and, 115,
    148–149
Access to information, *see* Informa-
    tion access
Accountability of Federal Reserve,
    173–175
  credibility of central bank and,
    174–175
  secrecy of central bank and,
    173–174
Adjustment credit, 46
Advances
  collateral requirements for, 269
  Federal Home Loan Bank
    (FHLBank) System use of,
    265–268, 276
  Federal Savings and Loan Insurance
    Corporation (FSLIC) guarantees
    of, 269–273, 276
  pricing of, 277
Aldrich-Vreeland Act of 1908, 35

Aliber, Robert Z., 19, 40 n. 1, 87, 88,
    89, 95 n. 20, 96 n. 22, 96 n. 23,
    106, 118, 121, 141
Anderson, William J., 95 n. 17, 165
Assets
  complexity of transactions with, 85
  costs of resolution and, 164, 165
  credit crunch and, 210
  delay in bank failure and, 162
  Franklin National Bank bidding
    package and, 221–222
  insolvency and values of, 10
  policy choices involving, 170
  securitization of, 85, 182
Avery, R., 93 n. 2

Bache Group Inc., 133
Bache Securities, 136, 144
Bache, Halsey, Stuart, Shields, Inc.,
    133, 245, 246, 249, 250, 252
Bagehot, Walter, 21, 22, 23, 24, 25,
    26, 27, 59, 101, 102, 103, 105,
    111, 112, 115, 146
Bank failures
  case studies of, 213–279
  "catch 22" situation in assistance to,
    163–164
  central bank neutralization of, 24,
    58, 59
  contagion and, 18–20

costs of resolution of, 164–165
creation of Federal Deposit Insur-
    ance Corporation (FDIC) and, 2–3
definition of, 12
delay in acknowledgement of, 161,
    162–163
delay in assistance for, 158–159, 164
domestic precedents for, 213–214
Franklin National Bank case study
    of, 217–231
information needs on, 104–105
international precedents for,
    214–215
liquidation costs and, 202–203
management changes in, 165–166
market discipline and, 167–168, 170
number of (1921–1933), 2 (table)
number of (1934–1987), 4–5 (table)
receivership for, 166
as a regulatory decision, 12
reorganization of bank in, 163
risk-taking incentives and, 113, 153
savings and loan association (S & L)
    crises and, 257–279
silver crisis case study of, 233–256
speed of assistance in, 99–101, 124,
    128–130
spillover prevention and, 108–110,
    125
stockholders and, 170
see also Savings and loan association
    (S & L) crises and specific
    incidents
Bankhaus Herstatt, 217, 219
Bank holding companies, 145,
    175–176
Bank holidays, 2–3, 38, 145, 196, 204
Banking Act of 1933, 42
Banking system, see Commercial banks
Bank of America, 86, 108
Bank of England, 2, 21, 22, 23, 25,
    26, 75, 106, 112, 144, 163, 229,
    230
Bank of New York (BONY), 51, 56,
    70–71, 82–84, 100, 103, 130,
    133, 140, 171, 196
Bank runs, see Runs on banks
Bankruptcy
    financial crisis and, 11, 135
    size of bank and, 66
Banks, see Commercial banks and
    specific banks

Barth, James R., 13 n. 4, 21, 22, 26,
    40 n. 1, 103
Baumol, William J., 98, 185
Beckhart, Benjamin Haggort, 40 n. 10
Bennett, 94 n. 12
Benston, George J., 8, 12, 40 n. 1,
    40 n. 2, 40 n. 3, 101, 113, 126
    n. 2, 147, 150, 162, 167, 186 n. 9,
    186 n. 10
Bernanke, Ben S., 39, 73, 94 n. 8, 209
Biddle, Nicholas, 113
Board of Governors of the Federal
    Reserve, 46, 47, 48, 54, 59, 60,
    62 n. 11, 63 n. 24, 83, 132, 134,
    136, 145, 155 n. 19, 224, 227
collateral requirements and, 50
comprehensiveness of coverage and,
    131, 132, 135, 136, 137
discount rate and, 54
discount window loans and, 47, 48
early Federal Reserve and, 36
indirect assistance from the Federal
    Reserve and, 131
public confidence and, 145
silver crisis (1980) and, 25, 255
Boorman, John T., 40 n. 4
Booth, James R., 85
Brevill, Bresler and Schulman, 108
Brimmer, Andrew F., 21, 22, 40 n. 1,
    135, 144, 156 n. 26, 186 n. 17,
    220, 224, 225, 231 n. 1, 231 n. 3,
    248, 255

Call reports, 89, 142–143
Capital
    bank holidays and, 204
    delay in bank failure and, 162
    Federal Reserve supply of working,
        137
    forbearance of, 203–204
    off-balance sheet liabilities and
        adequacy of, 75
    interdependency of banks and, 88
Cargill, Thomas F., 6, 257, 259
Carron, Andrew S., 9, 10, 155 n. 12,
    220
Cash insolvency, 11
Central bank
    advantages of, 207–208
    bank failures and, 214–215
    collateral accepted by, 25–26, 57,
        59–60

credibility of, 174–175
early history of, 28–32
effectiveness of, 99
evaluation criteria and, 98
future directions for, 193–194
lender of last resort concept and,
  22–28, 191, 207–208
lending freely for liquidity by,
  24–25, 57, 59
lending to all borrowers by, 25, 57,
  59
less developed countries (LDCs) and
  international debt and, 72
liquidity policy and monetary policy
  and, 57, 58
market assurances from, 27, 57, 60
monetary policy and, 180
moral hazard issues and confidentiality policy of, 173–174
penalty rates used by, 26–27, 57, 60
policies and procedures of, 146
prevention of systemwide failures
  by, 24, 58, 59
public confidence in financial systems and, 111, 146
responsibility to whole monetary
  system of, 23–24, 57, 58
risk-taking incentives for, 112–113
size of assistance from, 103
speedy and short-term assistance
  from, 23, 57, 58
Central Liquidity Authority, NCUA,
  31, 42, 43, 49, 160
Certificates of deposit (CDs)
  international debt and, 73
  managed liabilities and, 82
Charters
  First Bank of the United States, 28,
    29
  Second Bank of the United States, 29
  state banking systems and, 33–34,
    43, 44
Chatsworth Corporation, 95
Chicago Board of Trade (CBOT), 240,
  244, 245
Chicago Federal Reserve Bank, 55,
  145
Chrysler Corporation, 136, 165
Citibank, 72
Citicorp, 82, 94 n. 6, 95 n. 16
Clearing House Interbank Payments
  System (CHIPS), 69

Clearinghouses, and lender of last
  resort concept, 29, 34–35, 190
Clements, Bill, 263
Cleveland Federal Reserve Bank, 50,
  101, 128–129, 138, 139, 146, 184,
  276
Collateral
  central bank acceptance of, 25–26,
    57, 59–60
  collateralization ratio and, 50
  concerns and issues with, 159–160
  fairness in requirements for, 116,
    150–152
  Federal Home Loan Bank and, 152,
    159–160, 161, 269, 273, 276–277
  Federal Reserve and, 49–54, 59–60,
    150–152, 278–279
  Franklin National Bank and, 225,
    230
  guidelines on, 50–52
  information access for evaluation of,
    141–142
  liquidation costs and, 202–203
  non-depository financial institutions
    (NDFIs) and individuals, partner-
    ships, and corporations (IPCs) and,
    52–53, 150–151, 183–184
  policy choices affecting, 171
  pricing assistance and, 171
  savings and loan association (S & L)
    crises and, 185, 269, 273, 278–279
  valuation of posted, 151–152
Collateralization ratio, 50
Collateral Work Group, Federal
  Reserve, 51
Commercial and industrial (C & I)
  loan, 211
Commercial banks
  changes in financial markets and,
    177–178
  comparison statistics on concentra-
    tion in, 107–108
  complexity of financial transactions
    and, 84–87
  concentration of deposits in,
    106–107
  creation of Federal Deposit Insur-
    ance Corporation (FDIC) and, 2–3
  credit crunch and, 131
  discount window loan access by,
    53–54
  economy and role of, 90–92

electronic funds transfer and, 81–84, 178
failures of, *see* Bank failures
Federal Reserve focus on, 178, 179–180
financial crises and pressure on, 135–136
financial system safety net and, 42
information on collateral from, 134
insolvency of, *see* Insolvency
interdependency and, 87–89
as "lenders of next to last resort," 9, 210
less developed countries (LDCs) and international debt and, 72, 136–137
liquidity and, 180
market share to non-bank financial institutions and, 90, 91 (table)
mergers and, 203
monetary policy and, 179–180
need for lender of last resort by, 16–17
off-balance sheet liabilities and, 74–77
off-balance sheet risk and, 80–81
runs on, *see* Runs on banks
short-term business credit and, 90–91, 92 (table)
silver crisis and, 144
specialness of, 179–180, 210–211
standby letters of credit (SLC) and, 77–80
suspensions of, 204–205
tiering of, 19, 100
Commodity Exchange Inc. (COMEX), 144, 177, 240, 242, 244, 245, 246, 252, 255
Commodity Futures Trading Commission (CFTC), 155 n. 24, 188 n. 27, 237, 241, 242
Community Savings and Loan Association, 86
Competitive Equality Banking Act of 1987, 1, 176–177, 262
Complexity of financial transactions, 84–87
Comprehensiveness of coverage
evaluation criteria for effectiveness and, 101, 124
Federal Reserve performance in, 130–137

indirect assistance and, 131
individuals, partnerships, and corporations (IPCs) and, 131, 135–137
insolvency and, 101
lender of last resort and, 101
member banks and, 130–131
non-depository financial institutions (NDFIs) and, 101, 133–135
nonmember depository institutions and, 101, 131–133
Comptroller of the Currency, 43, 104–105, 106, 149, 219, 220, 221
Computer failure, and Bank of New York (BONY), 82–84, 100, 130
Concentration of deposits, 106–108, 121
Cone, Kenneth, 40 n. 3
Congress
bank failures and, 3, 12
clearinghouses and, 335
Federal Reserve and, 48, 102, 118, 174
Federal Savings and Loan Insurance Corporation (FSLIC) and, 262–263
financial and economic stability maintained by, 43
financial legislation of, 1
House of Representatives of, 61 n. 7, 16, 171, 187 n. 16, 251, 252, 253, 254
lender of last resort and, 28, 38, 105, 195
money creation and, 44
non-bank banks and, 176–177
Reconstruction Finance Corporation (RFC) and, 38
savings and loan association (S & L) crises and, 259, 262–263
silver crisis (1980) and, 253, 254–255
size of financial assistance and, 103
societal interests and, 117
state banking systems and, 33
Conover, C. T., 19
Constitution, 28
Contagion
bank failures and, 18–20
bank size and, 159
Federal Reserve efforts to prevent, 166–167, 208
Franklin National Bank and, 220

interdependency of banks and, 87, 89
spillover prevention and, 108–109
ContiCommodity Services, Inc., 240, 242, 245
Continental Illinois National Bank, 17, 19, 55, 74, 81–82, 100, 110, 129, 144, 149, 164, 165, 174, 199, 208, 213, 214
duration of assistance to, 102, 138
extent of assistance in, 176
size of assistance to, 139
Core deposits, 82, 83, 84, 121
Corrigan, Gerald E., 62 n. 23, 71, 84, 89, 133, 171, 179, 186, 187 n. 15, 188 n. 5, 254
Costs
bank failures and rescue and, 12–13
bank holidays and, 204
capital forbearance and, 203–204
complexity of transactions and, 86–87
concerns and issues with assistance and, 54–57
Federal Home Loan Bank System assistance and, 161
financial system safety net and, 168
lender of last resort (LLR) action and, 197–205
liquidation and, 202–203
mergers and, 203
penalty rates and, 173
recovery of an institution and, 199
resolution of insolvency and, 164–165
runs and, 197–201
societal, and fairness, 117, 153
suspensions and, 204–205
Credit
bank runs and, 209–210
commercial bank share of short-term, 90–91, 92 (table)
interdependence of banks and, 89
savings and loan association (S & L) crises and, 259–262
Credit crunch, 10, 131–132, 210
Credit unions, 46, 49, 54, 148, 180
Crises, see Bank failures; Financial crises, Insolvency; Panics; Savings and loan association (S & L) crises; and specific incidents

Dale, Richard, 3
Dallas Federal Home Loan Bank, 269
Dallas Federal Reserve Bank, 50–51
Department of Justice, 220
Deposit insurance
bank failures and, 3
contagion and, 19–20
financial system safety net and, 43
lender of last resort (LLR) services and, 208–209
runs and, 17, 208
savings and loan (S & L) crises and, 82
Depository institutions (DIs)
bank holidays and, 204
collateral requirements for, 151
comprehensiveness of coverage of, 101, 124
concentration of deposits in, 106–107
discount window loans and, 46, 49
financial system safety net and, 43
information access on, 183, 184
interdependency and, 87–89
lender of last resort coverage of, 15
liquidation costs and, 202–203
monetary policy and, 179–180
need for lender of last resort by, 16–17
reserve requirements for, 183
runs and, 17–18
spillover prevention and, 108–110
state charters for, 43
suspensions of, 204–205
uninsured deposits and runs in, 169
Depository Institutions Deregulation and Monetary Control Act (DIDMCA) of 1980, 1, 47, 48–49
Depression, see Great Depression
Diamond, D. W., 126 n. 1
Discount rate, 54–55
fairness in pricing of, 117, 152–153
flexible market rate structure in, 152
individuals, partnerships, and corporations (IPCs) and, 56–57
long-term borrowing and, 55
non-depository financial institutions (NDFIs) and, 56–57, 152
penalty in, 152, 171–173
policy choices affecting, 171
potential interest rate subsidies and, 55

setting, 54–55
unusually large borrowings and, 56
Discount window loans, 45–46
 access to, 46–47, 60, 130
 Bank of New York (BONY) and, 71
 categories of applicants for, 46–47
 cost of assistance through, 54–57
 discount rate for, 54–55
 extent of assistance from, 176, 177
 Federal Reserve role in, 47
 Franklin National Bank and, 220,
  222, 224, 227–228, 230
 individuals, partnerships, and corporations (IPCs) and, 47, 52–53, 135,
  179
 information access and, 141–142
 Monetary Control Act of 1980 and,
  49
 money supply and, 45
 non-depository financial institutions
  (NDFIs) and, 17, 52–53, 185
 nonmember depository institutions
  and, 47–48
 policy choices affecting, 171
 non-uniform access to, 53–54
 runs and, 209–210
 savings and loan associations
  (S & Ls) and, 132
 silver crisis (1980) and, 177,
  251–252
 size of assistance from, 140
 size of institution and access to,
  148–149
 special industry lenders and, 49
Discrimination, in access to lender of
 last resort, 114–115
Disintermediation, in savings and loan
 association (S & L) crises
 (1985–87), 257–259
Diversification, and risk, 85
Drysdale Government Securities, 133
Duration of assistance
 evaluation criteria for effectiveness
  and, 102, 124
 Federal Reserve performance in,
  138–139
 Franklin National Bank and, 224
 lender of last resort assistance and,
  138
Dybvig, P.H., 126 n. 1

Economy
 deposit insurance and, 209
 Federal Reserve crisis prevention
  and, 146
 role of banks in, 90–92
 silver crisis (1980) and, 234–239
Effectiveness, 97–114
 classic lender of last resort (LLR)
  components applied to, 123–125
 comprehensiveness of coverage and,
  101, 124, 130–137
 duration of support and, 102, 124,
  138–139
 equal access and, 114–115
 equity in, 97–98, 114–117
 establishing criteria of, 97–98
 Federal Reserve performance for,
  128–147
 frequency of assistance and,
  102–103, 124, 139
 incentives for appropriate risk taking
  and, 112–114, 125, 146–147
 information access and, 104–105,
  124, 141–143
 public confidence and, 110–112,
  125, 145–146
 size of assistance and, 103–104, 124,
  139–141
 speed of assistance and, 99–101,
  124, 128–130
 spillover prevention and, 105–110,
  125, 143–145
 trade-offs between effectiveness and
  equity in, 99, 118–123
 working capital provision and, 137
Eisenbeis, Robert A., 176
Electronic funds transfer, 178, 210
 Continental Illinois and, 81–82
 economic malfunction in financial
  system and, 67
 large-dollar payments systems in, 68
 runs and, 17, 81
 speed of transmission and, 81–84
Ely, Bert, 13
Employment Retirement Income
 Security Act (ERISA) of 1974, 42
England, Catherine, 13
England, see Great Britain
Englehard Minerals & Chemicals
 Corporation, 249, 251, 252, 253

Equity, 114–117
   classic lender of last resort (LLR)
      components applied to, 125
   collateral provisions and, 159–160
   comprehensiveness of Federal
      Reserve coverage and, 134
   concerns and issues with, 158–161
   delay in assistance and, 158–159
   direct versus indirect assistance and,
      121–123
   equal access and, 114–115, 120, 148
   establishing criteria of, 98–99
   fairness in treatment and, 115–117,
      125, 185
   Federal Reserve performance in,
      147–149
   geographic region and, 115, 149
   size of institution and, 115,
      148–149, 158–159
   societal interests and, 117
   trade-offs between effectiveness and,
      99, 118–123
Equity Program Investments Corporation (EPIC), 86, 108
ESM (broker-dealer), 128, 129
Eurodollar deposits, 214
European and American Bank and
   Trust (EAB), 217, 222
Evaluation criteria, 97–125
   classic lender of last resort (LLR)
      components applied to, 123–125
   comprehensiveness of coverage and,
      101, 124
   duration of assistance and, 102, 124
   effectiveness in, 97–114
   equal access and, 114–115
   equity in, 97–98, 114–117
   fairness in treatment and, 115–117,
      125
   frequency of assistance and,
      102–103, 124
   incentives for appropriate risk taking
      and, 112–114, 125
   information needs and, 104–105,
      124
   public confidence and, 110–112,
      125
   size of assistance and, 103–104, 124
   societal interests and, 117
   speed of assistance and, 99–101, 124

spillover prevention and, 105–110,
      125
   trade-offs between effectiveness and
      equity in, 99, 118–123
Evans, Gary, 13 n. 4
Extended credit, 46

Failed security agreement, 51
Failures, see Bank failures
Fairness
   collateral requirements and, 116,
      150–152
   evaluation criteria for equity and,
      115–117, 125
   Federal Reserve performance for,
      150–154
   pricing of assistance and, 117,
      152–153
   societal interests and, 17, 153–154
   valuation of posted collateral and,
      151–152
Fama, Eugene E., 180
Farm Credit System, 133
Federal Deposit Insurance Corporation (FDIC), 5, 76, 84, 107
   bank failures before creation of, 2–3
   bank failures after creation of, 3,
      4–5 (table)
   Continental Illinois and, 176
   duration of assistance and, 138
   extent of assistance from, 176, 214
   Federal Reserve action and, 167, 214
   financial system safety net and, 42,
      148, 195
   Franklin National Bank and, 217,
      221, 222, 223, 228
   information needs on runs and,
      104–105
   number of problem institutions and,
      6, 7 (table)
   resolution cost and, 165
   runs and, 17
Federal Deposit Insurance Corporation
   (FDIC) Act, 221
Federal Financial Institutions Examination Council (FFIEC), 71, 142
Federal Home Loan Bank Act, 166
Federal Home Loan Bank Board
   (FHLBB), 6, 42, 105, 132, 166,
      184, 263, 264, 266, 269, 273

Federal Home Loan Bank of Dallas, 269
Federal Home Loan Bank of San Francisco, 264, 269
Federal Home Loan Bank System (FHLBanks), 40 n. 13, 145, 264–273
  access to information from, 184
  advances used by, 265–268, 270–271 (table)
  collateral requirements of, 152, 159–160, 161, 269, 273, 276–277
  creation of, 26
  Federal Reserve assistance and, 132
  Federal Savings and Loan Insurance Corporation (FSLIC) guarantees and, 269–273
  legal authorization for, 265
  as lender of last resort, 38, 42, 43, 49, 157, 160–161, 273
  management changes in failing firms and, 166
  Management Consignment Program (MCP) of, 6, 166
  penalty rate issues and, 172, 173
  pricing of assistance in, 152–153, 213
  role of, 268
  savings and loan association (S & L) crises and, 157, 164, 263–273, 276
  size of assistance from, 140
  societal interests and, 153
  speed of assistance and, 129
Federal Open Market Committee (FOMC), 38, 57, 134, 136
Federal Reserve
  access to assistance from, 147–149
  accountability of, 173–175
  advantages of central bank for, 207–208
  autonomy of banks in, 37
  bank and thrift holding companies and, 175–176
  banks runs and, 37–38
  Board of, see Board of Governors of the Federal Reserve
  capital forbearance and, 203, 204
  classic lender of last resort (LLR) components applied to, 57–60, 123–125
  collateral requirements of, 49–54
  Collateral Work Group of, 51
  commercial bank focus of, 178, 179–180
  complexity of financial transactions and, 85
  comprehensiveness of coverage by, 101, 124
  concerns about performance of, 127
  contagion of runs and, 20, 166–167
  Congress and, 48, 105, 118
  cost of assistance from 54–57
  credibility of, 174–175
  definitions of money used by, 61 n. 11
  delay in acknowledgement of failure by, 162–163
  direct versus indirect assistance from, 121–123
  discount rate and, 54–57
  discount window loans and, 45–47, 60
  duration of assistance from, 138–139
  early years of, 30–31, 35–36, 191
  effectiveness of, 128–147
  equity of assistance from, 147–149, 158–161
  evaluation criteria and, 98
  extended credit and, 46
  extent of assistance from, 175–183
  Federal Deposit Insurance Corporation (FDIC) and, 167, 214
  financial system safety net and, 43–44
  flexibility of, 119, 149, 150
  Franklin National Bank and, 217, 229
  frequency of assistance to, 139
  future direction for, 193–194
  goals of, 36
  Great Depression and, 2
  handling of domestic crises by, 127–154
  incentives for risk taking from, 146–147, 157
  indirect assistance from, 131
  individuals, partnerships, and corporations (IPCs) and, 56–57, 93, 121–123, 178
  information needs on runs and, 104–105

interdependency of banks and, 89
as lender of last resort, 28, 31,
  41–60, 105, 157–158, 214
less developed countries (LDCs) and
  international debt and, 71–72, 136
management changes in insolvency
  and, 165–166
market-sensitive rate on long-term
  borrowing from, 55
membership in, 36, 158, 191
mergers and, 203
Monetary Control Act of 1980 and,
  48–49, 158
monetary policy and, 36–38, 145,
  179–180
money creation and, 44–45
non-bank banks and, 176–177
non-depository financial institutions
  (NDFIs) and, 56–57, 93, 121–123,
  178
nonmember depository institutions
  and, 47–48, 57, 101
non-uniform access to, 53–54
open-market operations and, 20,
  140–141
payments systems and, 70
policy choices for, 168–171
potential interest rate subsidies in
  loans from, 55
private sector participation in assistance and, 164, 211, 255
public confidence in, 111–112
recovery of an institution and costs
  to, 199
reserve requirements and, 44–45
savings and loan association (S & L)
  crises and, 139, 142, 144, 146,
  185, 193, 264
secrecy of actions of, 146, 157–158,
  173–174
silver crisis (1980) and, 177,
  251–256
size of assistance from, 103,
  139–141
societal interests and, 153–154
spillover prevention and, 109, 125
unusually large borrowings from, 56,
  103
Federal Reserve Act of 1913, 35, 36,
  45, 47, 50, 52, 53, 54, 101, 134,
  137, 154 n. 11, 191, 278–279
Federal Reserve Advisory Council, 37

Federal Reserve Bank of Chicago, 55,
  145
Federal Reserve Bank of Cleveland,
  50, 101, 128–129, 138, 139, 146,
  184, 276
Federal Reserve Bank of Dallas, 50–51
Federal Reserve Bank of Kansas City,
  51
Federal Reserve Bank of New York,
  81, 90, 92, 110, 133, 145,
  155 n. 25
  Bank of New York (BONY) and,
    70–71, 82–84, 100, 103, 171
  duration of assistance and, 138
  Federal Reserve policy and, 38, 134
  Franklin National Bank and,
    219–220, 223, 225, 226
  loans from, 51, 56, 133
  Penn Central and, 135
Federal Reserve Bank of Richmond,
  50, 139
Federal Reserve Bank of San
  Francisco, 51
Federal Reserve Board, see Board of
  Governors of the Federal Reserve
Federal Reserve notes, 36
Federal Savings and Loan Insurance
  Corporation (FSLIC), 6, 199
  Federal Reserve assistance and, 132,
    148, 152
  financial condition of, 262, 263
    (table)
  insolvency of, 262, 273
  resolution cost and, 165
  runs and, 17
  safety net provided by, 3, 6, 42, 195
  savings and loan association (S & L)
    crises and, 269–273, 276–277
FHLBanks, see Federal Home Loan
  Bank System (FHLBanks)
Figlewski, Stephen, 85
Financial Corporation of America
  (FCA), 110, 199, 264
Financial crises
  causes of, 7–8
  central bank prevention of, 208–209
  definitions of, 9–10
  duration of assistance in, 102, 124
  Federal Reserve handling of,
    127–154, 192–193
  indirect assistance in, 131
  interdependency of banks and, 88

lender of last resort (LLR) evolution
and, 192–193
open-market operations and, 145
silver crisis (1980) case study and,
233–256
see also Bank failures; Great Depression; Insolvency; Panics; Savings
and loan association (S & L)
crises, and specific incidents
Financial markets
central bank assurances and, 27, 57,
58, 60
changes in, 177–178
commercial bank share of, 90, 91
(table)
extent of Federal Reserve assistance
and, 177
financial crises and pressure on, 136
future directions for, 194
interdependency and, 87–89
non-depository financial institutions
(NDFIs) and, 182
open-market sales and, 140–141
public confidence in, 111–112,
145–146
risk-taking incentives for, 113,
167–168
safety net concept and discipline in,
167–168, 170
short-term business credit and,
90–91, 92 (table)
speed of assistance and, 100–101
spillover prevention and, 144
Financial services industry, 80–81
Financial system
causes of problems in, 7–8
central bank responsibility to,
23–24, 57, 58
complexity and sophistication of,
68, 84–87
costs and benefits of bank failures
and rescue and, 12–13
factors in economic malfunction in,
66–68
federal legislation and, 1
interdependency of institutions in,
68, 87–89
less developed countries (LDCs) and
international debt and, 71–73
magnitude and concentration of
economic activity in, 68

public confidence in, 110–112, 125
public or private responsibility for
safety net in, 13
redistribution of funds and perceptions of safety of, 73–74
signs of stress in, 3–6
silver crisis (1980) and, 255
size of banks in, 66–67
technology and, 65
tiering of banks in, 19, 100
unregulated areas in, 67–68
Financial system safety net, 42–44
benefits and cost of, 167–168
comprehensiveness of coverage in,
101, 124
concerns and issues about, 127,
167–168
duration of Federal Reserve assistance and, 139
evaluation criteria and, 98
federal activity in, 42
frequency of assistance and,
102–103
lender of last resort (LLR) within,
43–44
market discipline and, 167
risk-taking incentives and, 167–168
size of institution and access to, 149
societal interests and, 153
speed of assistance and, 100–101
state activity in, 43
timing of action in, 195
First Bank of the United States, 28,
29, 30, 190
First Dallas, 233
First Pennsylvania National Bank, 164,
174, 199, 207
Fixed rate mortgages, 21, 259
Foreign exchange
Franklin National Bank and,
218–219, 228–229, 230
interdependency of banks and, 87,
88–89
off-balance sheet liabilities and, 75
France, deposit insurance in, 3
Franklin National Bank, 55, 82, 138,
139, 154 n. 6, 213, 214
bidding package in, 221–222
case study of, 217–231
causes of failure of, 218–219
contagion and, 220

development of crisis in, 219–220
disposition of London branch in, 229–230
foreign exchange book in, 228–229
interest rate subsidy in, 225–228
international cooperation in, 229
international deposit outflows in, 225
lender of last resort (LLR) precedents for, 223–224
as model of resolution, 230–231
resolution of crisis in, 220–221, 222
size and duration of assistance in, 224
Frequency of assistance
evaluation criteria for effectiveness and, 102–103, 124
Federal Reserve performance in, 139
Friedman, Milton, 2, 3, 37, 94 n. 8

Garcia, Gillian G., 6, 13 n. 4, 13 n. 5, 55, 81, 95 n. 17, 101, 126 n. 11, 153, 154 n. 3, 155 n. 16, 161, 186 n. 7, 211 n. 3, 212 n. 7, 212 n. 8, 212 n. 12, 257, 259, 279 n. 2
Garn-St Germain Depository Institutions Act (GSGDIA) of 1982, 1, 132, 180, 259
General Accounting Office (GAO), 44, 61 n. 3, 61 n. 6, 95 n. 17, 105, 108, 126 n. 5, 138, 153, 154 n. 5, 155 n. 21, 156 n. 32, 164, 165, 166, 184, 185, 186 n. 6, 187 n. 12, 211 n. 5, 262, 263, 272, 273
Generally accepted accounting principles (GAAP), 6, 7
cash insolvency and, 11
Management Consignment Program (MCP) and, 166
off-balance sheet liabilities and, 74–75
savings and loan association (S & L) crises and, 260–261 (table), 262
Geographic region, and access to assistance, 115, 149
Goldfeld, Stephen M., 160
Goodfriend, Marvin, 13, 21, 209
Government securities, 131, 133, 150
Gramm-Rudman-Hollings law, 262
Gray, Edwin, 129, 184

Great Britain
deposit insurance in, 3
lender of last resort (LLR) concept and, 21–22, 190, 191–192
Great Depression, 127, 204, 207, 209
clearinghouses and, 35
contagion of runs and, 20
Federal Reserve loans and, 47
financial system safety net and, 42, 74
lender of last resort (LLR) concept and, 2, 28, 40
monetary policy before, 36–38
Reconstruction Finance Corporation (RFC) and, 38, 39, 191
Greenspan, Alan, 67
Guttentag, Jack, 40 n. 1, 113, 149, 170

Hackley, Howard H., 47, 48, 131, 137
Havrilesky, Thomas M., 40 n. 4
Herring, Richard, 40 n. 1, 113, 149
Hirschhorn, Eric, 221
Home Owners' Loan Corporation (HOLC), 28, 31, 39, 191
Home State Savings Bank, 128–129, 143–144
Hoover administration, 38
Horne, Karen, 155 n. 23
Horvitz, Paul M., 195
House of Representatives, 61 n. 7, 165, 171, 187 n. 16, 251, 252, 253, 254
Humphrey, Thomas M., 21, 22, 25, 27, 40 n. 1, 102, 115, 119
Hunt brothers (Nelson and William), 136, 177, 233, 239, 240, 242, 243, 246, 247, 250–251, 252–255

Incentives for appropriate risk taking
concerns and issues about, 161–173
evaluation criteria for effectiveness and, 112–114, 125
Federal Reserve performance in, 146–147, 157
future directions for, 194
management of failing firms and, 166
penalty rates and, 172
pricing policies of loans and, 147

Individuals, partnerships, and corporations (IPCs)
  access to assistance by, 148
  collateral requirements for, 52-53, 150-151
  comprehensiveness of Federal Reserve coverage of, 101, 124, 135-137
  discount rates for, 56-57
  discount window loans and, 47, 52-53, 135, 179
  discrimination in access to lender of last resort by, 115
  Federal Reserve and, 93, 121-123, 148, 178
  future concerns for, 175
  lender of last resort (LLR) assistance to, 179
  pricing of assistance to, 152
Inflation
  Federal Reserve and, 192-193
  financial problems and, 7
  public confidence in financial systems and, 111
Information access
  call report data and, 142-143
  collateral evaluation and, 141-142, 183-184
  comprehensiveness of Federal Reserve coverage and, 134
  concerns and issues about, 183-186
  evaluation criteria for equity and, 104-105, 124
  fairness in treatment and, 150
  Federal Reserve performance in, 141-143
  non-depository financial institutions (NDFIs) and, 143, 183-186
  policy choices for, 185-186
Insolvency
  "catch 22" situation in assistance to, 163-164
  comprehensiveness of coverage in, 101, 124
  costs of resolution of, 164-165
  definitions of, 10-12
  delay in acknowledgement of, 162-163
  extent of Federal Reserve assistance in, 175
  Federal Savings and Loan Insurance Corporation (FSLIC) and, 262, 273
  frequency of assistance in, 102-103, 124, 139
  frequency of occurrences of, 139
  information for assessment of, 134, 141-142
  generally accepted accounting principles (GAAP) and, 6, 7
  lender of last resort and, 16-17
  management changes in, 165-166
  market discipline and, 167-168, 170
  receivership for, 166
  regulatory accounting principles (RAP) and, 7, 11-12
  reorganization of bank in, 163
  savings and loan association (S & L) crises and, 260-261 (table), 262
  speed of assistance in, 100-101, 124, 128-130
  spillover prevention and, 108-110, 125
  see also Bank failures; Savings and loan association (S & L) crises; and specific incidents
Interdependency of financial institutions, 68, 87-89, 233
Interest rates
  delay in bank failure and, 162
  Franklin National Bank and, 225-228
  incentives for risk taking and, 147
  lender of last resort and, 16, 192-193
  monetary contractions and, 20-21
  Regulation Q on, 131
  sophistication of, 84
International banking
  bank failures and, 214-215
  Franklin National Bank and, 225, 229, 230-231
  interdependency and, 87-89
  less developed countries (LDCs), and international debt and, 71-73, 136
  off-balance sheet risk and, 80-81
  speed of assistance and, 100
  tiering of banks in, 19, 100
International Metals Investment Company (IMIC), 239, 248-249, 250-251
Isaacs, William, 61 n. 7
Israel-British Bank, 217, 219
Italy, deposit insurance in, 3

Jackson, Andrew, 32
Jaffe, Stephen, 268, 285
Jaffee, Dwight M., 160
James, Christopher, 210
Justice Department, 220

Kane, Edward J., 8, 12, 17, 44, 61
   n. 4, 65, 66, 67, 71, 72, 81, 87,
   89, 126 n. 8, 126 n. 11, 153, 154
   n. 7, 154 n. 8, 154 n. 10, 155
   n. 16, 167, 170, 186 n. 2, 197,
   232 n. 10, 268, 279 n. 2
Kansas City Federal Reserve Bank, 51
Kareken, John H., 170
Karmel, Roberta, 67
Kaufman, George G., 12, 20, 54, 62
   n. 22, 65, 73, 113, 126 n. 1, 147,
   170, 172, 208
Keleher, Robert E., 13 n. 4, 21, 22,
   26, 40 n. 1, 103
Kennedy, Susan Estabrook, 37
Kent, Richard J., 160, 268
Kindleburger, Charles P., 94 n. 9
Koehn, Michael, 94 n. 10
Koppenhaver, Gary D., 66, 77, 79

Lender of last resort (LLR)
   American concept of, 28–39
   availability to banks of, 15
   British concept of, 21–22
   "catch 22" situation in assistance
     from, 163–164
   causes of financial problems and, 8
   central banking and, 28–32
   classic components of, 22–28,
     57–60, 123–125
   clearinghouses as, 34–35
   collateral requirements of, 49–54,
     151
   commercial bank role in economy
     and, 90–91
   complexity of transactions with, 86
   comprehensiveness of coverage by,
     101, 124
   confidentiality of actions of,
     173–174
   contagion with bank failures and,
     18–20, 166–167
   cost and benefits of, 54–57,
     197–205
   criteria for judging performance of, 8
   definitions and themes and, 9
   development of concept of, 1–3
   discount window loans and, 45–48
   duration of assistance from, 102,
     124, 138
   early Federal Reserve and, 35–36
   effectiveness of, 98
   electronic funds transfer problems
     and, 67
   equal access to, 114–115, 147
   equity and, 98–99
   evaluation of, see Evaluation criteria
   evolution of concept of, 28
   extended credit and, 46
   Federal Home Loan Bank (FHLB)
     System and, 157, 160–161
   Federal Reserve as, 28, 41–60, 105,
     214
   financial system safety net with,
     42–44
   flexibility of assistance from, 149,
     150
   Franklin National Bank case and,
     223–224, 230
   frequency of assistance from,
     102–103, 124, 139
   functions and operating dates of
     organizations undertaking, 28,
     29–31 (table)
   future concerns for, 175
   Home Owners' Loan Corporation
     (HOLC) as, 39, 191
   individuals, partnerships, and corpo-
     rations (IPCs) and, 52–53, 56–57,
     179
   incentives for risk taking and, 146
   information needs and, 104–105,
     124
   interdependency and, 87
   magnitude and concentration of
     economic activity and, 68
   Monetary Control Act of 1980 and,
     48–49
   monetary contraction periods and,
     20–21
   monetary policy before the Great
     Depression and, 36–38
   money creation and, 44–45
   moral hazard issues and, 119–120
   need for, 16–17
   non-bank banks and, 176–177
   non-depository financial institutions
     (NDFIs) and, 52–53, 56–57, 179

nonmember depository institutions and, 47–48
non-uniform access to, 53–54
off-balance sheet liabilities and, 74
operations for, 45–48
origins of, 15–40
penalty rate for, 171–172
periods of evolution of, 189–193
private sector assistance in, 164, 206–211
public confidence in, 110–112, 125, 166–167
public or private responsibility for safety net in, 13, 190
rationales for action of, 196–197
Reconstruction Finance Corporation (RFC) as, 38–39, 137, 191
runs and, 17–18, 168–169
savings and loan association (S & L) crises and, 264, 273, 277–278
signs of stress and, 3–6
size of assistance from, 103–104, 124, 139–141
social accounting and, 205–206
summary of concept of, 27–28
technology in financial system and, 65
timing of action of, 194–197
trend away from bank financing and, 93
Lender of last resort loans, 46
Less developed countries (LDCs), and international debt, 71–73, 136
Liability management
complexity of financial transactions and, 84–85
dependence on, 82
Liquidations of banks, 202–203, 212 n. 7
Liquidity
banking without a lender of last resort (LLR) and, 33
banks as backup sources of, 180
central bank loans for, 24–25, 57, 59
clearinghouses and, 34–35
contagion of runs and, 19–20
Continental Illinois and, 81–82
interdependency of banks and, 88
lender of last resort and, 16, 23, 57, 58, 196

Reconstruction Finance Corporation (RFC) and, 38
savings and loan associations (S & Ls) and, 180, 259, 264
speed of assistance and, 100
Litan, Robert E., 170
Loans
clearinghouses and, 34–35
commercial and industrial (C & I), 211
commercial bank share of short-term, 90–91, 92 (table)
complexity of financial transactions and, 84–85
fairness in pricing of, 117
Home Owners' Loan Corporation (HOLC) and, 39
mergers and, 203
off-balance sheet risk and, 80–81
runs and, 18
Lockheed, 136
Longstreth, Bevis, 95 n. 19

Maisel, Sherman J., 156 n. 26
Managed liabilities, 82, 83, 84
Management
bank failures and changes in, 154 n. 6, 165–166
risk-taking incentives and, 167
Management Consignment Program (MCP), Federal Home Loan Bank Board (FHLBB), 6, 166
Manufacturers, Hanover, 110
Markets, see Financial markets
Martin, William McChesney, 137
Maryland savings and loan association (S & L) crisis, 13, 81, 82, 86, 108, 111, 132, 163, 184, 262
bank holiday in, 204
duration of assistance in, 102, 138–139
Federal Reserve action in, 142, 144, 146, 185, 193
political issues in, 174–175
speed of assistance in, 129, 130
suspensions of banks in, 205
McCall, Alan S., 91
McCullough, Huston J., 81, 197, 286
McLean, Kenneth A., 118, 159
Melton, William, 134, 135, 144, 147, 187 n. 17

Meltzer, Allan H., 22, 25, 27, 40 n. 1,
    103, 113, 114, 115, 128, 172
Mergers, 203, 278
Merrick, John, 85
Merrill Lynch, 245, 246, 248–249,
    250–251
Mexico, financial difficulties in, 134
Michigan National Bank, 19, 110
Minsky, Hyman P., 9
Miron, Jeffrey A., 46
Monetary contraction, and runs,
    20–21
Monetary Control Act (MCA) of 1980,
    47, 48–49, 101, 130, 132, 142,
    148, 158, 160, 181, 182, 192, 278
Monetary policy
    choices available in, 168–171
    Federal Reserve and, 134, 145,
        179–180
    frequency of assistance and,
        102–103
    before Great Depression, 36–38
    lender of last resort and, 192–193
    liquidity assurance by central bank
        and, 23, 57, 58
    social accounting and, 205–206
Money, definitions of, 61 n. 11
Money market, and credit crunch, 132
Money market deposits, 82
Money market mutual funds
    (MMMFs), 181, 257, 259
Money supply
    contagion of runs and, 19–20
    credit flows and, 73, 74
    before Great Depression, 36–37
    discount window loans and, 45
    large-dollar payments systems and, 69
    lender of last resort concept and, 22,
        208
    money creation and, 44–45
    national banking system and, 34
    open-market sales and, 140–141
    state banking systems and, 33
Moral hazard problems, 119–120
Morgan Guaranty, 233
Morrisey, Thomas F., 160, 268
Mortgages
    complexity of transactions and risk
        in, 86
    Home Owners' Loan Corporation
        (HOLC) and, 39

monetary contractions and, 21
securitization of, 182
savings and loan association (S & L)
    crises and, 259
spillover prevention and, 109
Mote, Larry R., 65
Multinational banks, 115, 220
Municipal securities, 131
Mutual savings banks, 148

Nash, Nathaniel, 67, 68
National Bank Act of 1863, 33
National Credit Union Association
    (NCUA), 42
    Central Liquidity Authority of, 32,
        42, 43, 49, 160
    Federal Reserve assistance and, 132,
        148, 153
    as lender of last resort, 160
National Currency Association, 35
National Housing Act of 1934, 42
National Monetary Commission, 35
Net worth, and insolvency, 10
New York City, financial crisis in, 136
New York Clearing House Association
    (NYCHA), 34
New York Federal Reserve Bank, 81,
    90, 92, 110, 133, 145, 155 n. 25
    Bank of New York (BONY) and,
        70–71, 82–84, 100, 103, 171
    duration of assistance and, 138
    Federal Reserve policy and, 38, 134
    Franklin National Bank and,
        219–220, 223, 225, 226
    loans from, 51, 56
    Penn Central and, 135
New York Safety Fund, 33
New York State Banking Commission,
    220
Non-bank financial institutions
    Federal Reserve assistance for,
        176–177
    financial markets and, 90, 91 (table)
Non-depository financial institutions
    (NDFIs)
    access to assistance by, 148
    collateral requirements for, 52–53,
        150–151, 183–184
    comprehensiveness of Federal
        Reserve coverage of, 101, 124,
        133–135, 137

discount rates for, 56–57
discount window loans and, 46–47, 52–53, 178, 185
discrimination in access to lender of last resort by, 115
Federal Reserve and, 93, 121–123, 148, 178
future concerns for, 175
information access on, 142–143, 183–186
lender of last resort (LLR) assistance to, 179
liquidity assurance and, 180
payments systems and, 70
pricing of assistance to, 152
reserve requirements and, 181, 182
runs and, 181, 182
specialness of, 181–182
spillover prevention and, 109
Nonmember depository institutions, and Federal Reserve, 47–48, 57, 101

Off-balance sheet liabilities, 74–77
Off-balance sheet risk, 80–81
Office of the Comptroller of the Currency (OCC), 43, 104–105, 106, 149, 219, 220, 221
Ohio Deposit Guarantee Fund (ODGF), 129, 143
Ohio savings and loan association (S & L) crisis (1985), 13, 35, 81, 82, 108, 111, 132, 163, 184, 196, 262
    duration of assistance in, 102, 139
    Federal Reserve action in, 139, 142, 146, 185, 193
    Home State Savings Bank and, 128–129
    political issues in, 174–175
    speed of assistance in, 128–129, 130
    suspensions of banks in, 205
Okun, Arthur M., 99, 118
Open-market sales, 140–141, 209
Organization of Petroleum Exporting Countries (OPEC), 237–238, 239

Panics
    British, 21–22
    central bank loans during, 24–25, 57, 59
    clearinghouses and, 34, 35

lender of last resort (LLR) concept and, 2
    see also Financial crisis and specific incidents
Partee, J. Charles, 254
Patinkin, Don, 180
Payments systems
    banking system changes and, 177–178
    Bank of New York (BONY) disruption of, 70–71
    Federal Reserve support for, 70
    risk in, 69
    services provided by, 69–70
    size of, 68–69
Penalty rates
    central bank loans with, 26–27, 57, 58, 60
    determining appropriate level of, 172–173
    Federal Reserve use of, 171–172
    penalty choices affecting, 171–173
Penn Central, 135, 177, 178, 180
Penn Square National Bank, 19, 95 n. 18, 104–105, 108–110, 139, 142, 144, 149, 163
Pension Benefit Guarantee Corporation, 42
Pension plans, 42
Placid Oil Company, 144, 177, 247, 250, 251
Plautz, Elizabeth, 55
Polakoff, Michael, 101, 153, 155 n. 6, 161, 211 n. 3, 212 n. 7, 279 n. 2
Political factors
    Federal Reserve and, 118–119
    interdependency of banks and, 87
    international debt and, 72
    savings and loan association (S & L) crises and, 174–175
Pratt, Richard, 61 n. 8, 132, 264
Pricing of loans, 213–214
    advances from Federal Home Loan Banks (FHLBanks) system and, 277
    fairness in, 117, 152–153
    incentives for risk taking and, 147
    penalty rate issues and, 172–173
    policy choices for, 170–171
Private sector
    bank runs and supply or credit and, 209–210

deposit insurance and runs and, 208–209
Federal Reserve and, 164, 211
lender of last resort assistance and, 13, 190, 206–211
silver crisis (1980) and, 233, 255–256
specialness of banks and, 210–211
Public confidence
contagion prevention and, 166–167
credibility of central bank and, 174–175
evaluation criteria for effectiveness and, 110–112, 124
Federal Reserve performance and, 145–146
information needs on runs and, 105

Quandt, Richard E., 160, 268

Real estate investment trusts (REITs), 220
Recapitalization of failing banks, 163
Receivership for failing banks, 166
Reconstruction Finance Corporation (RFC), 119
as lender of last resort, 28, 31, 38–39, 137, 191
proposal for re-establishing, 169
Region, and access to assistance, 115, 149
Regulation A, 49, 50, 52, 56
Regulation Q, 131, 144
Regulatory accounting principles (RAP), 7
financial crisis and, 11–12
off-balance sheet liabilities and, 74–75
savings and loan association (S & L) crises and, 262
Reid, Margaret, 106, 163, 231
Reorganization of failing banks, 163
Reserve requirements
access to assistance and, 182–183
banking without a lender of last resort (LLR) and, 33
contagion and, 19–20
depository institutions (DIs) and, 183
discount window access and, 56, 134
Federal Reserve control of, 44–45

less developed countries (LDCs) and international debt and, 71–73
Monetary Control Act of 1980 and, 48–49, 61 n. 10
money creation and, 44
money market mutual funds (MMMFs) and, 181
non-depository financial institutions (NDFIs) and, 181, 182
open-market sales and, 140–141
runs and, 17, 18, 208
Richmond Federal Reserve Bank, 50, 139
Risk
complexity of financial transactions and, 85–87
diversification and, 85
interdependency and, 87, 88
electronic funds transfer and, 67
financial system safety net and, 167–168
incentives for taking, *see* Incentives for appropriate risk taking
information needs on, 105
international debt and, 71
large-dollar payments systems and, 69–70
management and, 167
off-balance sheet liabilities and, 74–77
off-balance sheet risk and, 80–81
societal interests and, 153
standby letters of credit (SLC) and, 77
Robertson, Ross M., 29
Roosevelt, Franklin D., 38
Rosenblum, Harvey, 65
Runs on banks
ban on, 169
"catch 22" situation in assistance to, 163–164
conditions for, 17–18
contagion and, 18–20
credit supply and, 209–210
deterioration of bank after, 199–202
electronic systems and, 17, 81
Federal Reserve and, 37–38, 208
Federal Savings and Loan Insurance Corporation (FSLIC) and, 278
information needs on, 104–105
less developed countries (LDCs), and international debt and, 136–137

liquidation after, 202–203
monetary contractions and, 20–21
non-depository financial institutions
  (NDFIs) and, 181, 182
parties losing in, 198 (table), 199
permitting, 168–169
policy choices concerning, 168–169
possible outcomes of, 197–199
reserve requirements and, 17, 18,
  208
resolution of, 199, 200–201 (table)
uninsured deposits and, 169

Safety net, see Financial system safety
  net
San Francisco Federal Home Loan
  Bank, 264, 269
San Francisco Federal Reserve Bank,
  51
Santomero, Anthony M., 94 n. 10
Saulsbury, Victor L., 91
Saunders, Anthony, 179
Savings and loan association (S & L)
  crises (1985–87), 213–214
  advances in, 265–268, 270–271
    (table), 274–275 (table), 277, 278
  building up to, 259–264
  case study of, 257–279
  "catch 22" situation in assistance to,
    164
  causes of, 259
  collateral requirements in, 269,
    276–277
  comprehensiveness of coverage of,
    101, 131
  Congressional rescue bills and,
    262–263
  credibility of Federal Reserve
    actions in, 174–175
  credit crunch and, 131, 259–262
  delay in acknowledgement of, 163
  disintermediation and, 257–259
  equity concerns in, 160–161
  Federal Home Loan Bank (FHLIB)
    system and, 157, 160–161, 164,
    264–273, 277, 278
  Federal Reserve and, 26, 268,
    278–279
  Federal Savings and Loan Insurance
    Corporation (FSLIC) guarantees
    in, 269–273, 276–277, 278

FSLIC insolvency in, 262, 273
frequency of insolvency of, 139
Home State Savings Bank and,
  128–129
incidence of insolvencies in,
  260–261 (table), 262
information access in, 142–143
issues in, 273–277
lender of last resort (LLR) assistance
  in, 264, 273, 277–278
liquidity assistance and, 180, 264
management changes in, 166
periods of deposit losses in, 257,
  258 (table)
receivership in, 166
run resolution and, 199, 200–201
  (table)
societal costs of, 153, 205
specialness of, 180–181
speed of assistance in, 99–101, 124,
  128–130
suspensions of banks in, 205
see also Maryland savings and loan
  association (S & L) crisis; Ohio
  savings and loan association
  (S & L) crisis; and specific
  incidents
Savings and loan associations (S & Ls)
  cash insolvency and, 11
  crises in, 82
  discount window loans and, 46
  discrimination in access to lender of
    last resort by, 115
  Federal Home Loan Bank Board
    and, 184
  Federal Reserve and, 26, 49, 149
  Federal Savings and Loan Insurance
    Corporation (FSLIC) coverage of,
    3, 6, 42
  financial system safety net and, 42
  generally accepted accounting prin-
    ciples (GAAP) and, 6, 7
  holding companies for, 175–176
  number of problem institutions, 6,
    7 (table)
  regulatory accounting principles
    (RAP) and, 7, 11–12
  signs of stress in, 3, 6
  spillover prevention with, 108
Schwartz, Anna J., 2, 3, 13, 21, 37,
  40 n. 9, 61 n. 2, 61 n. 4, 63 n. 25,

63 n. 26, 65, 94 n. 8, 126 n. 3,
    170, 207
Seafirst, 110
Seattle First Bank, 19
Second Bank of the United States, 29,
    30, 190
Securities and Exchange Commission
    (SEC), 42, 188 n. 27, 239
Securities dealers, 133
Securitization of assets, 85, 182
Shafer, Jeffrey R., 97
Silber, William L., 160, 268
Silver crisis (1980), 111, 133, 136,
    144, 180, 214
  brokers and dealers during, 245–251
  case study of, 233–256
  economic fundamentals underlying,
    234–237
  Federal Reserve role in, 177, 178,
    251–256
  general economic conditions and,
    237–239
  influences on silver prices and,
    243–245
  investor demand for silver and,
    239–242
Sinai, Alan, 10
Sindona, Michele, 218, 219
Singer, Mark, 126 n. 7
Sinkey, Joseph F., Jr., 81, 218, 231
    n. 1, 231 n. 3, 231 n. 8
Size of assistance
  evaluation criteria for effectiveness
    and, 103–104, 124
  Federal Reserve performance in,
    139–141
  Franklin National Bank and, 224
Size of banks
  concentration of deposits in,
    106–108
  equity concerns and, 158–159
  failures and, 66–67
  Federal Reserve access and, 148–149
  lender of last resort access and, 115,
    120–121
Smith, Richard L., 85
Societal interests
  costs of resolution and, 165
  fairness of assistance and, 117,
    153–154, 161

Federal Home Loan Bank System
  assistance and, 161
  policy and, 205–206
  silver crisis (1980) and, 255
Speed of assistance
  evaluation criteria for effectiveness
    and, 99–101, 124
  Federal Reserve performance in,
    128–130
  Home State Savings Bank and,
    128–129
Spero, Joan Edward, 222, 224, 225,
    226, 227, 229, 231 n. 1
Spillover prevention, 202
  evaluation criteria for effectiveness
    and, 105–110, 120, 125
  Federal Reserve performance in,
    143–145
  moral "suasion" in, 144–145
Sprague, Irvin H., 149, 159, 164, 207
Standby letters of credit (SLC), 77–80
State banking systems
  access to information and, 184
  banking without a lender of last
    resort (LLR) and, 33–34
  financial system safety net and, 43,
    44
  savings and loans (S & Ls) and, 82,
    129
Steagall, Representative, 42
Stockholders, and bank failures, 170
Stock market crisis (1987), 110, 133,
    134, 140, 145–146, 192, 193, 209
Stoltz, Richard W., 85
Suffolk Bank of Boston, 33
SuperNOW accounts, 260
Suspensions of banks, 204–205
Syndicated lending, 80–81

Taxes
  recovery of an institution and, 199
  state banking systems and, 33
  suspension of banks and, 205
Technology
  financial system and, 65
  see also Electronic funds transfer
Texas, 262, 263
Thompson, James B., 89
Thornton, Henry, 21, 23, 24, 102,
    112, 113

Thrift institutions, *see* Savings and
    loan associations (S & Ls)
TICOR, 86
Tiering of banks, 19, 100
Timberlake, Richard H., Jr., 40 n. 6
Timing of assistance, 158–159, 164
Todd, Walker F., 89, 137, 154 n. 9,
    155 n. 13
Treasury, 61 n. 6, 69–70, 84, 141, 153
Treasury bonds, 70, 278

Unitary thrift holding companies, 176
United Kingdom, *see* Great Britain

Volcker, Paul A., 19, 61 n. 8, 67, 84,
    100, 111, 132, 133, 204, 207, 264
    silver crisis (1980) and, 233, 252,
    253
    spillover prevention and, 144, 145

Wall, M. Danny, 184, 263
Wille, Frank, 222, 231 n. 1, 231 n. 6,
    231 n. 9
Wolfson, Martin H., 134, 135, 144
Working capital, and Federal Reserve,
    137
World War I, 37, 207
World War II, 137, 192

Zweig, Phillip L., 104, 126 n. 7

ABOUT THE AUTHORS

Gillian Garcia is a member of the staff of the Senate Banking Committee on detail from the U. S. General Accounting Office. She is also an Adjunct Professor of Finance at Georgetown University. At GAO she directed an Economic Analysis Group, which conducted research on financial institutions for the U. S. Congress. Previously, Dr. Garcia was an assistant professor in the Business School at the University of California, Berkeley, and a consultant and senior economist at the Federal Reserve Bank of Chicago. She has written four books and numerous articles on financial legislation, financial institutions, monetary policy, banks, and thrifts. She was born in England, where she received much of her education.

Elizabeth Plautz also worked for the GAO's Economic Analysis Group, where she did research on issues related to the lender of last resort and international capital markets. She received her MBA in finance from Indiana University. Currently, she plans to pursue her doctorate in international finance.